Postmodern Journeys

THE SUNY SERIES IN
POSTMODERN CULTURE

Joseph Natoli, *Editor*

Postmodern Journeys

∽ა∾

Film and Culture
1996–1998

JOSEPH NATOLI

State University of New York Press

Published by
State University of New York Press, Albany

© 2001 State University of New York

For information, address State University of New York Press,
90 State Street, Suite 700, Albany, NY 12207

Production by Marilyn P. Semerad
Marketing by Patrick Durocher

Library of Congress Cataloging-in-Publication Data

Natoli, Joseph P., 1943–
    Postmodern journeys : film and culture, 1996–1998 / Joseph Natoli.
        p. cm. — (The SUNY series in postmodern culture)
    Includes bibliographical references and index.
    ISBN 0-7914-4771-5 (hc. : alk. paper) — ISBN 0-7914-4772-3 (pbk. : alk. paper)
        1. Motion pictures—Philosophy. 2. Postmodernism—Social aspects. I. Title. II. Series.

PN1995 .N36 2000
    791.43′01—dc21
                                                                                00-020339

10 9 8 7 6 5 4 3 2 1

*To all the students who have journeyed with me,
and especially to my teaching assistants
Mike, Susan, Steve, and Monica.*

Contents

Questions at a Book Signing

November 5, 2001

"The man making a sandwich over by the refreshment table."

"Could you tell us why, Mr. Natoli, you haven't updated your material? You knew when you were writing in 1998 that some of what you wrote in 1996 had changed or was no longer true."

"I see no sense in concealing the moment of writing. Or in concealing the fact that our writing is always of this moment, in this place, by this observer. I'm writing from within the flux of things at a certain time; I'm trying to capture that. I'm trying to avoid the pretenses of 'timelessness' and disinterestedness. I'm interested in a certain way at a certain time. And, maybe I wasn't alone in that kind of interest."

"Don't you think your interests go way beyond the expiration date? And people don't buy beyond the expiration date?"

"The shirtless man without shoes smoking over there by my mom and dad."

"So your stuff is dated before it comes out. What's the use or sense in reading dated stuff? Or about films we can't even remember or never saw? Who has time for stuff like that? Didn't you ever hear the expression 'time is money?'"

"Everyone who writes a sentence is in the revival business. Maybe I'm trying to revive stuff that's been destined for the discard pile. But who destined it? I mean, why is popular culture less liable to be meaningful at the present moment than so-called serious culture? The man in the cap who looks like Superman."

"That's the point—pop culture is all about the present moment that flies by, man, because it's weightless. If it gets heavy, it loses its popularity, its mass appeal. It loses profits."

"Did you ever think that perhaps the present moment perseveres because someone writes about it and someone else, in the future, reads about it?"

"Hey, man, no one in the future is going to care to read about Meet Joe Black *or about your trip to Sicily. You're writing about transient stuff, you know. Pop culture pops off, that's why it's called pop culture."*

"Mom."

"You really haven't answered the man's question, dear. What's to keep everything you're writing and writing about from flying out the window?"

"As long as I'm teaching, Mom, I hope to make all that required reading. You know if it hangs on a museum wall, it must be art and if it's on a required reading list, it must be worth reading. That sort of thing. Yes? The woman on the phone."

"I'm lost. I mean who cares what floats into your head when you see or hear something? Correct me if I'm wrong, but aren't you supposed to be objective?"

"I think I'm trying any way I can to show the overlapping of the personal and the social/cultural. I'm trying for honesty, not objectivity."

"I think that's despicable. I have more to say but I have a call waiting."

"The man in handcuffs way in the back there."

"You mix headline events with films and your own personal life and a lot of postmodern attitudes and the like. Is this a subject? And is there an argument in there that I've missed? If you've got a case, you haven't presented it to me, I can tell you that."

"We lived in certain cultural imaginaries during these years and what they might be comes out in all kinds of ways and all kinds of places. I don't have a thesis or an argument; I'm trying to trace a cultural history, but not the sort that tries to get this period of time 'right' but rather one that gets us to see how we ourselves knew and produced these years. And how those hook-ups are at play in the present moment."

"And what lesson has anybody learned here? Or, is there one? Where's the rehabilitation? You do ten years in Elevenworth, maybe you should write about some line of progress you've seen?"

"Yeah, well, I think we've been putting the world and ourselves together within a very observable hierarchy which leaves a whole hell of a lot of things out; I like to refer to the inconceivable but I don't know how you do that. But it needs to be done. Yes, the bald man with bells on his fingers."

"I'm interested in the journey this book is on or you think it's on. I expected more of a travel diary."

"And it is one, I think, but you can't write a personal diary because for me the personal is infused with the social/cultural. If you set out to describe how headline events play out in popular culture for a whole decade, you're writing a travel diary because you're on a journey, but it's the journey you're taking inside a culture. Yes, Dad?"

"And you say it's a postmodern journey. Why don't you make those connections between postmodern theory and the idea of a journey more up front. You don't get into the theory in a normal academic way. And sometimes you don't even show that you know what you're saying connects with an ongoing debate. You don't put your credentials up front, son."

"Sorry, Dad, but for me, this cultural history of the '90s, which I began with *Hauntings* and *Speeding to the Millennium*, is just normal evolution from my work in theory in the '80s and books like *Mots d'Ordre* and *A Primer to Postmodernity* where I go at the theory directly and try to prep myself to use it. I'm putting the theory into play in *Journeys*. And with each volume I'm learning something which I try to employ in the next volume. Yes, the woman in the dark glasses who looks like my ex-wife."

"If I'm hearing you correctly, you're not trying to write a reliable history of the '90s and you don't have an original thesis that would enable you to break new ground or come up with something original. And you don't believe you're writing about stuff that is timeless but only stuff that will last as long as you or somebody else requires it to be read. So, can you give me a reason for spending good alimony money to buy your book?"

"That's a good question. I didn't write it for a promotion because I'm an adjunct and not eligible ever to be promoted and I didn't write it with the idea that it would make me rich because as I think of that idea now I think immediately of writing an entirely different book about my travels. I began to write about the '90s in America via headlines and popular film because I thought it was going to be an important *fin de siecle* . . ."

"Are you answering my question? You'll have to tell me because it doesn't sound like an answer. It sounds like you're ducking the question, which is what I would expect."

" And I think it has been—I mean the decade—has been important . . . but important in a frightening way, the way that the three witches tell Macbeth what is important. And I wanted to take a postmodern approach to this important decade which I thought would open up new writing possibilities for others. My writing is in the cracks . . ."

"Don't you think that's where it belongs?"

". . . between journalism and scholarly writing, autobiography and film review, sermon and revery, fact and fiction, logic and imagination. So I had you in mind when I wrote it. I want more people to fall through the cracks of our commercially defined world. Rabbi?"

"Your answers here are like your writing. Mazy. Sometimes your essays start at one point, fork off to another and then yet another until finally the reader begins to wonder if there's some point to trying to lose the reader? I mean, is this style intentional or what? Movies are not Kabbalah. They're just movies."

"I have a friend who's always interrupting me to ask 'what's your point?'"

"So—what is the point of this book?"

"Oh, hi, Captain Clabber. I didn't see you back there. The Captain's always telling me that I'm getting off the point. I'm straying. He's a lifetime bureaucrat and has put through some effective policy in his time. His ability to keep to the point without straying has time and again been helpful and profitable to me. He's focused and knows how and when to be. I, on the other hand, don't trust my focus. I wonder where it comes from."

"That's because your writing is godless, like the writing of all people who say they're postmodernists. God provides focus. You should know that at your age."

"I often know what the point is, Rabbi, but more telling, I often know what the counterpoint is, because I'm always looking for the counterpoint. In short, I stray in my exposition because I'm trying to wander, to err, move away from an obvious point to an inconceivable one. Should I try doing this? Can you do this without losing or confounding a reader, or making their reading difficult? The easiest form of communication is redundancy: You repeat what the reader is already lined up to grasp."

"If you didn't wander, you wouldn't be liable to repeat. If you keep on and go straight ahead, you avoid redundancy. Try it. And don't put out any more godless books in that SUNY Press Postmodern Culture series. As a favor to the next generation."

"Nothing goes straight ahead. Unless somebody stacks the deck. Otherwise it's all side trips. I don't want to take another spin around the block with no side trips allowed. Mr. Data?"

"If it is all side trips then why do you have chapters designated as side trips? I would like to know what logic you employed to separate the side trips from what I presume are trips down the right road?

"Well, the main road pieces stick to what came down the road headlinewise and filmwise. So they're instigated by outside, public events. The side trips come out of the mental journey I myself was on in those years. But the public pieces are crisscrossed with the private, and the private pieces are crisscrossed with the public. So the separation between the two is confounded. What journey I was on was totally wrapped up in what was going on around me. My private meditations, so to speak, were always inside the public menu. Which makes it impossible to claim one is more significant than the other. What's the logic behind extinguishing the personal and private and pretending one's observations are disinterested observations of a world 'out there'?"

"A positronic brain makes that possible. A fact you may wish to consider in the future."

"Thank you. Monica?!?"

"If you know in advance what you're getting at, can't you delete the maziness and cut to the chase? I mean, if you write from real desire wouldn't you want to build to a climax and not just peter off in a lot of different directions?"

"In the beginning I never know quite what I'm getting at. To go back after I complete a piece and find that one objective, or perhaps two or however many, and rewrite in order to make a beeline to that . . . why then, I would have to believe that the destination is all and the journey nothing. I take the reader on the same journey I've taken. Borges called it a "garden-of-forking-paths" journey, not a superhighway journey, not a journey down the Golden Road to the Truth. You follow a mazy path in that garden. It's a style I'm just now entering. The woman with a call waiting."

"I've been following this history of the '90s you're writing. I mean, just the titles. In one we're 'haunted' and in another we're 'speeding' and in this one we're on a 'journey.' And what's the title of the next one? There is a next one, right? To cover 1999? So how do they all connect? Or don't they?"

"It's a classic American screenplay: We rush out to the car hoping to take a long journey from a whole lot of haunting issues. We take off speeding down County Road 99. Our eyes are glued to the road, white-line fever, the rush of something frightening behind us, not sure how far we have to go or where we'll spend the night. Or even sure we want to get to journey's end. We've got to be some place by midnight on December 31st. Meanwhile we keep glancing at the rearview mirror of our minds and the past, full of all kinds of undecidables that won't fade, blinds the present like high beams from a cop car and wipes out the future."

"*It sounds like a dark call waiting.*"

"Thank you all for coming and I hope. . . . If you run into any-one who has enjoyed the book could you tell them to e-mail me at natoli@pilot.msu.edu?

"*I did, son.*"

"Thanks, Mom."

Walk On!

"And sedentary species," she said, "like sedentary genes, are terribly successful for a while, but in the end they are self-destructive."
> —Bruce Chatwin, *The Songlines*

I was forced to travel, to ward off the apparitions assembled in my brain.
> —Arthur Rimbaud, *Une Saison en enfer*

The journey thus pre-empts the need for hierarchies and shows of dominance. The "dictators" of the animal kingdom are those who live in an ambience of plenty. The anarchists, as always, are the "gentlemen of the road."
> —Proust, *Guermantes Way*

You know, in a lot of ways—none of them having to do with my bank account—I'm ripe for the postmodern journey. I mean I'm somehow situated emotionally to take one. The composition of my consciousness is such that the idea of a journey to places I've never been to before resonates beautifully, like a soprano voice from long ago singing "Ave Maria" in the church of my childhood, Regina Pacis. Even my unconscious mind has me traveling cheerfully through a Borgesian garden of forking paths. No, my unconscious does not project fears of flying, of traveling, of instability, of nomadic wandering. It is only when I don't travel that still waters breed a mental pestilence. When an "order of things" becomes more than the barest, faintest circumference of imagination but presumes to stand for the world "just as it is" and myself "just as I am," then I have dark dreams.

Unfortunately, we spend most of our lives at rest; call it grounded, call it centered; call it home base, call it the still point, the contemplative heart of your being from where, like the Buddha, you sit in the lotus position, eyes half closed, and integrate the fury, solitary at the very center of the garden to which all paths ultimately lead. A sweet image, a

1

sweet story, that, like all stories, has its own "otherness." There is the emaciated Buddha as well as the fat Buddha; the dark soul journeying as well as the sedentary soul in peace, the Buddha whose last words are "Walk on!" The Hindu dancing Shiva is never at rest, enacting in his dance somehow the endless fluidity of time, space, self, objects, others, laws and dreams, desire and science, mind and world.

We are thrown into a world that is always already in motion and whose always alreadyness we immediately inherit. The image of ourselves, then, as quietly sitting someplace, or centered for dominating viewing in Foucault's panopticon, taking in a world that is somehow "out there"—that image and the story it spins encourages what I call a "modernist" way of journeying. How do you journey toward another story—let's call it the postmodernist—of how the world and ourselves exist and we "correspond" with each other, another story of how we travel, if you will, from self to world? It seems to me that you cannot do so unless you first perceive that you have been thrown into, say, a modernist *story* of things and not into the world itself. We are now living at the crossroads of both kinds of awareness, although only the postmodern awareness allows us that awareness.

In this last decade of the second millennium, we have our so-called cultural wars, the semiotics of such proliferating each day. Perhaps it is all about traveling, about the journey, not only—as Rod Serling used to say at the beginning of every segment of *The Twilight Zone*—of time and space, but of mind. Again, the Buddha: "You cannot travel on the path before you have become that Path itself." Some are secure and content, for whatever reason, and want to journey little from that contentment and security, except perhaps to augment it. Others are unsatisfied with their present lot and continue to journey toward a goal that promises what is yet not theirs. Still others have no journey in mind but are on the road because one place is as good as another: There is for them no place to rest. Perhaps, like Rimbaud, they are not going *to* any place but merely fleeing *from* "apparitions assembled in the brain."

But I say I am suited to journey in a postmodern way and I am not in any of these categories. Where am I then? I am "adjunct": Quite literally my academic title is "Adjunct Lecturer." But is there an ontological connection here, one that connects me to postmodern journeying? I want to describe what I will call an "adjunct *Lebenswelt*" or lifeworld in which one's connection with the center is marginal, and with the social order, subordinate and temporary.

Firstly, we have to consider that the lifeworld becomes important only because a separation between world and self cannot be maintained; in other words, we drift into certain connections with self and world that shape or sculpt future interactions. The lifeworld is a product of being thrown into the world, the site of our "throwness," by which I mean it is an accidental, "at this time and in this place," interfacer of the "everyday" out of which we can concoct and even hook up with grand, transcending "everydayness" stories. Paradoxically, these grand stories tell us that we are not accompaniments to the "flux of the everyday" but can transcend that flux. We live in the myth that we can remove the lens of the *lebenswelt* from our gaze and encounter our being severed from where it has its being (its state of throwness). We live in the myth that we can apprehend from "the outside" world as it is severed from it being always already caught in its own everydayness.

This is not a "war" that can be brought to closure through either peace or extermination; this is a true paradox. Either we are inevitably questioning what we are and what the world is from within lifeworlds already complicit with the everydayness out of which our questions arise, *or* we have already separated ourselves from both the lifeworld and the world's everydayness and are asking questions and getting answers that bring both the flux of being and the worldly flux to a stop. Baldly put: We can either tell a story of being "inside" things or are able to get "outside" things.

As soon as you say something that pretends to be outside the contingencies of self and world, outside the force of the everyday, you can say that only those contingencies at that time and the everydayness you are in at that time engender such a story of detachment. But in the modern world, we have been striving strenuously to transcend the stories of "always already" worldly attachment. We have been placing our bets on "methods of detachment" that winnow "storymaking" from "reality." Being "thrown into" the modern world means that we are thrown into a world in which such stories of detachment flourish—and since the Enlightenment and the "rise of Science," they do. Such stories are employed to transcend the stories of no detachment, of "always already-ness," the stories of being inseparable from world and world accessible only in its perplexing, changeable "everydayness."

Let me put the paradox on a less abstract level, in fact, on an everyday level: In order to test my theory that we journey in a different way as postmodernists than as modernists, that the postmodern take on the encounter between identity and difference necessitates a whole new way of "studying other cultures and peoples," I proposed to do a series of "study abroad" programs, specifically rail and hostel tours of Europe. While I proposed that our journey include stays in several European countries, I announced that mastery of the different languages, histories, politics, arts, literatures, folkways, and so on was not claimed by me, nor was it a goal of the program, although I didn't set the program up to discourage interest in any of these. Here's my argument in one long sentence:

> If the world is configured differently in different states of "throw-
> ness," different latitudes and longitudes of mediation, within each
> of which we "make" the world differently by enouncing different
> stories about it, and we have neither an unimpeachable rod by
> which to measure the value of each nor a foundation of prior
> absolute and universal judgment upon which to stand, then no one's
> mastery can stand unimpeached and each of us is compelled to
> "walk on!" both geographically and ontologically.

Indeed, what I hoped to reach through these journeys was a perception of what comprises our being-in-the-world as humans as well as, through a continual clash of identity and difference, what is shackled or rejected by the particular circumstances of our own societal and cultural throwness. In short, the journey was toward making conceivable what previously had no existence in the mind of the traveler and thus toward extending the panorama of human awareness, imagination, empathy, sympathy, understanding. We were traveling along the hermeneutic circle of contrastive, differently situated, and contextualized cultural interpretations.

My intent here was countered by a series of questions. While I had answers to all of these questions, my answers emerged from a postmodern way of knowing the world and that way produced the reasoning that made my "answers" answers. The questions, on the other hand, emerged from a modernist way of knowing the world and that way produced the reasoning that asked the questions and could not at the same time find my answers to be reasonable, or "good" answers. I was inferring that "reason" came out of the lifeworld and did not exist outside it or prior to it, although stories of what is reasonable vary according to time and place. So we were back to the lifeworld, to the notion of everything being sculpted or worded or sounded from within a personal, social, and cultural framing of the world, including our entire "critical reasoning" enterprise.

If critical, discerning reason came out of the lifeworld and the lifeworld was in motion with a changeable everydayness, was a result of our throwness here and now and not there and then, then I could make a case which countered the Western Tradition of Rationality and Realism mindset which produced the questions. I could question the presence of a reason operating outside or independent of the lifeworld. I could not, however, at the same time summon that sort of reason in order to negate the validity of the questions themselves. In fact, these questions that I call "modernist" are a greater part of that everydayness we are in and out of which we construe scenarios of being-in-the-world than are my postmodernist answers.

I, as a postmodernist, am in a dilemma that the modernist is not in. I face a paradox that the modernist has no trouble resolving. My seeing where the reasoning behind the questioning comes from does not enable me to discount that reasoning; it is in fact a reasoning I too am thrown into, although I resist the way a supposedly detached reason "self-reasons" itself out of any such throwness. I want to trace the semiotics of this reasoning, trace it to its social and cultural lifeworlds, to the horizon of a certain time and place, but I can't sever it from this web of interconnections. What I can do is deny its foundationalism, its Kantian transcendent credentials, but not its operating force within an everydayness we experience in ways this transcendent reason has produced for us. In other words, when I reason, I reason this way too; I am, like you, if you are reading during my lifetime, thrown into a world in which we have sculpted reason in this way. But as this world is already shifting into another way of "making" itself—a postmodern way—I am also trying to "reason" in a postmodern way.

What is needed in the end is a jump from one paradigm to another, one social/cultural/personal lifeworld to another, one way of perceiving, knowing, and therefore producing the world to another. William Blake writes of such epistemological alterations that have ontological effects, of moving across paradigms, or what he calls "visionary modes," from one-fold to four-fold perceptions. I have no trouble with this; as a postmodernist I first want to know what "reality frame" someone is in, or some society, or how many reality frames does this culture now express, and so on. What reality am I dealing with here at this time and in this place? What are the special circumstances of "being" in this world at this time? Into what are we here thrown, and how does this produce a state of throwness which we mistake for stable being, for the ineluctable conditions of human nature and existence?

But only a person who already has made the jump perceives the necessity of making the jump, or, perceives where one is jumping to and from where. If you already believe that reason and all its foundational artefacts are transpersonal (it's the faculty by which humans communicate and get to know themselves and the world, although they possess it to varying degrees), and transcultural (it travels even to cultures "steeped in superstitions" and irrationalities), then it certainly is transparadigm (it works within whatever theoretical frame you construct). If you take Kuhn's original notion that paradigms are not merely discursive, theoretical frames but cognitive/perceptual/affective frames that societies and cultures adopt at various times and then proceed to reality make and reality test within the parameters of those frames, and that, further, paradigms can follow each other in time but remain incommensurable, then the idea of a special faculty lying outside the influence of the paradigm becomes very moot.

One asks if such a free-floating faculty existed would not its thread, however faint, link paradigms, insure the commensurable within the seemingly incommensurable? And surely the thread is there—in the eyes of the modernist. At any point in time, one can go back and discern, with the necessary critical eye, the thread of continuity, of coherence, of unity. Whatever reason may be or has been, a postmodern would observe, it must in the present lay claim to its reasonableness by tracing its path in the past and from the past to the present. It must show itself working toward progress, however slowly, and overcoming obstacles to that progress. But what is the nature of this progress? We are becoming more reasonable, more civilized, more adept at controlling the irrationalities of Nature outdoors and Human Nature within. We are succeeding to do so through the steady implementation and instrumentation of our logics, our knowledge, our expertise, our technology, our science. In this way every reason in every state of historical "throwness" validates itself and renders, as Nietzsche says, an alibi by which it can perpetrate what in another more reasonable climate will stand forth as heinous, inhuman, irrational.

But the force of the paradox persists: If reason prevails in every state of throwness by securing its own reasonableness and tracing itself as a supracultural, supraparadigm faculty—otherwise it is replaced by a reasoning that can do so—then we are never free of an everydayness in which reason propounds the unreasonableness of paradigm-relative reasoning, of reason emerging from a lifeworld in motion. Thus, only the postmodernist will make the jump to another frame of reasoning, the modernist staying behind in order to critique and question the journey the postmodernist has undertaken.

The modernist also has a story of journeying, so in the present we wind up with conflicting stories of how we journey, which in turn tell different stories regarding the necessity of journeying, the effects of journeying on individuals, societies, and cultures, the stories we tell of past journeys—that is, our histories—and the journey into the future that we chart for ourselves, i.e. our notions of progress. But how do you choose what journey to take? I mean how do you take the postmodern journey—the journey that validates itself by saying that since we live in stories of reality we are bound to journey out of the limitations of our own stories by journeying into other stories—if you have no reason to do so? This story only becomes conceivable if we are already in a postmodern way of "story making" or "reality making." Or, what I think is more the case, we have already been shifting along with our American culture from one way of story making to another. We have, in short, already been thrown into the journey.

At some point, I, in the modernist paradigm, had no sayable reason to prompt me to recognize another way of journeying, yet clearly I had already been on such a journey. At some point I began to contemporaneously make the map that produced the journey and take the journey that made the map conceivable to me. I say "at some point" but I can't locate the point in time or space. I've already said I'm perfectly suited to make the journey, which means I was suited for the jump that had to be made first. But how am I suited? Let's fork back to the *Lebenswelt* because the answer is there—although it's an answer, once again, relative to a frame of real-izing. The journey, you might say, is from lifeworlds toward lifeworlds, yours to theirs, a society's to more of a culture's, one culture's myriad lifeworlds toward another culture's myriad lifeworlds. The lifeworld at the beginning and the lifeworld that the journey hopes to affect.

The lifeworld at the beginning and the lifeworld that the journey hopes to affect:

This "adjunct" lifeworld which I lay claim to intersects Victor Turner's sense of the "liminal," the postcolonial sense of "subaltern," the ethnic/racial/gender view of the "marginalized," the necessity of always being on the "border" between worlds advocated by Henry Giroux, and the Deleuzian view of the "nomad." The images are all of space: I am at the threshold of one reality peering into another; or, I am standing someplace below waiting to be recognized by the major players; or, I am on the periphery, at the border waiting to be granted access to the center; or, I am wandering in the vast empty spaces of a desert, the fires of civilization always in the distance.

But in my mind I'm not in any one place; I don't occupy space, only time. If I had a spatial sense of myself, of where I was positioned, of where others were positioned, where the things of the world were, I would be leading a sedentary mental life; I could only journey in the spatial configuration in which I already lived. You don't really take journeys within sedentary lifeworlds; you merely convert a new space into the blueprint of space you impose upon it. Syed Islam refers to the sedentary nature of Robinson Crusoe who shapes the alien island into an English "space" and thus translates a possible disrupting otherness into a comfortable English identity.[1] From the Enlightenment onward we have been very concerned about where the observer is positioned in space and have stood by the belief that that observer is distanced from the objects or subject he or she is observing, as well as aloof from the "variables" operating upon those objects or subjects. With enough distance we can observe without being observed, observe without being pulled into the field of observation, observe without fear of interaction which muddies the space of observing. When space outside the discrete space we ourselves occupy can be defined, then things in space can exist independent of us, are there to be measured and mapped and the whole world can exist as places already defined and circumscribed to which we can journey.

But this sedentary sense of travel and of space never leads to a journey in the way the nomad can journey. What is the nomadic, or postmodern, post-Enlightenment sense of space? Time. Time is already a factor in the sedentary, Enlightened sense of space: For instance, space has to be reified in this view, given shape, measurable proportions, so that we can apprehend and measure our distance from the world. But we need that distance because we need the time it takes to go from here to there in order to distance ourselves emotionally, subjectively. We become disinterested and therefore neutral observers of the world because distance gives us the time to put off our first impressions, our "in your face" volatility, our prereflective responses, the immediacies of look, tone, gesture. But time, in the postmodern view, does more than make spacing or distancing possible: It fills space with the stories that fill time, that make up time, that give us our sense of time passing—fast, slow, or not at all. Time moves in stories and stories configure space.

At any particular time the world will appear to us within the lineaments of that moment, or have the physiognomy of that time. Without the imposition of some story out of our own past, present, or future— which also of course intersects the stories of our cultural and social past—upon the world "out there"—the world mediated within some symbolic, narrative configuration of it—we cannot mark our place in the world and if we cannot do that we cannot mark where the world is.

Where is the empty space and the space for objects and ourselves if not first adumbrated in the way we occupy or dwell in the world at a particular time? In other words, we are in the world in a particular way shaped by a particular time, so that traveling in space is nothing more than travel between different temporal configurations of world, differing reality frames. And, since we are always already "thrown" into space configured within one or many timescapes and cannot step outside in order to see space, time, self, and world in their "essential" identities, we cannot justifiably map the terrain of any one privileged configuration, or maintain the transtemporal value of our own point of observation, or insist upon the virtues of journeying for the purpose of transforming "terra incognita" into the coordinates of our own privileged temporal mappings.

It is not possible for humans to consider space without temporalizing that space, without putting everything, including the notion of empty space, into place. Neither is it possible for us in the present to clone the configurations of past space, although it is very possible for some, including whole societies, to re-present in line with the perceptual frame of the present, past physiognomies of space or even future ones. Such correspondences may or may not be noted in the present. I think we can have little idea of when and how we are occupying space and measuring time in "old ways."

You can, however, conceptualize differences. You can contrast, say, a medieval, pre-Reformation sense of space with an Enlightenment one: Catholic dogma and ritual mystifies the space of the physical body, putting it into a subordinate relationship with an inner-dwelling soul that occupies no space, while Reason demystifies the spatial order of the Great Chain of Being, brings out weight and measure and finds laws of interaction between objects and planets. Wordsworth attempts to reconfigure all of Nature in terms of time, investing in Nature the epiphanies of past moments, reinvesting those past moments, "spots of time," in a world of objects that needs emotional redemption. Zola, following Claude Bernard, seeks the opposite, hoping to "detemporalize" and thus "destorify" or "deimagine" the worlds of his characters in order to chart the underlying laws which propel and compel their lives, the forces operating between objects which gives us this or that picture of "social life." Gingrich's *Contract with America* is no less than a set of coordinates by which to get the right spatial mapping of America at this time. The space the underclass and impoverished previously occupied within the timescape of Lyndon Johnson's Great Society—the poor stood like a challenge on the road to the American Dream and the whole society positioned itself to face the challenge—is now, in Gingrich's timescape, no longer real space but only mistaken space, correctable space, trivial space, vanishing space. The underclass no longer occupy space as real entities, but are now the remnants of a discarded matrix. Angels were so real in the Middle Ages their presence on a pin was not challenged, only the number of them was moot. The contemporary world provides no space for angels; we cannot dredge up stories about them to bring them to conceivability, to give them place and space. The underclass is going the same route, storyless in the present, the times make no place for them.

What has no identity and no place within one timescape, or narrative blend of time and space, may very well have identity and place within another. Thus, the necessity of making the journey from here to there, from one mapping of the real to another. But I have been suggesting that only when identity is viewed as a construct of throwness, of being-in-the-world within a certain array of timescape narratives, do we have the incentive to give up the sedentary sense of the journey—rediscovering the blessings of solid identity fixed securely in a true mapping of space—and become nomadic. And neither empirical nor rational methodologies, nor impeccable logics, can take us from the sedentary to the nomadic. But the nomadic constructs a lifeworld and is in turn constructed by a lifeworld. In a way, the postmodern, nomadic sense of journeying already abides in me because I am thrown into a world within which it already abides. In another way, American culture seems to me to be playing out its culture wars within the modern/postmodern paradox because I seem able only to tell that story and see that drama.

You can get at the intermix from either side: from either the cultural lifeworld or my own. But as the intermix or entanglement of myself and the culture is not available for "bracketing" or "surgical removal," we are never on one side without being on the other side at the same time. And in terms of the journey, we are never quiet, inputting observers traveling into the world "out there," but traveling already within a mental space, a geography of mind, a mental timescape, and into other and different narrative arrangements which penetrate us, bushwhacking us before we're ready. The "right" journey throws us into a clash from which we, as we were, never return. At the same moment, that is precisely the journey, from where we are now, that we would say is the "wrong" journey. In the present moment, we are either in a lifeworld that knows how to preserve its stability by avoiding clash, or we are desperately trying to shape a lifeworld that knows how to avoid clash.

The nature of the lifeworld is to promise the sedentary in a nomadic world, to fix the coordinates of time and space and mark our location at every point and moment. Through the lens of the lifeworld, which is always believed to be a crystal clear lens, we can take the proper measure of the world. This is a story we have been living in that we are not journeying out of but nonetheless we are journeying toward another and different story, the one I am telling here. If you want to take the measure of the world and yourself within it, you first have to get some sense of how the world is refracted through your own lifeworld, a mesh of personal, social, and cultural narratives, or timescapes. You have to, in short, take the measure of the lifeworld.

So how do you measure the lifeworld that is yours at journey's beginning? If we're talking about the "Big" journey—life to death—then you have to delve into personal, social, and cultural histories. Depth psychology has made much of the "personal" that we cannot recollect but yet lies buried in levels of the unconscious. Immediately the notion of a "collective unconscious" takes us into a cultural memory, a reservoir of inherited human archetypes that call us in various ways to reconnect with the shared stories of humankind. Whether one buys into this notion or not, the fact remains that this entanglement of the personal with the cultural marks a difficulty in separating the two that we cannot resolve. We can likewise hopelessly entangle the biological/genetic with the cultural, as do those biologists presenting the theory of self-organization or autopoiesis. Here is Francis Varela on the imbrication of social practices and biological structure:

> [O]ur human life, our experience right now, is but one of the many possible creods of knowledge, where the immense background of our biological structure [our internal coherences] and social practices [a creod resulting from a history of "natural drift"] is inseparable from the regularity we discern in both world and self.[2]

So we map our biological geography, if you will, culturally; or, in a different phrasing, our biological structure and our social/cultural world interactively shape each other so that our biological organization finds a commensurable, discernible organization in "both self and world." That compact Varela refers to as a "creod," which is not an absolute and universal "unified field theory" or some such thing, but "one of the many possible" configurations of human experience and biological adaptation. You might say that our own human biology comes out of the cultural lifeworld, which itself comes out of human biology, a situation that cannot be observed from any "external point of reference" as well as one that establishes ongoing dynamic and flux rather than stability and underlying order as the "rules of the game."

Let's move from the journey of the species back to the lifeworld that is yours at any point in your own journey. If we restrict our grasp of our personal history to what we recall, we may find that from the differing perspectives of differing times in our lives, what we recall and how we recall it may differ. The recollections of any present moment, however, may assert their own objectivity, their own truthfulness, accuracy, and reliability. Conflicting memories may be resolved by a present-based scrutiny of the past. Why? It's clear that we as humans don't tolerate confused and conflicting scenarios of ourselves and our past. We work hard to impose a veneer of understanding, of connectedness, of causality, a sequence of self-determining events. And if we can't do this, we need some outside help: Prozac, support group, the psychic hotline, meditation, TaeBo, spiritual healing, green tea, more soy in our diet, and so on.

Memories are subject to the predilections of the present; the present stands like the gatekeeper at Oz making sure that what is admitted into consciousness conforms to the order of the lifeworld presently in residence. Other people and their narratives, or what Niklas Luhmann calls "second order" observing, may problematize our own reading of our own past. On the level of the social order, you can say that the Third Reich, for instance, desperately needed to heed other observations from other social orders in regard to Germany's own memory of its own past. The future was at stake. More recently, White South Africa's memory of its own apartheid was finally effectively countered by other memories from all over the world. Perhaps this is the first and most crucial journey: the journey into countermemories, the narratives of your identity told by others. The caveat here of course is that the representation of others to themselves is itself the sort of tyrannical imposition that the Third Reich, for instance, imposed on Jews, gypsies, anarchists, and homosexuals.

To mark the sort of hand-in-glove relationship between the personal and cultural/social, Freud suggested that only the traumatized had memorable childhoods; everyone else's childhood sort of fell into an amorphous, public memory, one co-opted by the media, public schools, and church or temple. Nothing stands out on the horizon of the average, normal childhood; it's all a wash, a tabula rasa open to other hands. The other hands emerge from the social order, or the culture, the former emerging from the latter. But the traumatized assert their own "order of things," their own immoveable memories upon the social/cultural. There's a sort of ratio of imposition here: The more intense the trauma, the more the personal will elide the social/cultural. And if the trauma is frightening enough, time will stop for the traumatized and the lifeworld will not move. No journey can be taken. The present moment, no matter how different from one's past, can never overwrite the early trauma. The seductions of Madison Avenue go unattended; the Baltimore catechism shapes no moral conscience; public education teaches no civics, provides no socializing influence; family life goes on in the shadow of trauma.

The traumatized are thrown into the world of the trauma; everything connects to it; everything means and is valued in terms of it. For the untraumatized, meanings and values connect almost immediately to the social order and to various depths of the cultural turmoil. I attained a sense of the social order through my family, but at the same time I developed some sense of what a family *is* through watching "family" TV of my childhood: "Ozzie and Harriet," "Father Knows Best," "Leave It to Beaver," and "The Life of Riley." I went every Saturday to the Fortway and saw movies that revealed lifeworlds I adopted, movies like *Rebel without a Cause, The Blackboard Jungle, Knock on Any Door*. I was at the same time brought up with a Sicilian sense of family, as both my mother and father had been brought up by Sicilian immigrants. Since American culture is culturally heterogeneous, my Sicilian narrative of family was present in the culture but not privileged. In other words, there were other narratives of family out there. But I had to journey outside Bensonhurst, Brooklyn, which did in fact privilege a *mezzo giorno* culture. Chance has mostly propelled me over the years to other parts of the country and therefore into other cultural "hoods." And I've watched other TV shows and movies about family life, much influenced by David Lynch's "Twin Peaks" and *Blue Velvet*.

I don't want to diminish the influence of books I've read, conversations I've had, lectures I've attended, and experiences I've had—from traveling, to subsistence farming, to landscaping, cleaning and laying carpet, selling, buying, editing and writing books, teaching, throwing mail, working for the now defunct Department of Health, Education and Welfare, cooking, and just being unemployed. I still believe that the best journeys to be made into the fullest display of human lifeworlds are the journeys we make into art, from fiction and poetry to film and music. Theory, or discursive writing, gives one a sense of how to make sense or order of the lifeworld but it does not fill the lifeworld. And while our theorizing always pretends to transcend the present social and cultural frames, it is tied to them. However, the effort to transcend, universalize, generalize, normalize, and absolutize obscures the connection. The lifeworld is more composed within and affected by the everydayness of concrete particularized life shown on TV and radio talk shows, MTV, and popular film than by a National Book Award or Pulitzer Prize winner.

Should this be the case? Or, is this the case because public education and the family have failed in America and a sex and violence saturated media have taken over? The root problem here is a clash between a social order and a cultural furor. If we, for instance, could establish a social order in which preferred moral, societal, family, and economic values could be upheld and imposed and at the same time diminish the cultural dissent to those values, or at least put some sort of lid on them, then we could establish a predictable, calculable, and alterable connection between individual lifeworlds and society. If for instance the Soviets had been able to impose a Marxist order of things across Soviet society, then any individual lifeworld—with the exception once again of the traumatized—would be shaped within that order. The lens through which each citizen would see the world, find meaning, and determine value would be prefabricated. As it turned out, that Marxist order of things was eroded at the theory stage and the Soviets, from the very beginning, sought to impose various ad hoc arrangements, until the economics of fantasy gave way to the economics in play.

While a social order always wants to carve out certain preferred parts of the cultural mélange, that riot of cultural narratives yet remains, here and there, at one time or another, more or less available for lifeworld connection. The journey from modernity to postmodernity, a journey in which displacement replaces hierarchy, has proliferated the number of dissenting cultural narratives, expanded the geography of clash, and riddled the present with "culture wars" that have provoked a pressing need to reassert the social order of things. Of course, only one side feels that pressing need, while the other, the postmodernists, want to augment the number of cultural narratives and thus augment the maziness of the world through which we journey so that lifeworlds can never rest in their sedentary complacency.

Notes

1. Syed Mansurul Islam, *The Ethics of Travel*. Manchester University Press, 1996, 2–3.
2. Francisco Varela, "Living Ways of Sense-Making: A Middle Path," in *Disorder and Order*, ed. Paisley Livingston (Saratoga, Calif.: Anma Libri, 1984), 221.

Side Trip: Why Do Anything?

"Why do anything?" Brad asks when some of the group, including me, asks him why he would want to jump out of a plane with a bungi cord tied to his ankles.

Later on I am saying yes to Fred when he asks me if I will go funyaking with him. We go into white water with a small two-person kayak. I say yes because I think Brad's question is resounding in my head. Why do anything? Because you want to do it and because the Goddess Fortuna allows you to do it. But why do I want to do anything? Take away young Billy Clinton's ambition to be president and you just might have a catatonic. On the opposite end, Melville's Bartleby has lost the desire to do anything. Why do anything? he has asked himself. Desire. But he has no desire. He would prefer to follow through on his desirelessness. Desire masks a foundational absence of purpose and meaning. We want a big house and a big car and a big job, big success and widespread acclaim, and the quest fills our lives. One filler is as good as another, Brad seems to be saying. We are spinning the fabric of our days out of the loom of arbitrary whim and desire.

Desire is behind necessity, else there is no necessity to necessity. It is necessary to eat but both bulimia and anorexia are pathological desires that confound this necessity. Insomnia confounds sleep; hyperventilation confounds breathing; alcoholism confounds drinking. Is there a necessity to going to work? To raising a family? To paying your bills? To obeying the law? To investing for the future? To wearing a condom? To getting a degree? To bearing children? To saying no to drugs? If there is, it's a necessity that's been ignored countless times by countless millions.

Is the desire to bungi jump a crazier desire than, say, the desire to major in accounting because there are always good paying jobs for accountants? I say yes right off the bat but then I think perhaps after a lifetime of being an accountant, the retired accountant goes bungi jumping. Why? Desire. In this case, a desire it would take a novelist to describe thoroughly. But you can imagine. There is a greater possibility of having a truly up-scale life with a blossoming investment portfolio if one pursues certain occupations rather than others. Computer science, engineering, medicine, banking, finance, marketing, waste management, psychopharmacology, investment analysis, packaging, stock brokering, and corporate law, among others, are not desired occupations in themselves but for the money they earn. It may be that our global-market society has nurtured ten year olds who, when asked what they want to be when they grow up, chirp "I want to be a Wall Street broker" or "I want to do knee surgery at ten thousand dollars per operation and do six per day." The desire to be a certified public accountant and go over scores of numbers day after day is surely not a desire for the activity itself but for the money that activity brings.

And at the moment of our last breath was a desire to bungi jump or go canyoning or funyaking or hang gliding or mountain climbing a more senseless desire than to spend a lifetime doing what paid well in a particular society at a particular time? Maybe the successful arbitrager used his or her money to ski the Alps, or climb Everest, or—bungi jump. Some say money allows desire to be fulfilled. The view is that without money, desires are fruitless. But if money paves the road to desire, it is a road filled with perils because money is a cultural fantasy that replaces human desire with the best-laid plans of Madison Avenue advertising firms. Money doesn't allow desire; it replaces it.

In the end, there is no reason to do anything and the main task facing any society is how to commit itself and its citizenry to anything. Money has filled our days and our lives; it engages our day-to-day attentiveness; it gives us something to do. It gives us a purpose at daybreak and something to think about at day's end. Why do anything? I do it for the money. We do it for the money. In the absence of real human desire, which is fast disappearing from the face of the earth, we do anything for the money.

When we travel we are constantly being amazed at what folks in the distant past accomplished. We look up at the Sistine Chapel and cannot conceive how any one person could execute what we see. We are awed by the Roman ruins that perforate modern Rome; we marvel at the work that went into medieval tapestries; the scope of the Doge's palace in Venice, the marvel of the Eiffel Tower, the perfection of Venetian glass, the brilliance of the Monreale church, the architectural majesty of St. Paul's, St. Peter's, the palace at Versailles, the Duomo in Florence. We marvel at so much desire for beauty, for devotion, for truth, for honor, for love, for knowing, for creating—finally for what our own globalized desire for money has almost made inconceivable to us. Why did they do what they did? We know the answer to Brad's question, Why do anything? But what strange desires prompted our ancestors to do what they did? From a global-market point of view, much that was done in the past was merely an inefficient means to profit. Michelangelo supplied more quality in his product than the market could bear; medieval monks overelaborated their duplication processing; Mozart oversupplied; the Alhambra needs to be wired; Chaplin's films colorized. And so on.

We are fast traveling toward a moment when we won't know why we should do anything and won't be able to imagine why those who devoted their lives to doing something ever did what they did.

Side Trip

The U.S. Open?

We are fast traveling toward a moment when we won't know why we should do anything and won't be able to imagine why those who devoted their lives to doing something ever did what they did.

In the film *Tin Cup*, off-the-beaten-path golf range pro, Kevin Costner, explains to Rene Russo, his psychologist for the "mental game," that anyone is eligible to play in the U.S. Open—garbage man or billionaire. It's the epitome of democracy, a world of competitiveness open to all. Thus, a microcosm of global free market play within which we all have equal opportunity to play. Costner, the "Tin Cup" of the title, gets a chance to play, to compete, an unknown from a tiny unknown town in Texas, Salome, that the TV announcer pronounces as "salami." The question is can anyone in the audience repeat Cup's play? Can you get from "salami" Texas to a real chance at millions, your moment of fame on national television? And as you sit there in the theater, wanting what Cup wants—the TV fame, the millions, the beautiful Rene Russo—you keep hearing the voice of the TV production manager, a well-tanned, grey-haired guy with a voice of authority, a man annoyed at how things are going, who keeps saying "Heroes are what I need, not golf pros from nowhere." So how open is our own "open" democracy? Who can make the journey from Nowhere to televised heroism?

But the journey here is not that simple: Behind it all really is a "mental game," a mental journey, that's not a market-based journey to success. Is it Cup's journey alone? His own aberrant "mental game" that we can't identify with? That seems strange and incomprehensible to us? Why not "lay up," follow the clear logic of "winning"? Why detour down a path barely recognizable to most Americans positioned here at the end of the millennium? We get all sorts of hints of this strange kind of journey: Cup announces that he is in pursuit of his own self-defined mythic destiny, that the real contest here is between Cup's devotion to the game and the U.S. Open as a gateway to fame and fortune. Though "par is

18

good enough" to win in the public view, in Cup's view "greatness courts failure." In his mind, the millions at the end of the journey are not as important as the journey itself. This last becomes clear as Cup tries over and over again to "knock" it over a small pond of water that lies between him and the hole. He has a good chance of winning the Open if he "lays up," if he plays safe. But this is his quest, his "defining moment," and he follows his "inner demons" here and plays not conservatively but passionately, recklessly: He plays to meet his own inner challenge, to win in the way he wants to win; their millions and fame against his own sense of personal fulfillment.

He has all along been in the Open but on a different quest, and—to follow through on our market microcosm—he has been a player playing at a different game. When he listens to his brain, it tells him all about the logic of winning as it is defined in American culture at this moment; when he listens to his heart, trusts his feelings, forgets about the percentages, pursues his mythic destiny, follows his own desire, and so on, he courts failure in market terms but aims for greatness. There is a pride of self, of fulfilling an inner sense of destiny and achievement, a private quest, that counters money and fame. Is this a desire shared by others sitting in the audience? Is American culture at this moment about to break free of the hold of the impeccable logic of winning as written by the global market?

I don't know how far down the road we can go with this. After all, Cup puts aside one form of "self-interest" as globally defined for another personally defined. Cup sees himself taking chances, doing the heroic thing, not settling for "safe" play, which he fears will turn him into a "soul-less robot." He is vastly interested in the self, in a personal sense of fulfillment, although he doesn't subscribe to the current fashion in regard to what winning and success are. But he subscribes to an older American vision: the rugged individual not hampered by European values and traditions but going off and breaking a new trail. Cup is Emersonian self-reliant, Whitmanesquely a "man of the road," Thoreauvianly marching to his own drummer. We first find him with his cronies knocking out golf balls, drinking with the "guys," with the pack, of which he is the negligent, nonchalant force at the center. On one hand, there are all sorts of signals that this is a real community, a good fellowship of souls. On the other hand, this is not a community; his personal quest has nothing to do with others. He doesn't consider the impact of his actions on others. We have not really moved from self-interest to interest in others, from a Wilhelm Meister apprenticeship to travels toward and into otherness. All we've really done is exchange a global-market determination of how self-interest is pursued for a personal, idiosyncratic one.

Cup is the kind of rugged individualist who elicits the admiration of some men and women, the envy of some, and the bafflement of others. But he plays a lone hand, without considering the impact of his actions on others. Paradoxically, the film seldom shows him without his friends. Could it be that America in the midst of its competitive individualism is once again yearning for the utopian fellowship of community? He has a sidekick, Cheech Marin, who is loyal, who wants to see Cup achieve what his talent promises. But Cup quickly dismisses Cheech's concern and advice in pursuit of his own "inner demons." Those demons have no connection to market values but they also have no connection to other people. Cup, therefore, is not rising above self-interest and reaching toward "common dreams and hopes." Indeed, if you continue to follow him down his path of self-interest, you will wind up intersecting the same sort of self-interest that propels the market.

All personal mythic destinies detached from the shared destinies of the human race augment personal bank accounts, literal or figurative. Bill Gates, Rupert Murdoch, Ted Turner, Michael Milken, Warren Buffett, Ross Perot, among numerous others, are all fulfilling self-defined "mythic destinies" that have them journeying down solitary paths, the effects of what they do and accomplish somehow extending to others, but the precise logistics of that an insignificant matter, not to burden the solitary quest. The narrative of American rugged individualism, of eccentric yet noble quests, of standing firm in your isolation by Walden Pond, or cutting trails across the wilderness in an independent spirit, is the very stuff of global-market social Darwinism. The intrepid competitor in the global arena, unfettered by governmental restraints and "entitlement" taxation, is the new rugged frontier hero, the adventuresome mountain man, facing all challenges and obstacles, but persevering, and winning in the end. The "winning" here is strictly defined and not the idiosyncratic mystification that it is in Cup's case. He's fulfilling a personal sense of victory, of winning, that others find difficult to grasp. So while Cup is a free-floating agent wandering down strange paths toward self-fulfillment, our global entrepreneurs are venturesome within well-known rules of the game. Everybody here knows what winning is. Everyone knows when to "lay up," play the percentages, maximize one's chances of winning, and so on. Except Cup. He seems to come off in this film as a brand new kind of player.

Is he? Cup's actions replay the theme of rugged individualism which seems at first to be a refreshing resurrection of personal values in the face of global-market values, of self-generated rather than market-generated desire—until we realize that the Montana Freemen and the Arizona Vipers and the Unabomber are awaiting us down that road. In this

last decade of the century, of the millennium, there is a fitful expression
of a desire to break free of *something* constraining, some sinister, widespread web of control which threatens our individual freedom—is it the
federal government? Is it some United Nations cabal? Is it growing
"Pacific Rim" economic hegemony? Is it some lethal remnant of Liberalism? Is it a dehumanizing technology? Is it the media? Is it the legacy
of liberal Supreme Court decisions? Is it the "de-Christianizing" of
America engineered by secular, public education? Is it the gangsterism of
unions? Is it the weight of foreign immigrants on our national resources?
Whatever it is that threatens individual, personal freedom and choice, it
is organized, structured, cabalistic, having to do with the social and not
the individual, with the aggregate, with commonalities and solidarities,
with joint, cooperative unions, with bureaucracies, laws, protocols, regulations, licensing, limits, and so on. So Cup strikes the right tone even
though what game he's really playing and why his choices seem so odd
to us continue to mystify us.

Well, here you have an entire society finally feeling the effects of
"global-market logic" in the form of a widening gap between Haves and
Have Nots, and they are beginning to look around to see who's causing
the bleeding in their own lives. Some are already blindly striking out at
the supposed offenders cited in the previous litany of threats. The individual is being slowly but aggressively disenfranchised: economically
and therefore politically, socially, culturally. Everything here is translated
into the story of rugged American individualism fighting it out with
some "communizing, mind-controlling" menace. In terms of this
uniquely American narrative, what needs to be done is to stand up for
individual freedom, to get all the collective efforts at eroding that freedom off our backs, to stop at every point the politics of control and
domination, most likely centered in Washington D.C., or maybe in New
York with the United Nations, or in Brussels with the European Union,
or in Baghdad with Sadam Hussein.

Except for a very brief moment when Pat Robertson in the 1996
presidential campaign went after the Fortune 500 as the possible villains
in the piece, as the force behind a "profits-not-people" mission that had
indeed succeeded in putting the majority of the American population in
a state of diminishing status and possession, the market entrepreneurs
have never been marked as a threat to individual freedom. The discourse
of market free play, of heroic entrepreneurs competing with foreigners
to reap rewards for all Americans, of angry, tough, practical, and
shrewd businessmen battling with federal bureaucrats and regulators to
preserve "free choice" for us all—this discourse permeates the culture
and makes it impossible for Americans to find the source of their bleed-

ing in the headquarters of the transnationals. These remain the bastions of individual free choice, of the individual and not the commune, of democracy in action and not some form of socialism. So these intrepid entrepreneurs are as opposed in their hearts and minds to social, governmental, and personal restraints as is Cup. Hell, entrepreneurs have the same sort of frontier spirit, of cutting trails into new and unknown territory as Cup himself exhibits. He does it his way, unregulated, unfettered, willing to take chances, not a follower but a creative force for change. And so on.

Transnational power, however, does not accrue because loose organizations of loose canons, that is, Cup-type employees, are in a steady state of breaking all the rules and following their own "visionary quests" with some inconceivable, yet very personal, goal in mind. The maximization of profits to share holders is not a nebulous quest and neither does transnational power come from a global network of individuals all pulling in different directions, each and every person deciding for themselves when to "knock it on" and when to "lay up." The corporate critique of the federal mindless and inefficient bureaucracy is actually a critique emerging from another highly organized and structured locus: the corporate organization. The federal bureaucracy is only "mindless" to another form of equally elaborate organization which is only "single-minded," by which I mean that the EPA, for example, wants to mind the environment and not profits, and therefore its actions, its *raison d'etre*, seems "mindless" to the corporate organization. In the same fashion, governmental efficiency is not calibrated within only one set of criteria—have profits been maximized?—but rather may involve numerous goals all demanding a different set of criteria of evaluation in order to determine "efficiency." The post office, for example, is often criticized as inefficient, but the private sector cannot make it more efficient without limiting the goal of personal daily delivery of mail, including so-called junk mail—to each household. Other governmental agencies and departments have no purpose in the world of profit and therefore would be annihilated if profit were made the only organizational goal. And some governmental ventures—like education—tax corporations for benefits they can now get globally for nothing, that is, employees educated elsewhere.

Nevertheless, transnational corporate organization has the reputation—call it a positive semiotics—of championing individual freedom when in point of fact it is quickly reducing the majority of Americans's choices by placing them on an "economic" reject and discard pile. If you defined freedom as the proliferation of choices you can afford to make at your local merchandiser then about 1 percent of the popular are enjoying individual freedom and the rest are seeing it vanish. Of course, that is a notion of freedom promulgated by corporate values. At the same time, economic diminishment ultimately affects the quality of every aspect of human existence. Ultimately even Cup's "mythic destiny" and "personal quest" can be sidetracked by the market's dispensations, although the Hollywood side of this film displays honesty, comraderie, integrity, and just plain fun in being down and out, barely getting by, living in a world of debt. I mean that no matter how enchantingly mystical, high romantic, visionary, and just plain Thoreaulike Cup's quest and vision may be, they're bendable to the point of breaking, or turning sour, angry and bitter, dazed and confused, marginalized and silenced. Genuine eccentricity awaits Cup, a misunderstood oddball and loser playing his own style of golf in a world that rewards another style of golf.

What I perceive is that Cup needs his friends, other people, solidarity, connection, common dreams shared and pursued, concern, sympathy, empathy, a breaking free of the individually concocted quest to meet the needs and desires of others. Competition and winning is not everything; Cup shows us this but the mystique of one man as an island standing alone pursuing a personal quest overwhelms the mystique of community, of no man or woman standing alone. The inadequacy and nebulousness of these community goals are not simply Cup's; they are shared at this moment by most Americans. In an antisocialist climate, a fear of the collective, as well as a sense of victory over common dreams, the notion of displacing individual quests for the common, collective good is hopelessly ensnared in a "negative semiotics." The admired form of organizing others for a common purpose is the transnational corporation and it's purpose has nothing to do with the "common good" and all to do with the gradual stockpiling of wealth—in a sort of *Monopoly* game fashion—by a minuscule proportion of the global population. The insidiousness of this is obscured by a rhetoric of entrepreneurial heroes challenging the restraints upon individual freedom imposed by governmental regimes, by all-out governmental efforts to brainwash the individual into blind submission to the will of the group.

The journey the rugged individualist makes therefore may follow several paths and adhere to variations on the theme: We have the Montana Freeman variety wanting to knock "the government off our backs"; we have the market entrepreneur full of good old Emersonian self-reliance competing boldly in the global arena; we have the romanticized *Tin Cup* quixotic, Cyrano type whose image comes straight out of fiction and Hollywood and who seizes the "defining moment" to fulfill a "mythic destiny"; and then we have a vast number seduced by some narrative of individual freedom daily threatened by all the usual suspects—suspects, I might add, rounded up by market strategists intent on replacing notions of egalitarianism and social justice with the notion of individual freedom and choice. Unless the one displaces the other, the view down the road is clear: Political equality can only be *said* to exist in a society in which most of the wealth and therefore power is in the hands of a very few.

Economic dispensations therefore must be scrutinized closely. Is our preferred economic system delivering its rewards and its damages not only in a fair manner but *not* in an arbitrary manner? Do certain planned and calculated actions—say, four years at a university majoring in such and such—produce in some reliable way a fixed effect, an anticipated result? This is of vital importance since the entire fabric of democracy is grounding itself on the premise that a field of equal opportunity—that is, no inherited hierarchies or resident oligarchies or privileged participants—cannot be eroded by gross economic inequality. A democracy, therefore, must be vitally interested in the way wealth is garnered, distributed, consolidated, and employed to gather even more wealth. Global-market "logic," unfortunately, cannot free itself of contingency, of the mere play of chance, of its vulnerability to all manner of irrationalities—rumor of a crash is sufficient to produce a crash—and compelling greed and selfishness—a decrease in unemployment will cause the market to plummet. Democracy, therefore, grounding itself on political equality that can be preserved only if some modicum of economic equality is preserved, has grounded itself on the casino logic of the global market, on the play of chance, and on self-interest and desire narrowed to the calculations of profit. Despotic regimes in the present and the past have had as wide a gap between rich and poor as America presently has and have survived without compromising their own despotic natures; however, history provides us with no examples of a self-professed democracy attempting to survive although profoundly unequal economically. America is making a maiden voyage here.

Where Are We Going in Fargo?
And How Do We Get There?

We have already gone too far from Fargo . . . but it is also clear that within our cultural imaginary we have not been able to get very far from Fargo at all.

It's agreed: We're on a mental journey in this last decade of the second millennium A.D., a journey from one way of configuring time and space, stuff and things, self and others, seeing and knowing, chance and order, individual and society, memory and dream, fact and fiction, progress and decline, words and world, mappings and journeys.

Once consciousness conceives of itself interacting in a different way with the world, the world takes on the shape of that mental conception. This is so regardless of the fact that consciousness is always already embedded in the world in certain ways that have all to do with all prior sculptings of consciousness/world interrelationship. From one perspective, you can say that consciousness is never free of the ways in which it has been conscious of the world. Francisco Varela refers to it as something like a natural drift of mind into world. From another perspective, you can say that the world's stuff is surely there but the "thereness" is only there if it is mediated in some way by consciousness. If there is no such mediation, what is there is invisible, although at the very same moment or, at some past time—it may be, or, has been, visible to some *other* imbrication of mind and world. What James Joyce referred to as "epiphanies" may be interpreted this way: a sudden bringing into one's range of conceivability what previously did not exist, although of course it was always there.

The primal journey, then, is from one configuration of world to another, from one mapping to another, not merely from one set of coordinates on the same map to another set of coordinates, but a shifting of the gaze to another map. The intermediate journey you might say involves a double focus and therefore a certain blurring as the eye fol-

25

lows a path to one place on one map to the same place on another map
with different paths. Or, on the new map, there may be no such place at
all. Or, a place and no paths to it. A very unsettling experience, which is
precisely what many people take travel to be: so potentially unsettling as
to be avoided. One's own, homegrown mind/world wedding cannot,
from its own sense of realism, see any benefit to journeying elsewhere,
into the unfamiliar, into space on a new map that is clearly configured
in an "alien" way.

How the world comes to meaning for the "alien other" is to various
degrees "inscrutable," empathy is only forthcoming within the prescribed boundaries of one's own mental landscape; only a high Romantic sense of a transcending imagination frees imagination from its local
moorings. Even Coleridge and Wordsworth couldn't ascend to that level
for very long. Understanding is always the product of interpretation carried on within one's own perspective; appreciation depends on homegrown criteria of judgment and valuation. Love, however, crosses
boundaries and makes the journey from home to elsewhere, from identity to difference, bypasses, if you will, the values and meanings construed on our own mental mapping.

Something less appealing than love—accidental confrontation and
disruptive clash—can rudely jostle us into awareness, into a whole new
terrain of mind. A judge sentences us to death, a doctor says we have six
months to live, a soldier is sent into battle, a loved one passes away, a
blood test reveals the HIV virus, our heart attacks us. It is more difficult
to theorize good fortune, for the very fact that it is "good" implies that
it has already been valued positively within a resident mindset. It's good
because one can see the fulfillment of possibilities already inherent in
one's resident reality schema. You don't jump from one mental mapping
to another when you win the Irish Sweepstakes: You merely use the
money to put into effect all the dreams already dreamt in your world.
Of course, one can be a survivor of the Oklahoma Bombing and come
out of that with a whole new mapping of self and world. But that is a
disruptive clash first; good fortune in surviving makes a paradigm
change possible. And of course the sweepstakes fortune can maximize
your opportunities to travel and thus the possibilities of falling in love
outside your ken as well as experiencing accidents that disrupt your
complacency, your "peace of mind," which is no more than the peace of
a mind that stays home, that fears the journey outward for fear of running into something that will disturb that peace.

You can say that there's a sort of reason that propels the journey so
one can understand the necessity of journeying: Since the world comes
into being within the parameters of our consciousness; that is, spatial or

worldly geography comes to us through the mediation of mental geography and mental geography is always configured within the worldly geography that is already there to be mediated. It makes sense to want to have more of the world by seeing more of the world, by journeying to the edge of one's mental mapping and then into another. The mind is always in a box that in turn boxes in and boxes out the world. There is no "boxless" encounter with the world, but, there is a sort of "deboxing" and "reboxing," what Giles Deleuze refers to as "deterritorializing" and "reterritorializing," that can occur. The idea of expanding and augmenting in some linear, incremental fashion is replaced by a dynamic of continuous divesting and revesting which parallels the flux and fluidity of the mind/world dynamic itself. Sedentary moments are moments of inertness, alluringly stable and purposeful, but out of step with the nomadic wanderings of mind into world, world into mind.

All this is mere preface to saying that to make the journey into *Fargo* requires a rerouting of one's mental mapping, quite simply put, from modernity's mind set to postmodernity's. But let's say you hadn't read my prefatory matter here, or have read it and dismissed it, either because it doesn't make sense or you believe that an opposite view holds more sense. At any rate, you are not disposed to taking a journey on any other terms but your own. You are not inclined to put in quotation marks as possibly provincial and provisional all your most comfortable connections with the world and take on with enthusiasm what appear to be indecipherable connections. You don't see yourself starring in *The Truman Show*. You are not prepared to see *Fargo*, then, except in the way in which you see the world and the world you see confirms the validity of your way of seeing. In other words, you don't see yourself caught in a vicious circle of knowing the world in a certain way and continuing to produce the world within that way of knowing. Instead, you see yourself on a clear road to greater and greater understanding. And your hope is that this film will take you further down that road, will reveal in a dramatic, entertaining, and profound way a bit more of what lies on the worldly terrain, the map of which you have at hand.

The question then is: Does *Fargo* itself draw you into its own difference because it shapes that difference in a compelling, provocative way? You don't get it, but you like it; you can't say what it's about but it's about something that draws you into it, stays with you, works at you, challenges you, or more precisely, the ways in which you value things and things come to meaning. You have nothing intelligible to say yet you consume and respond to the film on unsayable levels. If this is so, then the argument long made for art—that it can make conceivable to us that which is beyond our discursive grasp—here presents art as a vehicle through which to journey from one paradigm to another, from one mental landscape to another. The form of difference is shaped by the imagination, the senses, and the emotions, as well as the intellect. A very Blakean notion.

Since, however, this ineffable grasp cannot answer the question, Where are we going in *Fargo*? it stands vulnerable to an already existing readiness to provide an answer. And that mindset is modernity's, a mindset we may be journeying away from and we may be journeying away from at warp speed—there's no way of knowing from our present position—but certainly the mindset that grounds our society and its practices, institutions, and privileged discourse. The answer ready at hand is this: This film gets sidetracked, has no focus, no center, no theme, no sense, needs a screenplay that stays on track and builds toward a definite closure, needs editing that cuts out unconnected banal stuff from the main story and so on. Verdict: a poorly made film not worthy of further consideration. The fact that the film hangs on your mind and won't go away finally gets settled as your annoyance with the broken, fractured, unresolved, unintegrated, trite, confused aspects of the film. You want to make it coherent and continuous in your own mind, according to the rules of the game that the film should be following. You continue to impose those rules until the journey the film offers you fades and you take that circular journey in your own mind that you were already on before you saw the film. And that's not any sort of journey; that's merely rotating, or spinning within the spin you came in with.

Unfortunate. Now let's try to take the journey to *Fargo*.

We journey into two radically different lifeworlds in *Fargo*. If we consider them first on the level of personal lifeworlds, we have Marge and Norm Gunderson, sheriff and bird painter respectively, and then Karl and Gar, kidnappers and murderers. But Marge and Norm also share a social/cultural lifeworld in the town of Brainerd, Minnesota, home of Paul Bunyan and Babe the Blue Ox. There is a regional vibe here, revealed in vestiges of a slow, melodic Scandinavian speech rhythm; we are in a cultural enclave within America, one of the many differing cultural lifeworlds that yet are part of the American social order. We're in "The Brainerd Show," into a special box of ice and cold. From the perspective of the "mainstream," "normative" America that TV has shown us for the past fifty years, the Brainerd world is different, loaded with funny provincial mannerisms, slow-paced, a Mayberryish unhipness, out of step with the times, not in the '90s, not thinking globally but only acting locally, marking time not digitally but by *The Farmer's Almanac*. "Gotta eat breakfast," Norm tells Marge. "I'll fix you some eggs." And he does so and later on Marge tells her deputy that Norm fixed her some eggs. The old protocols, the old traditions of life faring apply here; there are no fads and fashions around to challenge them. It is as if here in these cold northern regions of the Midwest, no one has heard that reality has been replaced by simulacra, that the hyperreal has buried the real.

Maybe Brainerd hasn't heard, up to this moment, but now in this Coen brothers' film, Brainerd nevertheless comes to us packaged and ready for nationwide simulation. I can see the Norm and Marge dolls now, Marge's "Jeez, that's a surprise" exclamation making its way to the comedy clubs. But this lifeworld was already caught in the hyperreal; it already had been "disneyed" as part of the Americana myth, the land of Paul Bunyan and Babe the Blue Ox, the world of Ole Rolvaag's *Giants in the Earth*. These folks are living in and in turn producing their own mythos, their own cultural/social lifeworld. They had a mental geography of their lives and lifestyle before the Coen brothers ran into it. They were storymaking before the film was made.

This lifeworld for all it hokeyness and seemingly slow-wittedness has yet something appealing about it. I suggest it has the same appeal for us that Salome, Texas, has in the film *Tin Cup*: Both places reveal community off the beaten path, lives not marking digitalized time, not listening to what E. F. Hutton has to say, not in each other's faces on talk shows, old-fashioned lives, quiet, peripheral lives following their own drumbeats. And no desire to show up on "The Jerry Springer Show." A very appealing note played at the edge of a new millennium that promises . . . what? Bill Gates's road ahead into cyberspace? Bill Clinton's bridge to more GATTs and more NAFTAs? Newt Gingrich's contract with America? More family values brought to us by moral czars like Bill Bennett and Ralph Reed? Opportunities for all Americans to give up Medicare, Social Security, public education, public libraries, public radio and TV, financial aid for college tuition, endowments for the arts and humanities, and on and on in order to "compete freely in the global market" and join the 1 percent of the population that controls 44 percent of the wealth, or become "symbolic analysts" and join the top quintile? Or, become like Bill Gates and earn as much money in one year as the bottom quintile of the American population? Or, does the future hold nothing but a dark insecurity for at least 80 percent of the American population on the eve of the millennium?

Here in Brainerd there is no such anxiety, no such insecurity. Could such refuges out-of-global-time exist now in America? So for all its strange comicalness, I think we hook up positively with the Brainerd world, with Marge and Norm. They become romantic configurations of local peace and sanity in a world rapidly overwriting local harmonies and replacing them with the Global Inchoate, an amorphous order where it is hard to see where one can live out one's life with an eccentric, personalized, detailed, minutely particularized flourish.

The Brainerd cultural lifeworld, however, is part of a larger, pluralized American culture, one filled with narrative worlds that openly challenge the social order that is always desperately trying to maintain itself within the cultural morass. That order is preserved in Brainerd, even though the Brainerd "whole way of life" is little and local, peripheral, filled with folkways and mannerisms that are never played on the east or west coast. Marge Gunderson, as quaint and small town as she is, is the sheriff here, the enforcer of a rule of law that is no different here than it is on the east or west coast. She doesn't have the police style of Sipowitz on "NYPD Blue" or Pembleton on "Homicide" but she "gets her man" nonetheless. The clash then is not on the level of the social order—although the kidnaping and murders have us on that level—but rather within the larger American cultural turmoil. Karl and Gar enter the Brainerd world like sociopathic/psychopathic snakes in the Garden of Eden. Lifeworlds taking entirely different journeys run into each other, and, although I want to talk about how this happens and what ensues, what is significant here is the disruptive, crisscrossing, accidental, mazy nature of the postmodern journey. The Brainerd world has its own mapping of a world it makes itself; Karl and Gar are going down roads on entirely different maps; but within each geographic enclosure there are yet other mappings, other worldly configurations, roads not shown, home routes and inconceivable pathways. The world is construed through and within narratives, narratives that tell time and mark space, and therefore any one world can fracture into multiple lifeworlds, different timescapes emitting actions we cannot fathom from where we are, words that have little or no meaning, values that have no hold on us.

Although he lives in Minneapolis, Jerry Lundegaard, the car salesman and instigator of the film's plot, is of the Brainerd cultural lifeworld, but within that world he occupies a different space and marks time differently. He is not the only citizen of this world whose personal lifeworld has distanced him from the social/cultural lifeworld of Brainerd. Later on in the film, we'll meet Mike Nagageeta, who also only *appears* to share Marge and Norm's cultural lifeworld, while in actuality he is taking some personal journey not in Brainerd and never explicable or conceivable to us. When Karl asks Jerry why he wants them to kidnap his wife and seek ransom from his father-in-law, Jerry only replies reluctantly "I'm in a bit of trouble." And when pressed, he simply says "personal matters." In this we hear nothing but the echoes of a personal lifeworld that is shaping its own cultural imaginary, some personal trouble or trauma overwhelming the Brainerd cultural "norm" and mapping its own journey.

Both Mike and Jerry conceal their personal lifeworlds, the journeys they are personally taking, the mental mappings that they follow. Both, however, possess a kind of jumping-bean reactiveness and volatility, as if what they were suppressing within is breaking through a thin veneer of assumed behavior. Mike clearly makes a move on Marge in the restaurant, some sort of repressed sexuality breaks out there but Marge checks him and he then erupts into a fount of lies, concocts journeys on the spot never taken, never real at any moment. And when at the end of the film, the cops knock on Jerry's motel door, Jerry answers calmly "Just a minute." They don't wait, break in and grab him halfway out a window. And then Jerry simply goes ballistic, screaming wildly, finally breaking out of the Jerry, good husband, salesman, father, son-in-law that he has been. We don't see Mike in a head-on collision between his own aberrant lifeworld and the cultural lifeworld of Brainerd, but we get a chance to see Jerry's. We do, however, get a chance to see Marge's reaction to the news that everything Mike told her was a lie. We get a chance to see how the Brainerd cultural order of things responds to the realization that it had just encountered an alien world, a world whose terrain it had no map of and could not journey into. Marge's response to the news is a wonderful understatement that expresses how rapidly a clash with total otherness, inexplicable difference has been transformed into a Brainerd reactive mode: "Jeez, that's a surprise."

Marge's scene with Mike Nagageeta serves no plot purpose, but only a more significant purpose: It's an encounter between alien worlds, between lifeworlds following different roads and on different journeys. Where we are going in *Fargo* plotwise pales in interest compared to *how* we are going and how others go in *Fargo*. And we go in accord with our own maps, our own timescapes, our own lifeworlds. On a path to solving a crime, to finding murderers and kidnappers, we nonetheless live in a world in which people are on other paths and taking different journeys. At 11:30 at night, Mike Nagageeta, a voice from the past, calls us up and wants to get together. Ironically, of course, Marge and Mike only appear to get together; in actuality, they fly past each other. He remains a mystery to her; she solves the murder mystery, but Mike remains a mystery. She can't go from the Brainerd cultural lifeworld to the Nagageeta personal lifeworld. She has no problem hooking up with husband Norm, whose daily life mystifies me, and neither one of them have any problem with any of their Brainerd neighbors. They all hook up on the same mental mapping; but Mike throws her for a loop. She's surprised that nothing Mike told her turns out to be true. Surprise is not clash; she doesn't journey toward Mike. She stays in Brainerd. In the same fashion, Mike's inexplicability throws the viewer for a loop: The scene doesn't make any sense in the murder plot; it's mystifying; it's a surprise. If you put the surprise behind you as something senseless and pick up on the murder plot that you have a map in hand for, then you didn't go very far to Fargo; you wind up taking the murder mystery journey in "Murder She Wrote" and winding up someplace with Angela Lansbury. You followed her map.

Peter Stormrak's Gar, the flaxen-haired, Marlboro-smoking, silent psychopath has just as inexplicable a personal lifeworld as Mike Nagageeta and Jerry Lundegaard. Neither the Brainerd social/cultural world nor the mainstream world "we" in the audience know—by which I mean, once again, TV-Disney-Film-Media-Madison Avenue "mainstream" reality—have had any affect on Gar. He doesn't belong in the Brainerd world but nevertheless he drives through; Brainerd runs into him. He and Karl are stopped by a highway cop for not having plates on their car. They have the kidnaped Jean Lundegaard wrapped up in the back seat. Karl compounds the offense to Brainerd's "order of things" by attempting to bribe the officer, who is, of course, not "reachable" in this way. They may be corrupted, wherever they're from, but he's not. And Gar reaches across, pulls the cop toward him and shoots him in the head. As Karl is dragging the body off the road, a couple of other Brainerd folk drive by, stop and stare at the scene, and then, finally realizing they are witnessing murder, drive off. It's pure chance that they've run into these aliens to their world but they can't escape the consequences. Gar chases after them; they spin off the road; one flees the car and Gar calmly shoots him in the back and the other, pinned under the car, is executed, just as calmly, by Gar, the "monster."

Let's contemplate the other felon, Steve Buscemi's Karl, for a moment. Unlike Gar, Karl is voluble; he narrates everything he feels and he feels a lot of hostility. His sociopathy has to provide a running, angry critique of the world around him while Gar's psychopathy feels no need, silent at the center of its own uncontested grasp of the world. "I guess you think you're some kind of authority figure," Karl tells a parking attendant, who unfortunately for the parking attendant, is wearing a sort of uniform and has insisted Karl pay his parking fee. Uniforms, orders, and demands spark Karl's ire. Described more than once in the film as a "kind of funny-looking guy," it becomes clear that Karl suffers under such appraisal from without. The little, weird-looking guy who bites back at the those who mock and belittle him, a small man who hates the big world. Unlike Gar, who doesn't need to prime himself to murder, Karl has to work himself up with his own invective, his own profanity, an angry spew of words flung in the face of imagined provocateurs. He's so vicious and ill-tempered that you believe that he can be brought into line only by being slapped down. You can't reason with him; he's rabid. But when you do see him viciously beaten and reviled at one point in the film, flung around the room like a hapless skinny kid, kicked over and over again, you begin to think that being slapped down like this has made a vicious dog of him. And when this vicious sociopath is in a face-off with Wade Gustafson, Jerry's wealthy father-in-law, we see that the only person to ever break through Wade's entrepreneurial imperiousness is the sociopath Karl. For Wade, this exchange of money for his daughter is a business transaction, something he not only knows about but is a master of. The "funny-looking guy" facing him is clearly a "loser," a man without a portfolio trying to break into a "winner's" coffers and take something for nothing. Wade knows how to deal without liberal compassion with these kind of people and he knows how to "make the deal." Or, thinks he does. His entrepreneurial lifeworld has no sense of what anger drives Karl, what irrationalities that lie outside "good business practices" propel a sociopath like Karl. Once again, one man's journey jumps tracks, goes off the map, and crashes in unknown territory.

The biggest clash of bodies going in different directions is made by Marge and Gar. In the end, when Marge accidentally comes upon the kidnappers's hideout and Gar pushing a leg through a woodchipper, it is Gar who is the loser in the sudden confrontation. He flees across the ice, Marge slowly takes aim, misses him once, and then hits him and he falls to the ice with a bullet in his leg. She was slow to fire not because she was enjoying the chance to kill, as Gar did with his victim, but because she was aiming just to stop him, not kill him.

Maybe Gar in his unspoken, immoveable way understood the Brainerd lifeworld, the lifeworld of the two he killed on the side of the road, and the lifeworld of Jean Lundegaard who he kills because she gets noisy. As he is as wordless as Iago at the end of *Othello*, we have no way of knowing what he knows. But Marge tells us that she has run into what mystifies her. As Gar sits handcuffed and bleeding in the back seat of Marge's police car, a protective metal screening between them, Marge checks his blank countenance in the rearview and sends out a message from the Brainerd world: "There's more to life than a little bit of money, don't you know that?" To which observation Gar is more imperturbable than ever. As we sit there and watch this, we wonder if Marge is driving past the million dollars that Karl has stashed in the snow. That's more than a little bit of money. The kidnaping and ransom money resonate for a moment for me within the film *Ransom*, where kidnaping, ransom, and sociopathy also appear. The biggest fear of the wealthy few in South America is kidnaping, being kidnaped by those from the multitudes of "have nots." Is that fear moving north as America "Brazilianizes"—two classes: the ultrarich and the ultrapoor—in the fashion predicted by Michael Lind? Maybe it's only a Hollywood defense mechanism, a self-preserving spin, that psychopaths and sociopaths are the only ones who would think of kidnaping the rich for a million bucks.

Marge tries once again to reach the alien mind, the mind that the Brainerd mind finds inconceivable: "And here you are and it's a beautiful day. I just don't understand it." She's right: It is hard to understand a psychopath like Gar, a mind lost in its own twisted connections to the world, traumatized somehow far beyond Brainerd behavior and comprehension in a chink-proof armor of self-construction. We only see Gar, running into and clashing with others, being affected by chance, but we are seeing from the outside, imposing our own seeing. In actuality, he encounters nothing, clashes with nothing, sees nothing, and chance distracts him from his course as little as does a fly colliding with a moving vehicle. True, a bullet in the leg physically stops him in the end and we reach him and cuff him, but his personal lifeworld has not been reached. He also is not moving, taking no journey, locked into what he alone contemplates.

Marge returns to Norm and the two lie in bed. Norm's painting of a mallard we discover has been accepted for a three-cent postage stamp. But Norm isn't happy: "Don't much use the three-cent anymore." But Marge, the Marge who has just clashed with Gar the psychopath and won, tells Norm reassuringly that a lot of people use the three-cent stamps when stamp prices go up and folks need the little ones to add to the big ones to make up the new price. And this makes Norm feel better. "I'm so proud of you, Norm," Marge tells him. "I love you, Marge," Norm tells her. "I love you, Norm," Marge tells him. In its own Brainerd way, as inexplicable a bit of human interaction as we have seen in the film. Maybe Marge survives by not bringing the "bad stuff" home and focuses on the little, three-penny stuff of everyday life to heal the wounds inflicted "out in the world," where Karls, Gars, Jerrys, and Mikes hang out. Maybe Marge sits in bed watching bark beetles battle on TV because she can't take the real news of the world when she's "off duty." I think this is all telling but at the same time I want Marge to make an effort to journey further, to not fall back in Norm's three-penny world, to make an effort to understand what lies beyond that world, to benefit from chance encounters with nonBrainerd realities. Paradoxically, I also feel I don't want Brainerd's own reality construction to be run over by the globalizing stampede, I don't want Brainerd to go online. I want that world to defend its own right to exist, to journey in its own way, to be interrupted, intersected, interpenetrated, but not torn down and rebuilt "for the '90s."

Honey, Be Glad We're Not Rich

Maybe it's a Hollywood defense mechanism, a self-preserving spin, that psychopaths and sociopaths are the only ones who would think of kidnaping the rich for a million bucks.

What journey are we on in the film *Ransom?*

A journey to justice by way of revenge, a desperate journey of an intellectually gifted man who has risen no higher than being a street cop, spending his life among petty criminals, hungry and rapacious like wolves, his own talents dissipated among the dissipated; he tries to journey out by putting a death hold on a rich entrepreneur whom he thinks has lost his Darwinian instincts and will part with the ransom money easily to get his son back.

When the superintelligent find themselves with the rats in the sewers and society seems to give them no means to travel from there to the penthouse, to what is their intelligence directed? The bottle? Drugs? Gambling? Crime? Salvation? Pathology? Family? Job? Friends? Lovers? The past? Scapegoat? Dream? Future? Hope?

You get a very mixed portrait of rich and poor, winners and losers, entrepreneurial energy and rebellious energy. Gary Sinise's detective has all the fiery rebelliousness of Blake's Orc, a wild-eyed, angry revolutionary out to topple the order of things that market hegemony has dispensed. He is full of resentment, a man "with issues," striking out against an unjust world that has denied him the status, the money and power, that he feels his superiority to other men merits him. No serial killer he, no psychopath playing out desires perverse and distorted because of some personal trauma. Sinise's battle is with the resident social valuing of power and riches, worth and reward, circumstances and achievements. Sociopaths are made, not born. At least that's the story in this film.

We see Sinise briefly on the streets, dealing with crime and criminals that he no doubt feels should be there because neither their intelligence nor their imaginations prompt them to take a journey upward and out.

35

He is contemptuous of their lack of resentment; he is filled with resentment because he sees the difference between the life he has now and a
life that he knows other people, less talented than himself, possess. But
it is 1996, New York City, and he may be, as a cop, as far down the road
as he will ever get. Intelligent eyes that gaze down the road lose track of
where it is leading. He doesn't see anything less than what we see: At
some point if your life is on the streets of a city like New York in the last
decade of the millennium, the way out of there, or upward, the rise to
the top, the climb up the mountain, the journey from inconsequence to
consequence, from the lowly to the high, from rags to riches, from
anonymity to fame—that road has no markers, that road has no hurdles
to jump, that road is no longer paved, that road ends in darkness. And
the other road, the new road to the top is somewhere in an alternate
reality, a different time and space dimension and it has all to do with digital transfer of capital on a global scale by agents of capital owners
whose capital proliferates like maggots on dead meat in the sun, and
whose lives take capital journeys that someone in the street can no
longer see nor even conceive.

What happens in a democracy when the Have Nots can no longer
even conceive of how the journey to where the Haves are can be made?
In previous times, revolutionary ideologies would fill the minds of the
intelligent but dispossessed. But Lester Thurow is right; we can no
longer conceive of any form of socialism, either in its extremes of anar-
chism or communism, or in its moderating guise as social democracy, as
anything but a failed experiment, laughable, extinct, no longer feasible,
conceivable as real paths to justice only by the old and inane. Even the
obviously nonradical liberalism is no serious counter to the justice that
global-market free play dispenses. There is nothing progressive about an
ideology that cannot put a dream of the future in the minds of the many,
a dream that challenges what an ethos of greed promises. Why fight for
an equal playing field lying somewhere ahead when turbo-charged capitalism tells us we already have it? Nevertheless, although ideologies fail,
we yet live at a time when the dream of journeying from mean streets to
penthouse cannot be dreamed. In the absence of any revolutionary ideology that shows us the road ahead, that plans the journey back to social
justice, to social mobility, to some connection between great brains and
talent and success—in the absence of all this, intelligence must take a
detour. Perhaps to God or to higher consciousness or to Calcutta with
Mother Theresa or to duplicate bridge or to Las Vegas or the office—or
crime. Only crime puts one on a social journey; all the others are personal journeys. You can be building a replica of the entire city of New
York in match sticks in your basement, or taking Yoga classes, or vol-

unteering to give out turkey dinners to the poor, or studying scratch sheets for winners, or whatever—but these do not rock the social and economic order of things.

The last option of the dispossessed in a global-market order is crime, and if there is passion and a desire for revenge plus enough intelligence to see that this is the only way the journey up and out can be made, then kidnaping is the crime of choice. Why? Because—if you're clever enough and lucky enough—you get your two million and you also get into the personal life of those people whose lives are so distant, so different that there is no longer a personal connection between one human and another, between our intelligent, angry detective in the streets and our young entrepreneurial, penthouse dweller. It's not hard to see what besides the money is motivating the superintelligent but salaried detective Sinise portrays.

Let's talk more about the global-market order, an order which has disconnected personal assets from financial assets, has indeed just about finished making the new world order digital allocations of wealth, allocations which the continued use of electronic financial dealings on a global scale will increase geometrically while at the same time making it less and less possible for those without funds to climb aboard and make the same journey. This is a brand new state of affairs that the world has not seen before. While wealth has been accumulated before in narrow corridors, they were national corridors. Now the super wealthy deal with each other globally; they are on the same journey; they cross paths. And while an order of things which supports the few on the backs of the many has historically always faced possible overturning, that option, as I have suggested, has never been less conceivable than it is now. The world has also never before seen the instrumentation that a global market now has at its command: The telecommunications industry looms large on the horizon not simply because it has state-of-the-art electronic "infernal devices" through whose agency stocks, bonds, certificates, currency exchange, futures contracts, and the like are manipulated, but because the same electronic agency can come into the homes of people like Gary Sinese, the angry detective, and lull him into submission through gadgetry, from virtual reality to home shopping. He can be put on a numbing diet of Bread and Circuses.

But not our detective. He walks the streets of New York and sees all the roads out blocked for him; he can't get a fix on the right map coordinates that will take him to the penthouse. He desperately wants to take the journey but he can't see any way to start that journey except through crime, through reaching out and grabbing some part of a rich man's life. Maybe the crime of kidnaping does this and only this: Through grabbing the son he connects with the father, the man on the street who can no longer suffer life on the street reaches out and takes hold of the rich man, which he can never do, except through kidnaping the son.

There is no other reason as to why the film builds toward the final confrontation of Gibson and Sinese. It has never been about money; only about the journey from one place to another, from one life to another. It's a desperate jump, not a journey at all, not a real journey. So futile, so desperate, so sad.

Side Trip: Resentment

"I'm not going to present myself as a hero. Or a victim. And I can't hide what you'll see: that my life has left me damaged goods, not as bad as the Unabomber. But bad. It's all different. I shouldn't refer to other guys, somebody else's life. Nobody's problems are like mine but I don't say mine are any bigger than yours. I just played the cards dealt me differently.

The other night I saw a TV show documenting the life of the mobster Frank Costello, and they said that if he hadn't gone into a life of crime, he had the brains to be just as wealthy and powerful, a legitimate success. Reverse of that situation is Nixon as an underworld 'Prime Minister,' which is what they called Costello. Both hypotheticals seem to work. Listen to Elvis on the Sun recordings; you can hear what he was before he became Elvis The King. Now think that that trip to record a song for his mom on her birthday just led to that. And nothing else. And for his whole life Elvis, who never became The King, knew he was The King in his own heart but still had to drive a truck, or cut lawns, or work for the city, or flip burgers, singing on the weekends in small, local venues, waiting for his break. Not coming.

That small elvis doesn't die on a bathroom floor of a mansion; he winds up in his late fifties with cancer racing through his body from where God only knows. Maybe it's the resentment that starts it off; knowing that he's got something but he can't get inside with it. He gets close but he keeps getting swallowed up by things he can't control. He had his moment back then in the mid-fifties but he didn't hook up and then things passed him by and he just sounded like somebody who was passé, wasn't really with it. Somebody else carried the ball across the goal line. Somebody else was crowned King. Think about it. Then think that that happened to everybody Elvis knew back then. Everybody he ran into, everybody he saw, everybody he spoke to. None of them became King and they all lived the rest of their lives in resentment.

Put Clinton in Gary Hart's time and place and Clinton vanishes as a viable presidential candidate; Anita Hill hits Clarence Thomas with a sexual harassment suit back when Thomas first hit on her. Ross Perot reaches the height of his popularity a day before the election. JFK's older brother Joe isn't killed in the war. Lee Harvey Oswald isn't killed by Jack Ruby but lives to tell us who hired him. Reagan starts the move toward oligarchy in this country in 1981 and Congress gives him a firm No! The electorate knows in 1988 that Willie Horton is a race card being played by Bush's handlers. Somebody videos Monica Lewinsky giving Clinton a blow-job and sells the tape to ABC. You have to be impressed by just how big a player the Goddess Fortuna is.

I get drafted in 1966 and spend five days in a Naval hospital with wounded from Vietnam, but I don't go in because somebody misreads my medical charts. I go to graduate school instead. One third of my working-class neighborhood doesn't come back from that 'conflict' or comes back haunted.

I've just seen a movie called Good Will Hunting about a young guy from Irish working-class South Boston who's got this mathematical genius. He's a janitor working at MIT but he can solve math problems none of the students can. To our surprise, he's not anxious to break away from Southie and his life there with his buddies. He doesn't care if his math genius is a ticket out. He's got a 'so what/don't bore me/I don't give a fuck/drop dead' attitude. Resentment. The kid reeks of resentment. He's an orphan and he's already been fucked over so he doesn't care what else the world out there has to offer. There's shit out there. At the top of the ladder there's a black hole. When NASA wants to hire him for 'national security' reasons, he wants to know what they're intelligent about? What purpose does your intelligence serve? Is there some big humanitarian goal it's heading for? He sort of asks the questions Ted Kacynzski would have asked NASA had they been trying to recruit him. But Will doesn't want to turn his brains into an instrument employed by NASA. He resents them and everybody else in power for what they've already done to the world. This kid resents all the duplicity and greed that's wrapped around the globe like an extra-tight athletic support.

What's my point? My point is on the end of this: If society wants to produce a war of all against all and says drop dead to caring about people from cradle to grave, then I say let's rock. And don't talk to me about rules of the game when they're already set up to benefit those already winning. When I was a kid and we played King of the Mountain, the first thing I did when I got to the *top was do everything I could to keep everybody else off. Now my opinion is that Bill Gates fast talked some poor slob out of his own creation; I think all the millionaires in Congress are there because they're millionaires; I think all the Ivy League brats are there because their parents went there or because they had pentium-chip computers at home and their parents were literate and taught them how to think and their houses were loaded with the 'classics,' and the vacations they took gave them a perspective on the world that a kid, say from Southie or from Bensonhurst, wouldn't have.*

Warren Buffet makes money by having money; Rupert Murdoch IS Frank Costello without the mob ties; Michael Milken is like the tip of the iceberg: There are more crimes in the suites than in the streets but 'no trespassing' signs keep them out. Now Mayor Giuliani's cops are out walking in every inner city, looking into everybody's window. Where are the cops looking in the windows of the lobbyists in Washington? Why don't they sit in the boardrooms of Disney, Solomon Brothers, Merrill Lynch, ADM, Microsoft, TCI? How much money that belongs to American citizens winds up in some fatcat's Swiss account? What about the corporations dying to giving up their loyalty to this country so they can operate 'transnationally'? An American worker is not a hero to them; an American worker is a deficit: too expensive, too vocal about rights, and a potential threat when they get laid off. What's the difference between 'downsizing' a whole fucking town and throwing a bunch of people too old and stuck in their ways to 'adapt' into a downward spiral toward a personal hell?

How many divorces, how many kids lost to drugs and crime, how much rage, how much resentment comes out of a 'downsizing' that not only boosts the stock options of the executive class but sees a rise in the value of that company's stocks? Fire forty-thousand workers, crush a strike, close a plant, out source, cut benefits, fight health care, block governmental agencies overseeing food and drug quality, environmental protection, and worker safety, fight a raise in the minimum wage, replace full-time workers with temps, contest unemployment rights, falsely advertise products, maximize services to the wealthy while cutting back on 'economy,' revise tort law and get rid of contingency-based legal assistance—this is a bloody attack force; this is bloody war; call it the new world order, call it the free play of the global market, call it 'show me the money!' call it entrepreneurial competitiveness, call it hardball.

Look at it this way, Ted K the Unabomber was playing hardball, so were Tim McVeigh and Terry Nichols. Stupid hardball but hard-

ball. *Nobody wants to see where it comes from. Those guys are just nuts; it's all personal; no social tie-ins. Like burgling Watergate didn't have a thing to do with Nixon, it was all those guys breaking in being personally fucked up. The Unabomber has been sending us all a bombogram but he doesn't know how to send it or where it should go. You mail something to somebody. It's personal. A totally innocent guy—maybe a guy two weeks away from being downsized for his own good, maybe a guy who just got 'liberated' from welfare—opens the bombogram. Who's it meant for? Not those guys. There's no way you can use door-to-door personal delivery that the U.S. Post Office offers to fight the war the Unabomber thought he was in. The trick is to see the connection between the personal and the social, the individual and the corporation, act so that the personal is affected but the action is impersonal. Unabomber gets an F on this.*

The two jerks who bomb the Oklahoma building think they're bombing the Federal Government. They don't like the Federal Government because it's taking away their personal freedoms. Of course, it's not the feds that are foreclosing on the McVeighs and Nichols but the banks working within a global investment network which shuffles money to where it can do the most good. And to hell with the people who are not on the profit end of those ventures. Some day a lot of money in the pockets of the global super wealthy will benefit the Nichols and McVeighs. There will be jobs for them, jobs that might be downsized at a drop of a hat, jobs that might go south, jobs that won't pay medical or retirement benefits, jobs that technology can replace. Jobs for the losers. For awhile. And then another job. And then another. So Nichols and McVeigh played hardball on the wrong court and played against guys on their own team. It's not Microsoft that is going to bring an antitrust suit against Microsoft; it's not Dow or Scott or GM that are going to tighten up EPA regulations and expand the power of that agency; it's not Merck or Food Lion that are going to fight for more food and drug inspection.

I could go on and on but I'm full of resentment. And it burns you out. I get sick when I think of how vicious this war of all against all is, how tough the hardball game is, and how nobody but the exploiters know how to play it. They're the only ones who know where the game is being played and who's playing it. Everybody else is mesmerized by Dow Jones figures, Disney fantasies, and Madison Avenue seductions."

Resentment is a personal thing, arising from a personal life-world, but the "personal" in that world is tangled up with the social and cultural. Resentment has its critique; it deserves its moment. Sure, it's easy for resentment to reduce complicated social/political/economic problems to the individual level, a face-off, hand-to-hand combat. But the ease smells of the ease of the *ad hominem* attack in philosophy: We know it's inappropriate. And yet, at the same time, personal lifeworlds are victimized and exploited, seduced and repressed, and others are victimizing and exploiting. And the resentment that comes from that is not inappropriate.

There is not a unique, personal journey nor is there a separate distinct world we are journeying toward, one that determines our destiny. There are only stories of such. Nor can we know anything more than a story of a Destiny that determines our journey. The journey our American culture is on and the journey we take personally are enwrapped, the one within the other. What we imagine as culture and personal are never for a second apart. Every story, then, of self is a story of culture; every story of culture, is a story of self. The grandest purpose of the postmodern journey is to journey off one map of both culture and self and toward another, toward what is yet unmapped, inconceivable to the present state of our imaginations. Beyond latitudes and longitudes we already know. Beyond even resentment.

Side Trip

Walking Down Main Street U.S.A.

I don't want Brainerd to go online.

The *Odeon* is packed by the time I arrive there at 6:58 for the 7 P.M. showing. And why not? It's a hot summer night, too hot to take an evening stroll after dinner. A couple of cool hours at the *Odeon*, bag of canola-ed popcorn in your lap, and a "serious" movie, an old-time movie with good characters and a good story, is up there on the screen. Advance notice: The critics have admired Peter Fonda's performance in *Ulee's Gold:* He hasn't been this good, they say, since he was Captain America in *Easy Rider*. Now twenty-seven years later, he's just a former 'Nam vet who has followed his father's and his grandfather's occupation of beekeeping.

It's an older crowd at this showing, old enough to have seen *Easy Rider* open in the theaters all those years ago. Besides escaping from the heat, they're also escaping from the Hot Summer Blockbusters! The films fully loaded with hyperkinetic, digitalized action scenes, highwire shootouts between two gun heroes and villains, cinematic Magical Realism that is neither magical nor real. This *Odeon* crowd here didn't earn their spurs playing endless hours of PacMan, graduating to Superintendo, or Super Mario 2000. The whole eye-brain-hand accord doesn't go on with these *Odeon* folks, myself included, at digital speeds. We're not even really at TV remote speeds; we're at page-turning speed: 33 and a third, long play, no jumping the needle please, continuous, connected visuals and sound only. It's too late for us to develop fractal imaginations; we see the way Euclid wanted us to: point to point.

This is a fork in the road worth taking: From the Digitalized Generation's point of view, this *Odeon* crowd is running on an antiquated processing system. There's no "Intel Inside!" pasted on our foreheads. It's not just a case of speed but of a different system, say a "tube" mental processing vs. a microchip one. Fed on impulses which do not play the notes between linkages but maximize alternative linkages, the digitalized mind is more in the "actively engaged" mode than in the "mulling" mode. There's no space left for backtracking the steps of a linear continuity because that linear continuity is always breaking off and going down another pathway. Gaps and fissures, disruptions and interruptions demand response. The play of stimulus/response almost elides consumption and digestion, by which I mean an internalization of a perceived pattern, a continuous line of thought or imagining or feeling. A measured stimulus-response, stimulus-response pattern that therefore allows for the "politics of incorporation" (you may comply, defer, or resist within the beats) suffers immediate overload if you switch to a computer game, joy stick in hand processing.

Now, while we all have been "billgatesed" enough to know that traveling down the electronic highway is infinitely better than horse and wagon, and that cyberspace is the place to be, we are yet dealing with observations made by someone at some time. The original Defense Department development of computers had a clear purpose: to enable them to process incoming data fast enough to defend against First Strike. So the Cold War narrating of the world, you might say, contained a key chapter called "First Strike" and computers became a part of that chapter. Market interests are more complex: New technology means new products means a new cycle of consumption means greater profits. But more cleverly what happens to us on the electronic highway is that a rush of bits pushing products and services packages the world for consumption and sets us at a speed where the world-as-*other-than-consumption* has neither time nor place to come into being. Why more direct buying isn't going on on the Net at this moment may have something to do with how the generation with the most buying power—and this *Odeon* crowd is representative—remains resistant to the seductions of Net mental traveling. To put it in terms that I am introducing here, the *Odeon* generation is traveling in a way that does not distract them from seeing that they live in a world to be consumed *and* a world that has nothing to do with consumption. In traveling with students through Europe over the years, I have had an opportunity to see how new places come to meaning for them as potential "buying sites," places to go on a "shopping spree," places that offer products at the volume and speed of American delivery. This first engagement with a different country—a product and services engagement—doesn't last—and making that transition happen is part of the intent of our travels. What I'm trying to do is take them down other highways of worldly interaction. I guess I'm taking them to the *Odeon*.

The world is not solely mediated through products and services; and if that is the case with the Digital Generation, it is only because they have been thrown onto an electronic highway overstimulating their con-

suming desires. Although the world is available for all sorts of processing or modes of traveling into and through, we are packaging it for
quick and easy consumption and market needs have mapped the electronic highway to achieve this. It is of course possible to believe that this
is the inevitable road to progress, or that the Net offers as many opportunities to see the world as-other-than-consumption, as a place where we
can all escape the Tyranny of Big Government! These are heavily advertised and marketed beliefs and I do admit they are hard, once you have
a joystick or a mouse or a remote in your hand, to resist.

We're back at the *Odeon.*

I'm saying that we're here seeking relief and refuge from films like
*Batman & Robin, Con Air, Fifth Element, Lost World, The Saint,
Face/Off, Speed 2,* and a swarm of others that are supposed to enliven
the dog days of summer. Digital hijinks of these films only produce a
blurred vision; being activated by digital cinematic hijinks proves
exhausting and the lack of any return, of something coming of this
besides the display itself, the lack of anything that remains on your
brainpan, leaves you outside the film, marveling perhaps at all this, but
not inside the film, engaged. This crowd tonight is here to be engaged;
they're hoping for a deep response; they're hoping for a real view of real
life; they want to be moved toward each other; they want to be transformed, for the film to make a difference in their lives. They want to
remember it the next day and go around and tell their friends how this
film moved them. The film might make them shed a tear, or laugh, or
cringe, or grab someone's hand tightly; it has permission to do all these
things, everything but leave them with nothing but wondering what the
next technical wonder will be and how the last one was done.

This is a crowd raised on stories with meaning, not melodramati-
cally overplayed as the Bette Davis/Joan Crawford films of the Boomers'
parents generation enjoyed, but replete with all the hookups of a generation born into a Cold War world, suckled on sitcoms like "Ozzie and
Harriet," "Leave It to Beaver," and "Father Knows Best," exploded into
a counterculture generation, and now mostly enjoying the financial
fruits of professionalism, of all those graduate degrees pursued to escape
Vietnam paying off in the post-Reagan meritocratic America. Whatever
this mindset turns out to be, toss it in the blender of a present American
cultural imaginary. This generation is like Jean Brodie—it's in its prime.

In regard to *Ulee's Gold,* all I can apply here is a preference for
tight-lipped taciturnity, best out of the mouths of actors and actresses
who have been where the Boomers have been, closeups of fast-disap-
pearing lifestyles, and an atmosphere of some kind of developing wisdom. What is "deprivileged" is computer arcade pacing, closeups of fin-

gers at a computer keyboard or on computer screens, more interest in new software than in human consciousness, out-of-focus conversations and monologues of the disaffected, scenes with drug dealers with attaché cases full of money, and an atmosphere of blank memory regarding the past. With this *Odeon* crowd a sense of realism is attached to what it prefers and a sense of annoyance is attached to what it doesn't prefer. Reality rides in on such noble discriminating.

Ulee's Gold lives up to its reputation: It's a small "gem of a slice of real life," one of those narrow-focus, life-in-the-raw, up-real-close films where character is all. The cinematography frames everyday moments as if the glory of what lies behind the everyday was there shining through, as if every bit of slow delivery had the deepest consequences. Biorhythmically, Peter Fonda's Ulee Jackson is the polar opposite of Jim Carey's Jim Carey, and the film itself is like what Hackers call "vinyl" and Boomers call "LPs." There's no sign of a TV or even a radio in Ulee's house. No CD collections in sight. Needless to say, no one in the film, even the young people, are surfing the net, either literally or mentally. It's not surfing at all; it's diving into the depths. Supposedly. Like *The English Patient* and *Shine* and *Breaking the Waves* and *Secrets and Lies*. It's going beneath the surface of the everyday and bringing up some eternal truths, some stuff that ennobles the human spirit, that expands human horizons, that warms the human heart. Etcetera. I am not mocking this; this can all be done if folks at some time and place believe that it has been done. When they stop doing so, the "gem" loses its sparkle and disappears. Unless, of course, a lecturer assigns it to his or her students. I show *Citizen Kane* on a fairly regular basis to students and I don't think I've ever gotten a class that would sit through the film if it wasn't part of my course and if I wasn't commenting on the film as we were watching it. In other words, they can't walk out. The film is being held up by the whole elaborate economic structure that keeps students enrolling at university: degrees mean better jobs mean more money.

There are a whole lot of reasons the Digital Generation wouldn't, if they were free to do so, choose to sit through *Citizen Kane*. But foundationally what it comes down to is this: They'd rather surf the surface for values and meanings than probe for foundations, maybe because they have been suckled in an antifoundation atmosphere, one created by their parents' generation, the Boomers themselves. Now the Boomers are themselves trying to reerect what they helped tear down. Of course, the generation was split; while some were "countering" others were "legislating." What the Digitals face is the split, the rift, the war we call the culture wars in all its many guises. But the very presence and prevalence of the conflict drives the Digitals toward an indifference to the terms of the game.

The tug of war between those pulling us toward a Golden Age of Absolute and Universal Values and Meanings, and those pulling us toward a "we construct the reality that constructs us" Age is just that in the eyes of the Digitals—a game. A post-Reagan generation observes that both ends of the rope always and only go where the market wants them to go. Truth, reality, meanings, values, progress, are all sought with the same software—the software engineered by the market. The Digital Generation surfs the game master itself; all the products and services of the market become the search engine chosen by this generation to journey into reality. Reality is products and services.

Now my *Odeon* crowd, including me, is, each and every one of us, somewhere in the game that has emerged in American culture between discovering or constructing values and meanings. We're Progressives or Conservatives, Libertarians or Social Democrats, Pro-Lifers or Pro-Choicers, Wise Users or Greens, Devolutionists or Regulators, Privatizers or Socializers, Homophiles or Homophobics, and so on. But what overwhelms and subsumes all these differences right at this moment, what has brought us here, is a desire to touch the hard ground of reality and escape the high-wire acts of high-speed movies, of life as a huge warehouse of cheap bulk products or an electronic screen manipulated by a mouse. Out of the hundred TV channels at home, none of us can surf up some lasting fare. Among all the direct advertising mailers we get each day, none of us can find an old-fashioned product meant to last a lifetime. And I think this is the point: This generation is aging; this generation has a fascination now with what lasts, with what endures. If not anything in the world around them, then with themselves. It is as simple as that. Does human consciousness display now its own capacity to be more than a receptor of market-driven stimuli? Do we yet have a capacity to yearn for what makes us more than just a product ourselves? Can we be deep? Can we suffer the slings and arrows of outrageous fortune and be something more solid than a blip in cyberspace? Can we come to something in the end? Have we come to something? The nets are out and trolling. We come to the *Odeon* for the catch.

This is what I observe in the net: Peter Fonda has assumed a Henry Fonda role and played it through without a misstep. It's Henry Fonda as Tom Joad in *The Grapes of Wrath*—taciturn, observant, reflective, considerate, somber. A good man in a bad time, a good man tested by hard times, a man trying to be a good man, a fellow traveler, a man filled with dependable, hard-won virtues and loyalties, a man of truth, a man who will hold the course, accept consequences, give folks a chance to change him but not blow in the wind, a man of serious intent, unseduced by fads and fashions, a man of good heart who recognizes a good heart in others, a man concerned with others in a sincere, open way, a man for all seasons, a man whose integrity transcends the integrity of his times. He's solid; he's not about to morph into Jim Carey, or seek reality in Cyberspace. He won't ever receive an e-mail or send one. He's a throwback, a man fast becoming obsolete who pursues a trade fast becoming obsolete. No one wants to work so hard he tells his neighbor, for so little in return. But his father was a beekeeper and his father learned from his father. And at film's end, it is clear that when his son comes out of prison he too will become a beekeeper. What endures is the gold of the bee's honey.

The film wraps us in a way of life and that ironically becomes what we have plunged the surface for. Though Ulee stands for Ulysses and his dead wife's name was Penelope and his daughter-in-law's name is Helen, there is no symbolic, subtextual level to this film. Plot doesn't set a central conflict in motion; no theme slowly builds and transports the film to an interpretive level filled with abstract nouns. It's all about feeling the texture of life; this is not virtual surface but textured terrain, from faces to rooms to hives to honey. So while you might be arguing what Homer's *Odyssey* is really all about, what eternal truths it reveals, what lasting dimensions of human nature it explores, you might find yourself meanwhile lost in Homer's exploration of the terrain, of the texture of the journey. So too with this film. Ulee is a man on a journey that will take him beyond his mourning state, outside the fences he has built around himself, past the security of how he thinks he knows the world. But the film doesn't mobilize itself to be all about this. Rather, some time spent in a meticulously created world, some time journeying across this terrain of work, duty, ritual, crisis, conflict, reconciliation, will fill the nets we throw out in hope of finding what lasts, what enriches, what makes us feel we are, as humans, after all, on a special journey in life, maybe even a quietly, unpretentious noble one.

At a time when I daresay at least half the audience sits many hours in front of a computer screen, Ulee is out in the world, driving from one beehive location to another, performing a variety of tasks in the light of day, daybreak till dusk. Thomas Carlyle's advocacy of work and renunciation a hundred and fifty years ago are the guiding principles in Ulee's life. "Only simplify" Thoreau tells us from Walden Pond, only cut away the excrescences of modern life, of consumeroid existence and live "naturally." "I understand the bees and the bees understand me," Ulee tells us. He's at one with the bees; he's never been stung. It's not just a matter of smoking them to calm them down. Bees can sense a "bad vibe," a type-A personality, just anybody uncomfortable out there in Nature.

Ulee is very comfortable in a natural setting: Only peace and quiet of the Florida woods, fields, and marshes surround him. And though we see him dog tired, stretching down on his dining room floor to ease his aching back, we envy the intensity, the realness, the refreshing simplicity of his life. After all, it's an antiquated life, a life that you can find on the screen and in museum tableaus with descriptive notes alongside. At the moment when we are ready to plunge head first into the virtual realities technology is promising us, we look back and see Ulee there in the woods with his bees, doing a job of work with skill, with sweat, with a sense of accomplishment as he draws a sample of pouring honey and examines it in the light. It's an everyday moment but a special one nonetheless; it establishes the real connection between Ulee and the honey. The movie is slow enough for such moments, another being Ulee's request of his daughter-in-law for a glass of water from the faucet. She watches him drink it and so do we. It's a simple scene but it establishes a connection between her and Ulee. But between Ulee and the water too. Water and honey: simple, natural, good; and Ulee has time in his life to be with them. The honey is tupelo honey, a quality honey, a honey that bees have garnered from the tupelo blossoms that last only a couple of weeks. It's honey of the moment, a moment that you anticipate, that comes and then passes. Like the tupelo, it's golden. "Here now I'm living," you say. Ulee is living, living hard, and with his share of troubles, but this is not Disneyland, this is not simulation, this is not programmed, this is not virtual. We feel that everything in his life is "natural" and "real." And it's lost to us. We are too far gone to retrieve it. We are especially vulnerable then to the way Ulee has his being-in-the-world.

In a world seduced by simulacra of all kinds, from Vegas and Disney to Microsoft and MTV, inexplicable depression lurks and grows. Some blame this depression on postmodernity, on its attack upon what's really real and its reveling in simulacra. But what postmodernity actually does is allow us to see the lopsidedness of one reality construction in terms of another. In terms of this film, we are talking about a juxtaposition of Ulee's honey, representing a simple, hard, natural way of life, and Eddie and Ferris's stolen money, representing a "show me the money" way of life. Now even though Eddie and Ferris crawl about on the screen as if Ulee found them under a log in the swamp, they are more representative of the *Odeon* crowd than is Ulee. I mean that I would bet that the majority of the audience is closer to wanting $100,000 the easiest way they can get it, a very short-term profit, than they are to taking up Ulee's life as a beekeeper, despite the fact that Eddie and Ferris are thieves and sociopaths and Ulee is Henry Fonda. America is not advocating a return to beekeeping, to hard work close to the land, close to nature, but rather sitting back at a terminal and letting your investments work for you. Eddie and Ferris may be just as antiquated as Ulee in that they went out and robbed a bank. Only losers order a bank teller to show them the money; real players, the winners, know more legal and acceptable ways of getting other people to show them their money. Both are caught nonetheless within a "show me the money" attitude, and the political nature of legality, its expansion for the sake of the corporate rich since 1980, for instance, shows us that while bank robbing is always illegal, "doing business" often gets away with murder and only sometimes gets busted. I'm simply saying that there are more of us here that will go after Eddie and Ferris's "gold" than Ulee's. In fact, there are more of us that already have.

Eddie is polite and shows all the signs of being reasonable and wanting to be reasonable and wanting to keep things on a polite level. Nevertheless, you get the feeling that if he's opposed in any way, this facade will crack. Ferris's meanness is there to run into; he's not bright enough to conceal it or see the usefulness in concealing it. Two sociopaths that Ulee has to deal with, two from the market discard pile, two who can't find a place in the new entrepreneurial America. We're not ever meant to think of rednecks and gangbangers and "street" people as anything but criminals. But they belong to the underclass, an underclass that may have twenty years ago been the middle class. They are poor, they are working class. They may show up on TV tattooed and without shirts but they may also be unemployed, homeless, union members, underemployed, drug addicts, on parole, partially schooled by partial illiterates. When they show up on TV or in the movies they show up as sociopathic or psychopathic. The whole lumpen proletariat has become sick, deviant, criminal, threatening. Maybe they're born to be bad and born losers, or maybe they just want short-term returns on their investments like the rest of us and have nothing to invest with. They should do what Ulee does: Renounce desires they don't have the means to fulfill and just work their asses off. But this is not a culture that promotes that attitude, no matter how big we are on telling the underclass to "assume personal responsibility" and announcing a "work not welfare" philosophy. This is a consumer culture where identity is closely linked to shopping. These boys want to shop on the Net. This is also a society that wants to switch immediately from being a working-class and middle-class democracy to being a meritocratic democracy. All blue-collar workers, factory, field, and assembly line, go south of the border or go out of business. All "symbolic analysts" come forward. Eddie and Ferris are just as scheduled for extinction as beekeepers; but while we wax sentimental and nostalgic over Ulee, these boys should be imprisoned without parole. Maybe beekeepers will go out of business in America, but how do human lives go out of business? How does a whole underclass go out of business?

The question that Eddie asks Ulee—"You haven't had much of a life, have you Mr. Jackson?"—gives Ulee a chance to say that thanks to having met Eddie, he now knows how much of a nothing his life could have been. Eddie and Ferris take the hit for us here because otherwise without their presence Ulee would be addressing us. He might have thought he had a nothing life as a beekeeper until he got a look at what we had done with our lives. We live such plastic, nominal, consumeroid, digitalized, under-glass lives that when we see Ulee out there in the woods with his bees, we wish we could be out there with him. Who wants to get up from their computer terminal and spend a day with Ulee? Of course, Eddie and Ferris's down-and-out presences bring us to our senses. We can't stop going after the money because we'd wind up like them: losers. We'd wind up without the means to fulfill our acquisitive dreams. We might get so frustrated we'd go out and rob a bank. Or hold someone for ransom. It's easier to satisfy our desire to be like Ulee by taking up beekeeping as a hobby.

Or maybe we can someday go to a "Beekeeper Resort" where we pay to be beekeepers for two weeks—meals, tennis, golf, and aerobics available. We can buy what he's got. We can get the gold without the work.

Journeying Out of Illusion

This is also a society that wants to switch immediately from being a working-class/middle-class democracy to being a meritocratic democracy.

I am anticipating a film called *Inventing the Abbotts* because it's about class in America of the '50s. The film has just been released now, in the spring of 1997. What's it like now? The stock market had suddenly gone bearish after breaking all previous records for Bullishness, and is now apparently going Bullish again, welfare recipients continue to be "liberated," luxury items like $140,000 wristwatches have grossed better than all nonluxury items combined, and the Heaven's Gate 39 have taken a charter suicide flight off a planet where "the weeds have taken over the garden and truly disturbed its usefulness beyond repair—it is time for the civilization to be recycled—'spaded under.'"

Strange journey to rendezvous with a spacecraft hiding behind the Hale-Bopp comet—to escape an unrecuperable world. A more normal-seeming journey would be one back to the '50s to escape something apparently undigestible in the present but somehow managed and handled in the past. I'm talking about class. And I'm as interested in the trip out of here in *Inventing the Abbotts* as I am in the trip out of here taken by the Heaven's Gate 39. Both are journeys back to this moment, back to the present, journeys you might say that never leave the present nor the planet, although I am more liable to believe that Applewhite & Co. performed the trick than I am that America in this last decade of the millennium can escape class warfare.

Which journey is more significant in terms of telling us something about the journey American culture is making to the millennium? One tells us something we already know and the other may tell us something we don't. The Heaven's Gate mass suicide is yet another sign in this decade that there is something seriously wrong with the American cultural imaginary at the edges. Koresh at Waco, Randy Weaver in the Montana foothills, the antigovernment mania of the Montana Militia and the Arizona Vipers, the Oklahoma Bombing, the Amtrak derailings, the Rodney King South Central Riot and Revolt, the Million Man March, the racial split over the O.J. criminal trial verdict, the persistent 42 percent poverty level for black children, the continued collapse of real income for the working class, the growing antipathy (lack of concern? compassion? empathy? understanding? humanity? altruism?) of the Have's for the Have Nots, and now the Heaven's Gate cult, tell us that although the market has hit a record high for Bullishness there is anger and hate erupting in violence at any moment; there is despair and desperation leading to unspeakable tragedy. We have sown the continent for early profit and now reap the whirlwind. Or, at this millennial moment, we think we are in for it.

The question is: Where did we go wrong? Where did we make a wrong turn, mistake a dead-end road for a golden road? In his heyday Newt Gingrich boldly declared that we made that wrong turn in the '60s and now he was presenting the country with a proper map to get us all back on the right road. He called that map *The Contract with America*. For a very short period of time it was spread on every cover and screen in the nation. Then it became clear that this wasn't a mapping of lateral, crisscrossing roads but a blueprint of an estate with all the entrances blocked. You could cut the grass and deliver the groceries but you couldn't get inside. That plan to keep the wealth with those that already had it became an embarrassment to those who had sung *The Contract's* praises. Bill Clinton in his 1996 presidential campaign spoke over and over again of a bridge to the future but he hung back from presenting a map to that bridge. There was no prepared map, no a priori formulation, no already existing template. We were to navigate and negotiate our way mile by mile, from one fork in the road to another. There was no saying beforehand what new context time would build for us and therefore how we would be swayed and turned in the future. What seemed to remain unimpeachable though was a sense that the invisible hand of the global market had to be kept at our back. There would be no crossing into the future if we tried to drive into those mighty winds. Somehow, Americans could always rise to meet the requirements of those arbitrary and capricious winds of market play. When hi-tech, computer-type expertise was needed, the American worker would shuffle off the skin of factory assembly-line work and retrain himself or herself. And if they didn't, they could wind up in a couple or three different places: nonunion work south of the border, five to ten in an American prison, or serving Happy Meals at McDonald's. In one generation, they would be gone, extinct, and only the symbolic analysts would remain. An American meritocracy.

What is the relationship between meritocracy and democracy? Between egalitarianism and meritocracy? What is meritocracy in a Brazilianized country? If most of the "capital gains" finds its way into the hands of that 1 percent of the population who are shareholders, then what is needed are professionals to build, market, and advertise shareholders' houses, cars, boats, and planes, mend their bodies and minds, broker their money, and lawyer their disputes. Southern California formerly needed its illegal aliens to cook shareholders' food, wash their dishes, cars, and clothes, cut their lawns, and work in their sweat shops. Now those jobs are wanted by desperate Anglos who forgo union representation, medical and retirement benefits. And out-sourcing has enabled American entrepreneurs to use cheaper labor elsewhere and forgo the unpleasantness that having illegal aliens around creates for those enjoying "top of the line" lives. Nobody cruises to the Caribbean to see its poverty, or ever went to Cuba before Castro to do anything but be waited on by the indigenous people of that island. Now that immigrants, legal or illegal, don't make economic sense, we want America for Americans.

This is the kind of rankness out of which grow the weeds that the Heaven's Gate group saw filling what once had been the garden of America.

If you look through a clear windshield you can see that you have to drive against the domination of market values and meanings in order to reach the damage point, the accident that has us stalled. It may be that art and literature and music will refine our sensibilities and chaperone our profit-orientated responses to the environment and each other. It may be that religion and morality will put a personal moral compass in our hand and guide us toward conscionable thoughts and actions. It may be that education will tame and civilize our appetites and instincts and make us socially responsible citizens. And it may be that all of this will accelerate our travel from poverty to money in the bank. But each one of these has been eroded and corrupted by the values of immediate profit: self-interest and the amorality of competitiveness.

When America faced this convergence of wealth in the hands of the few at the very beginning of the century, labor unions emerged to counter the money/power nexus and siphon profits downward and outward. The egalitarian prosperity that was celebrated at midcentury is the product of, among other things, union activity, a progressive income tax, luxury, inheritance and capital gains taxes, antitrust legislation, contingency-fee legal representation for the masses. At the end of the twentieth century global-market forces and transnational, computer-facilitated financing has made an end-run around the power of unions whose power has rarely been exercised on even a national level. And the political climate beginning with Reagan and Thatcher and continuing into the present has fostered the rapaciousness of global-market play, or, in the case of Clinton, has bowed to its unassailable power. Liberal progressives, libertarians, and conservatives have all joined together in inventing an America of Haves and Have Nots, a world of conspicuous consumption, selfish competitiveness, disdaining intolerance on one side, and a world of insecurity, anxiety, envy, anger, frustration, revenge, and despair on the other. This latter world of too many jobs, too many consuming desires, and decreasing real wages is a doomed world within a global-market landscape in which only continuous reinvestment of capital, of working with surplus capital, of employing your money as your medium and not your hands, is the way out. Minds are employed in investing, brokering, advising; those who own the tool of production: money. They are also employed in designing the homes, cars, gardens, boats, and planes of the wealthy, tending to their bodies and minds, tending to their legal affairs, and handling the computers. If we are headed toward the meritocracy that Clinton's administration has settled for in place of an egalitarian democracy, we must all either fit into the space at the very top or find our place as "symbolic analysts" for those at the top. Everyone else goes on the discard pile. We're inventing this sort of world right now. What time is it?

In terms of the film *Inventing the Abbotts*, we are inventing the Abbotts, the family that lives in the big white manor house on the hill, and the Holts, the working-around-the-clock family that lives below in a house not to be distinguished from any of the other houses on the block. Class is a very hot topic precisely because it is the suppressed malefactor in American culture right now. Talking about it is "nonproductive" and "inflammatory." Such talk does no one any good; leads to a "no-win/no-win" situation. In whose eyes? In the eyes, of course, of those who are already spending fortunes on personal and property security, privatizing their personal lives in gated, protected communities, living within secluded wombs of luxury designed to keep them safe and private. Our American Abbotts are already living as if a war was going on between them and the Holts—the majority of the American population who are working harder and harder for less and less. The growing frustration of these Americans—which amounts to no more than their rising anger at not being able to buy at the rate desires instilled by the market have instilled in them—does not need to be fueled by a discourse of class warfare. Besides, there already exists a countering discourse which says class warfare leads to socialism which leads to Big Government which leads to the welfare state—and all that has been proven to have been a mistake, a view based on an erroneous conception of human nature and the needs of society. At the very worst, class warfare talk might lead to some fools once again believing that Marx is the answer. And of course that road leads only to collapse. Witness the former Soviet Union. Thus, there are many reasons why we can't talk about class.

But can we film it? Touching upon class in a film is touching a cultural hot spot. Does that pay off at the box office? Only if the film doesn't sidetrack itself off the mainstream, popular film path. And only if something more amenable to our culture surrounds the issue of class and ultimately consumes it. What better matter than young love? A double stroke here: love can transcend and conquer class difference, but at the same time the young now are falling in love with what lies beyond their grasp. Jacey Holt, the older brother who is seeking to strike a blow against the wealth, privilege, and prestige of the Abbotts, expresses the range of love early in the film when he points to one of the Abbott sisters driving past in an expensive sports car and says: "The difference is driving that and driving this." He points to the beat-up Studebaker that is the Holt family car. Love, you might say, is now gated; there are places where young love cannot go. The princess is in the tower where she's always been and the young peasant who loves her is in the country where he's always been. The only change now, however, is that the country is saturated with desires to consume everything, including the tower and the princess, while the opportunities to fulfill those desires are diminishing. For instance, in the year 1957 both Holt boys are able to go to the University of Pennsylvania, although Doug does so on a scholarship. Now in 1997, I'm not sure who from that Midwestern town of Haley, Illinois, is going to have the wherewithal to go to Penn. I question whether they will be able to afford the twenty-five grand a year but also whether their small-town high school has upgraded their online technology to competitive levels. Computer technology is not only facilitating the instantaneous manipulation of capital for the benefit of those who have capital but it is also widening the chasm between the Haves and Have Nots. A seven-year-old Abbott in 1997 is happily surfing the Net or playfully interacting with stimulating computer programs while a seven-year-old Holt in 1997 is depending on a public library which is now opened only every other day.

The love of things plays alongside young love because what's of interest here in the present is having all the things that go along with a certain successful lifestyle. Money brings cars and big houses and it can bring a beautiful wife. One is more liable to feel frustrated if toys are not acquired than in love simply because today's credo is "The Guy with the Most Toys at the End of the Race Wins." And "It's Show *Me* the

Money!" and not "Show me Love" because the assumption is that money can bring love but love can't bring money. In the game of competitive hardball that we're all encouraged to play, money trumps love, along with everything else. Because our own greed for toys, our own Fall-of-the-Roman-Empire-type material decadence, is as repressed and suppressed a matter as class warfare, this film does more backing away from the issue than displaying it. But when it comes down to "druthers," Jacey would rather think of his mother having betrayed her love for her dead husband by having an affair with Lloyd Abbott than think his father had been stupid enough to give up a priceless patent for a used 1937 De Soto. A father who has his hands on the gold and then gets outsmarted is more offensive to Jaycee than a father who couldn't keep his wife's love. And what makes this loser father even more of a pathetic figure is the fact that he takes that same 1937 De Soto and loses it on the bottom of a frozen lake, along with his own life, in trying to win a twenty-dollar bet with the man who coaxed him into trading his patent for that ill-fated automobile. The father who could have possessed the house on the hill and bequeathed to his sons all the toys now owned by the Abbotts is a more disturbing image for Jaycee than the mother whom he thinks had an affair with Lloyd Abbott.

One of the ways of keeping Jaycee's relentless revenge on the wealthy Abbotts in a nonincendiary position is to have the younger brother, Doug, who tells us "I would never let the Abbotts matter to me," narrate the film. He is recollecting the story for us and it is through his eyes that we enter that world. He doesn't understand what makes his brother tick and when he finally does, it is because his brother's revenge plot has extended to the Abbott whom Doug is in love with, Pamela. From the very first moment we encounter Doug we see that he is not guarded but open to the fads and fashions around him. He draws Elvis-like sideburns on his face and postures like a moody James Dean. He is open to romance like any normal, red-blooded Midwestern youth. The scenario of revenge on the wealthy Abbotts that clouds his brother's youth does not touch Doug. He remains outside this obsession, this dark war between privilege and poverty, and thus becomes the perfect companion for the viewer, who like Doug, and unlike Jaycee, is ready for romantic optimism rather than destructive antagonism. Popular film has nurtured our notions of young love, of romance that sparkles even in the darkest of moments. And we in turn look to popular film to carry us away romantically. *Inventing the Abbotts* is as much about this and as dedicated to this as it is to fingering the rankling issues of class, privilege, and greed. And by having hot, young stars like Liv Tyler, Joaquin Phoenix, and Billy Crudup in key roles, the film sidles away from those rankling issues and moves the youth who will be attracted to the film toward a romantic attraction to its stars. In this way, love and romance make rich and poor seem like sad, adult concerns; love spills into the audience where presumably Holts and Abbotts are romancing without any difficulties.

The film however does more than overwrite class concerns with Hollywood romance. It becomes proactive on the behalf of the Abbotts. And here's what I mean: we are told that "If the Abbotts didn't exist, my brother would have had to invent them" and that it is part of the human lot to live in lies, to live in illusions. This last statement refers to Jacey's erroneous belief that his mother had had an affair with Lloyd Abbott and had given the patent to him. Now while the notion of living in stories of our own making is a very postmodern notion, its assertion here is not on behalf of postmodern ends. If it were, we would be led back to a suggestion made earlier: that America today has *invented* for itself a "logic" of winning and losing. If we humans inevitably live in illusions— or what postmodernists would call mediations of reality—then why adopt a credo of a war of all against all? Why settle for as much wealth in the hands of three men as in the entire bottom quintile of the population? Why settle for a story of personal success that owes nothing to no one nor to the play of chance? And why not, if we inevitably live in illusion, counter the ill-effects of one illusion with the ameliorating effects of another? Why not counter, for example, the illusion that the poor can become wealthy by simply choosing to become entrepreneurial with the illusion that the poor need government assistance in order to become entrepreneurial? Why not counter the illusion that those at the very top are the best and the brightest and deserve their desserts without them being redistributed to the less fortunate with the illusion that those at the top owe their success as much to the goddess Fortuna and the labor of others as they do to their own talents?

We are not meant to travel down this postmodern path. Rather, we are meant to see that if we choose to live in the illusion, as does Jacey, that the Abbotts' wealth is undeserved, despotic, and victimizing, we are indeed living in an illusion, living a lie. We are placed in the position that Doug is placed in at the very beginning of the film when his mother asks him whether he realizes that the sideburns he has drawn on his face look false. He tells her he does and that he is still prepared to go to the party as he is. He is accepting the lie and going ahead with it. Are we accepting the lie that wealth is a problem, that we must wage a war against it, and going ahead with that lie? Or, will we take the more noble American course and observe the Midwestern mean as Doug does and never let the Abbotts matter to us, never allow the illusion of class warfare to affect our lives? Only when the film rises to this level of eternal verities untainted by the messiness of class warfare—namely, that we adopt illusions and lies at our peril—does it safely distance itself from the potentially society-shattering topics of class and greed that the film raises.

Jacey's war on the Abbotts leads him to seducing all three of the Abbott girls in the hope of tearing that family apart. His own brother is hurt in the process but Jacey can't let this stop him. The high ground that the narrator leads us to at the end of the film—that the Abbotts went on living the lie of blissful family life and Jacey went on living the lie of class warfare—is, of course, the high ground we should all rise to. Living in illusions and lies seems to be the lot of humankind but a film like this shows us that we can dissect those illusions and rise above them. There is only a bitter battle between the Haves and the Have Nots if we delude ourselves into thinking so; and if we do, we become the sort of possessed, twisted creature that Jacey becomes. And even if we tend not to dismiss all of Jacey's actions as self-deluded, even if we see the Abbotts' wealth as a potentially unjust force in a democratic society, we need only recall that this is what was in 1957 and not 1997. Just as we have left Marx's idea of class warfare behind with the collapse of the Soviet Union, so too have we left behind—somewhere around 1957— naive notions that wealth garnered by the few ravages in every way the well-being of the many.

In a postmodern view it is inevitable that we live in stories. There is no high plane of nonillusion, no realm of eternal verities that the "best that has been thought and said" rises to. But there is always an "on the other hand," a countering story, an opposing "truism," a story told from a different reality frame, that has the potential to pull us out of our own reality take and draw us toward another. None of this sounds very grand if we say we are leaving one story of reality to take up another. And if we oppose stories of reality with the hard truths of reality, if we oppose fiction with fact, living in stories is living in illusions. But consider that our sense of illusion derives from the Enlightenment presumption that we can ascertain what an illusion-free reality is, that we talk about the "actual" nature of things, or of how the world *is* in a totally objective, nonsubjective way. Some illusions—that goodness wears a white hat and rides a white horse and can clearly be distinguished from evil, for instance—or that women have some inherent hysterical proclivity that prevents them from reasoning in an unemotional way—win the general approbation of the day only to come under suspicion another day. A fabrication of reality which loses in the battle of fabrications is thereafter called an "illusion." It may, however, reappear at another time and place; it may be refabricated under different circumstances. It will then neither be called a "fabrication" nor an "illusion" but "reality."

We are presently living at a moment when we do not deny the reality of the Abbotts who have and the Holts who do not have. What is an illusion is that this situation in a democracy has no pernicious effects; that power remains unabused. What is still in a state of contestation is whether or not the Have Nots will struggle to be rich endlessly and never declare war on the Haves. *Inventing the Abbotts* attempts to preempt that contesting by showing us the disastrous effects declaring war on the Abbotts has on the life of Jacey. Paradoxically, the film is all about that warfare and the paradox is not of 1957 but of now.

Side Trip: Feeling the Glitch

July, 1997

When I left the States in mid-May, spring had not arrived. A heat index of 100 greets me in Washington D.C. upon my return. I am having a hard time getting back into the flow of events, following the hooks the headlines are throwing into the culture. An American "cultural imaginary"? I seem very far from where that might be. A friend picks us up at the Detroit Metro airport. "How was the weather?" he asks me as we head west on 94 in the early evening haze of heated exhausts. "Where?" I return. "Anywhere," he replies, shrugging his shoulders. It's all the same to him. Europe. The European Union. It's all one. And then he tells me about the family of turtles that have shown up in what he calls a "pond" on what he calls his "farm."

I listen but in my mind I'm sitting at a corner café in Leiden with a windmill moving behind me, bikers, cars, pedestrians, and buses negotiating reality in front of me without traffic lights or stop signs. I am walking down the narrow cobbled Rue Mouffetard in Paris on a very early Saturday morning, stopping at flower cart, fish peddler, boulangerie, and then my favorite café where the locals enter and greet the woman behind the bar with kisses on the cheek. I am on my way to my dinner at the inn in Aschach on the Styr in Austria, past the church at the center of the village where I attended Claudia's wedding. And listened to the choir sing "I Will Follow Him" with a lead singer that sounded like Ronnie Specter. It's after midnight and I am breaking away from the group in Fussen, in the Bavarian Alps, and walking across town toward the rail station, so dark that I can't see what's in front of me. And quiet except now, right across from the rail station, the sound of a woman moaning. At first, I think she's in trouble but then quickly I realize she is in ecstasy. I feel stupid at misinterpreting. I walk faster because somehow I am invading the privacy of the two making love somewhere to my left, behind the bushes. Where do the locals go late at night to make love? Behind the rail station. Our hostel is about a mile beyond the rail station and I think that for most of the way I can hear her; so high up the stars are close and I begin to laugh as I walk. I don't know precisely what I'm laughing at: perhaps being startled by the unseen but audible lovers. I had been thinking: "What if I run into some trouble and I have to run? How can I run if I can't see the ground?" I don't know this route well enough to know what's ahead. I am barely, just barely, finding my way back to the hostel.

In Zurich, we are tired and wandering in the old town looking for a place we can afford. A young man who has the look of so many young men you see on the street in Amsterdam, wants to know if he can help me find my way. "Not unless you can tell me how to get back to New York City" I snap back with Joe Pesce ferocity. "Are you talking to me?" I DeNiro. The kid falls back and lets me pass. He's heard that kind of American in the movies and he knows in those movies a kid like him might get whacked if he messes with the wrong people. I fall back on a lot of movie New York style when in Europe when I am on the streets. I give off an "I am the wrong people" vibe. Here in Zurich I am tired and the prices of the hotels are tourist prices and I am cursing myself for letting a heavy rain keep me from getting off the train before it arrived in Zurich. I don't like skinheads. But maybe I jumped the gun. Maybe the kid was just trying to help. Maybe he had a bald head and no fascist, racist notions.

On my way north from Brugge, Belgium, biking to the sea, I have a flat tire and in a small village find an old man who very adeptly patches the tube, with some help from his wife who hands him what he needs at just the right moment. He doesn't want any money but I give him francs. My fellow bikers wait for me at a cafe, sitting out in the sun enjoying the local beer. Later on, just a short distance from the sea, the tire goes flat again and my friends go on ahead and I run and walk the bike back. I reach the same small village just before a thunderstorm and I retreat into a cozy-looking bar, leaving the bike outside. I sit near a window where I can look out at the bike and I order a thick soup, bread, and beer. The rain doesn't let up and I stand at the bar drinking beers and talking to the barkeep, who turns out to be the owner of the place. "If you buy that man there a beer he will drive you back to Brugge," the owner tells me, after having spoken to two men at the other end of the bar. "You'll have to leave the bike and come back tomorrow to pick it up." But no, the bike it turns out will fit in this man's car. He drives me back to Brugge; I offer him some money but he refuses. Another beer? No. And he's off. Inside the Brugge Bauhaus hostel I find one of my group at the bar with another local, a local who has driven him and his bike back to Brugge. Shawn, of my group, had been hit by a Vesper from the rear and had been sent flying. "Not hurt" he had proclaimed, getting up immediately. But the man had driven him back and now was seated drinking beers. "I can't believe how kind this guy's been," Shawn tells me. "You talking to me?" I say but don't say. He's fallen on his head and his eyes looked glazed and he tells me he knows he doesn't have a concussion. "Don't fall asleep in the next several hours," I tell him, not as confident in his knowing as he is. Without being able to rely on our knowing we are stranded but only other people know it. I know it for him. What I like about traveling has a lot of do with knowing that someone else will always know where we are stranded.

It's late June and we're driving down 94 in mid-Michigan but I'm not back. I'm stranded. My mind is wandering elsewhere. My mind is still going down other paths. For the next few days, European experiences overlay present American visuals. What I'm losing quickly though is the close-ups of me and world; I don't seem to be able to get in tight with what's around me. And then I realize it's because there's a manufactured distance between me and my surroundings. I'm living at some degree of remove; I'm walking around places where no one walks around, except in the evenings to walk a dog, or to do an aerobic jog, or older couples with cross-trainers on walking out their golden years on a mentally well-marked route. It suddenly becomes clear to me that we're walking in stories of where we're walking, and that I'm still straddling European and American stories, although I am rapidly getting reintroduced to the American ones. Our American stories, I am beginning to see, manufacture a distance between us and the world. Something is put in between us and the "world" and we then proceed to get at the world through these cultural productions. At the same time, we're already in the world and the world is in us so the world gets at us and we get at the world in "nonmanufactured" ways.

We can sometimes feel the glitch between manufactured ways of being-in-the-world and nonmanufactured ones. But since the latter can't be brought to words, to a level of representation, to a story level, we can't express the disjuncture. If you go into other stories of worldly connection—the kind I've found in Europe—you do so only because there is room in the world for other stories. The American stories don't exhaust the possibilities of being-in-the-world, nor do the European ones. Nor can we say that if we add up all the known ways of cultural being-in-the-world we will arrive at the wholeness or the truth or the reality of our imbrication in the world. All we can say is that we think we've tabulated all the cultural ways of being-in-the-world that can be observed by some observer at some particular time and place.

On one level, then, it's not an America/Europe thing, a Henry Jamesian contrast of callow and wise and so on, but of the "other" story—whatever it may be—making it clear that "our" story is indeed a story and not the whole story. As the "other" story is therefore an attack upon the "reality" of "our" story, it bears all the deficits of the "alien," the "foreign," the "unusual," and so on. It also, paradoxically, will bear all the assets of the "new and exciting," the "exotic," the "stimulating." And because it appears to be exposing where we've been before and how we've been there as merely cultural and not "real," we begin to grasp the "other" as really "real." So when we return from those "other" stories of what the world is like to the "old" stories, all we can experience for awhile is a sense of loss. We've been thrown once again out of Eden. Now Eden as we relate it—photos and video supplementing our words—to the ears of someone who has not made the journey into the "other" ways, sounds like so many blank spaces to fill in with something they know, say, the sudden appearance of a family of turtles at the "pond up north on the farm."

Nonetheless, while the traveler who has returned lives in this liminal state, the concocted nature of the "old" stories comes into sharp focus. The drive along route 94 from the airport back to my home exemplifies the way we drive into the world in America. It's all routed for the automobile; the internal combustion engine takes you from here to there. We shape the earth's surface to accommodate the wheels an engine rotates. The vastness of space in America has allowed this amplification: individuals walking on two feet that don't need superhighways or paved roads for that matter, to autos moving along at about five-to-ten miles above the speed limit. And that speed limit here on 94 is now 70 mph. Only when we have a flat and have to walk several miles, perhaps toward a place with a phone you never knew existed, do you get into a different story. You are walking surely but you are also changing stories of how we travel, how we live, in the world. America is manufactured for the car because America has to manufacture cars to be the America that we have—since Ben Franklin through Henry Ford,

General Electric, and Ronald Reagan and up to Gordon Gekko—told ourselves we want to be.

The idea that the way we live in America is of commercial manufacture simply means that we have our being-in-the-world within commercially generated stories. We have to get to the world—which means other people, Nature, and ourselves—along roads that are marketed for a profit. If a particular way of attending to the world has no marketing potential—that is, there is no material profit in it—then it's not advertised, not promoted, not, finally, adopted by a society that is trying to order its spaces—both internal and external—in commercially profitable ways. The world, ultimately, is to be purchased, consumed, driven over on our way to short-term profits. Mammoth malls lying at both ends of a collapsed centre ville, strip malls spotting the terrain, fast-food drive thrus and the like fit the "drive through" story of how we are in the world. We journey out in our cars to these sites and only stop if some signage along the way detours us into unexpected consumption. We vacation by taking long treks to consuming sites, like Disneyland's Epcot Center, where we walk around a simulated Europe.

Now, American terrain is shaped for the car but the car itself is shaped by a drive to generate profits through technology, to employ technology to create new desires which good marketing can quickly shape into new needs. Computer technology is now shifting us toward a new revolution in profit making; potential consumers can now travel along digital highways and never leave the comfort of their home, a home filled with products purchased on the Internet. If this Third Revolution does occur it will override the old mental mappings with a new one; we will be walking into the world through yet another story. Ironically, this digitalization of human consciousness will replace a literal walking in the world with a virtual one. We'll all be so much closer to each other because we'll all be intersecting on cyberspace highways, shopping and chatting on the Internet, and ultimately enjoying our own holodeck programs of virtual creations in the comfort of our own living rooms. Highways, superhighways, and freeways studded with strip malls and bypassing inner cities will themselves be bypassed. There won't be much need to go out into the world anymore, perhaps to go to your local fitness club where a half hour on an exercise machine will sum up your physical engagement with the world. You might be working at a computer in an office building but chances are the overhead of an office building will be bypassed and you will be at a computer at home getting the job done.

Bill Gates is anxious for us to speed down the road to this new way of being-in-the-world. But I'm not wherever he is right now. I'm still going down route 94, heading back into the auto-demarcated reality of America now, while in my mind I'm walking, stopping, gazing, sitting—being-in-the-world in a different way in Europe. What are the stories that support these different mental mappings? These different walkabouts?

Put blankly, it's profitable for the Europeans to be in the world in old ways; it's what tourists come for. If there is a centre ville in which shards of the distant past create the ambience, there is no reason, not even an economic one, for knocking it all down and "modernizing" it. Places which a Southern Californian strip-mall mentality hasn't reached—very few in America now—are very many in Europe. There is, it is true, less distance to be traversed; more concentrated populations. But it's the configuration of streets and houses, configured by slow accretion, often engineered by time and not blueprint, arrangements predating the automobile, which draws you in close to the world. Its the ideal geography for idle strolls, for people watching, for idle chat in the morning with café latte, for dreaming on park benches in inner cities too impressively aged to flee, talking over the day's accomplishments with friends at dusk in a corner bistro. On the corner of the Rapensburg Canal in Leiden, I sit on a worn stone bench, other idlers on both sides, and watch a world designed to first accommodate bikers and pedestrians. The world is set here at biker's speed, not the racing bike or the challenges of the mountain bike, but a sort of clunky, durable family-model bicycle. Neither space nor time nor velocity bow to the supremacy of the automobile. Real in-the-world walkabouts engender a comparable mental geography, a framing of the world that brings us into face-to-face encounters, puts us close enough for hands-on experience. It's the terrain of the mental walkabout: you need good shoes, time passing at a walker's pace, walker's distances, frequent watering holes, a willingness to see everything beyond its functionality, and an attitude for companionship and not isolation.

Older stories of being-in-the-world are extant in older places in the world. It's not just the configuration of space "out there." What is "out there" creates a physiognomy of mind, of consciousness. And vice versa. If I wanted to be cynical, I could say that all this is still in Europe because it attracts tourists, and tourism is a very profitable business indeed. But surely the economic incentives of tourism have

Side Trip

driven us in America to "overwrite" the past in ways that we think will be more "tourist attracting" and therefore more profitable? If the past is not packaged by Disney or one or another theme parks, it is repackaged in places like Williamsburg, Virginia, the Alamo, Boston Market, New Orleans promenade, Olivera Street in LA and so on. Clearly, all space in America is mapped within profit stories that have no grasp of living in the world in, relatively speaking, unprofitable ways. I cite the status of utter inconceivability within which the current American cultural imaginary greeted the Branch Davidians and the Heaven's Gate group. Both groups, interestingly, sought to enclose a living space for themselves, close encounters on a daily basis not limited to the workplace. Walkabout space still exists in Europe because walkabout stories still exist. There are places where no tourist goes to, which have no sense of interacting with people in a car going eighty miles an hour, or town centers abandoned to an underclass they fear, or suburban shopping malls that stand in for churches, family pubs, and local inns, or time told by a speedometer, or quality of life measured by convenience shopping. You can go into any small town in America now and find its space configured for easy consumption and time wanting to move like it does within a film the folks have seen about LA.

I am aware now that most of the cars passing us on the left lane are new cars driven by young people going at least 80 mph. I don't see any signaling of lane changes; I see cars going 80 mph no further than a foot away from the car in front of them. In spite of the 100-degree heat index, everyone's window is up. Air-conditioning is the norm. Cool, quiet interiors. Most cars have no passengers; just the solitary driver, probably listening to their favorite music on a CD. Cars don't ride like my old VW camper anymore; that van made so much noise there was no sense putting the radio on. And the windows had to be left open in hot weather because there was no air-conditioning. You felt and heard every bump. Little chance of withdrawing into a private enclosed space. And the engine always let me know when I was approaching 70 mph. You sort of struggled with it. But I see clearly now on my return to America that the car is the private womb and within that womb there is no sense of real speed, there is no sense that at 80 mph the car ahead of you is an object that you can touch, that the scenery you rush past is moving in its own slow time and is something you can walk into, touch, smell, look deeply into. The world now is a rushed blur: if the highway doesn't go through it, it doesn't exist. When you get out of your air-conditioned car, you curse the hot weather and rush into

a Seven Eleven for something cold. Other people in other cars are
not people but cars first: the Cutlass Supreme, the Merc Marquis,
the Ford Taurus.

A story of success and prosperity, of protected private property, of secure existence, drove us to abandon the inner cities. More
profits were to be made if you could get people to give up walking
and buy cars. There is no profit for anyone but the walker in walking. More profits were to be made if you could centralize your consuming centers and enable people to drive and park there conve-
niently. There was no incentive to keep people in close
communities, up close and personal in contact, walking to the
stores, to the movies, church, school, club meetings, parties, restaurants, and so on. Driving about proliferating buying opportunities;
instead of walking every day to the local grocery to buy milk and
bread, now you jumped into the car and drove to a shopping plaza.
And on the way, you spy a shop just opened. And in the shopping
plaza you buy more than milk and bread. And on the way back you
drive into a fast food restaurant. You drive home in time for the
soaps, where people are always running into each other, where personal encounters multiply each and every episode, where people, in
short, are walking about and being-in-the-world in a way that you
sort of envy, solitary now as you are in front of the TV screen, solitary behind the wheel of your car, faceless in the malls, lost and
wandering. Driving fast but never journeying. I think of the chick-
ens who once "ranged" but are now caged in buildings where the
lights never go out so that they can produce eggs on a twenty-four-
hour cycle.

I am going down route 94 in Michigan; I'm going home but I
think this highway is taking me no place, taking me only to a still
point, a motionless, sightless, soundless place where all I can do is
buy the world through the way we've manufactured it. It's not a
place in which I can be in the world and the world in me.

Side Trip

Walkabout: America on the Verge of a Walkabout

August 1997

> *. . . to be at or approach the border or start of condition, state or event.*

The aboriginal walkabout mystifies us: is there a psychopathology attached? Why suddenly walk away from one's normal routine, from one's everyday life? How can you just go without a destination? Maybe one morning you wake up and it's only a dark sun emitting opaque rays and you have to walk off that deep, ontological depression. Angst puts us on a road away from angst.

Maybe it's more colloquial: like the guy who goes out for the newspaper and never comes back. Why, I once asked my mom, doesn't he ever come back? Maybe it's something he's read in the newspaper. "Gold Discovered in the Yukon!" Something in a film inspires you to head the car away from home and keep driving until what you see on the side of the road becomes more like what you've seen in that film. Maybe she's left the kids with her husband for one night and goes out dancing and then suddenly decides to dance away from husband and kids forever.

There are reasons then, but reasons that go back so far and twist in so many directions that when you pick up finally and leave for good there's no hope of tracing a reason why. It just may be that here in America where "progress is our business," we can't be so heavily into goals and objectives, plans and schemes, purpose and direction without sometimes running from our obsession with all that. Our walkabouts are not positive, but merely collapses from our ideals; we can't live up to a present and future we've mapped for ourselves. A walkabout is a fall, a fall from a state of right being, a state of long-term planning and investment, the modern replacement of the medieval state of grace. At the end of the road of this American walkabout is a "homeless" existence, wandering about pushing a shopping cart, your pants held up with a rope, dark crusts of blood on your elbows. The break from the prescribed order of things is unsightly.

I suspect that the Australian aborigine's walkabout is a positive and not a negative thing; an ineffable sort of replenishment, a walking off the path well trodden and well scheduled to other paths uncharted. Difficult to map: not a walking away from what one no longer has the stomach for, or from responsibilities one can no longer bear, and not a walking toward what appears to be a better life or what offers some relief, some possibility of forgetting, of starting all over again. The magical conundrum of the walkabout lies in its disconnections with both a past that one is trying to escape and a future that one is yearning for. Rather, the aborigine just takes a first step in another direction, walks into a different movement of time and a different space. The move is physical but ontological as well, a move toward a different being-in-the-world. One walks off the map one has been on. And it's not the coordinates of the past nor the future that chart the journey. It's not "If I run away now I can escape the consequences of what I've done." Or, "If I quit my job and head for Hollywood, I'll be discovered." Nor is it the coordinates of the present as in "My life is unbearable; I'll hop a freight."

What the aboriginal walkabout does is unlink itself from context, from the circumstances surrounding its "birth." It's not the present story of being-in-the-world that inspires the walkabout; nor is it a future story. It's an abrupt, discontinuous break with the present. Anything less would make it no more than another chapter in a present narrative, a product of a present order, a detour down a road on the map already in hand. And the aboriginal walkabout is not this.

Perhaps it begins with a call from a world unmarked, the world that has not been seen as we walk face forward day after day. What is behind us? To the left? To the right? Over our heads? Beneath us? You suddenly turn about, at a moment unscheduled, and walk the other way. And keep on walking the other way, not remembering where you were going or the protocols of the world you were in. At the same time, paradoxically, never forgetting, because when it is time, you will return. When is it time? That's like asking for the itinerary of the walkabout. When there is an itinerary, there is no walkabout but only a planned tour, perhaps planned by your local travel agent who will take you to places where you can find relief,

Walkabout

relaxation, pleasure, and fun—only in accord with the way your life-world identifies "relief," "relaxation," "pleasure," and "fun." Even cruises to a "mystery island" cannot wind up mystifying you, cannot clash with your sense of what "fun" and "pleasure" this "mystery island" will offer, without going out of business very quickly.

All this is preface to saying that I think that either one of two things is happening right now: either I am on the verge of a walkabout or America is. I want to say we both are on the verge of a walkabout because I share the American cultural imaginary. But it may be that I am ready to say goodbye to my Midwestern life and live in Europe. In that case, everything I connect as signs of America on the verge of a walkabout really refer to my readiness. There is no way to settle this; there never is. Concealing my lifeworld doesn't solve anything or make things better. It's merely duplicitous. If this is all indeed "me" then all I can offer as a way back to you is to say that my "me" has no hope of extricating itself from the American cultural imaginary. I am on a verge the culture has placed me on, on a border the culture itself has erected.

What are the indications or signals of "being on the verge"? What are the signals that an aborigine is about to go on walkabout? On one hand, there must be none, because if there are signals, then there's some causality to walkabout and I've been arguing for an a-causal relationship. If the present propels the walkabout, then it plans the walkabout and one may be traveling to a different place but nothing, ontologically speaking, is different. On the other hand, if walkabout can't be reduced to an empirically determinable event, and "being on the verge" can be witnessed in other than an empirical/rational way, is there nothing left to observe? What I'm saying is that the walkabout is an irrational act from a particular point of observation. It's not irrational to the aborigine; in fact, the notion of what comprises rationality and irrationality is quite beside the point, not computed, within a world that knows and produces walkabout. So a person can "be on the verge" of success, of suicide, or madness, or a stroke, or a nightmare, or a desire, and there may be no means at hand to tabulate, predict, or determine all these events.

A whole culture may "be on the verge" of a crash, a crisis, a revolution, a war, an earthquake, a golden age, a plague, a famine, or an apocalypse, and even after the event the causal chain may be impossible to describe, the rationality of what actually occurred may defy the rational protocols of any one discipline. We surely were on the verge of the '60s Counterculture but we can neither go

Walkabout

to 1950s tabulations nor 1950s editorials and scholarly articles to find a description of what the '60s became. Nor is it even possible to go back now and bring that cultural walkabout within "textbook" grasp. Ditto the Vietnam "conflict," the war between the states, JFK's assassination, the O.J. trial, the death of Julius Caesar, the execution of Sacco and Vanzetti, the meaning of *Hamlet*, and, most aptly I think, the collapse of the Soviet Union.

The moment of walkabout for the aborigine begins without rhyme or reason—within one sort of observation. To another sort of observer of that aborigine something else is involved—context, environs, setting, horizon, culture—world. Let's say the earth is traversed with what Bruce Chatwin calls "invisible songlines," a terrain crisscrossed with stories that the traveler knows and retells. To walk through the world is to sing it or narrate it into existence; to bring out the imbricating dimensions of earth and human, to bring both into a dialogue, a communion, a "worlding." The act of singing the earth into a human frame is at the same time an act which brings the human into the "unframed." The "unframed" doesn't sing or narrate nor does it mark itself but there is no singing or narrating without it. When objects and consciousness, terrain and song, intermingle to produce a "worlding" then what we call "world" is filled with the signs of the human lifeworld as well as the physical world. We live neither totally in our songs and narrations, within simulacra, virtualities, signifiers, nor do we live close to the bone of the "objective reality as it is in itself."

The mental geography of the aboriginal songline intersects the mental geography of what I call "the cultural imaginary." Neither empirically generated facts and statistics nor mathematical models capture or grasp this "cultural imaginary," our very human act of interweaving ourselves, others, things, time, and space into a "worlding" within which we live. If we are culturally "on the verge" of a walkabout, we are at once on the verge of walking into a different "worlding" and at the same time we are also on the verge of a "worlding" we are already in. And we must be on the verge within our own cultural imaginary; we must imagine ourselves to be on the verge and our "worlding" must reveal that imagining. Indeed, the act of worlding is an act of imagining ourselves at a certain time and place into existence. Or, from the nonhuman side of things, it is an interruption of that imagining accomplished by the mere presence of what lies outside human lifeworlds.

The aboriginal walkabout is not unsung within the geography of songlines. An American cultural walkabout is not unimagined

Walkabout

within the landscape of the "cultural imaginary." These statements hardly give me a methodology of approach or any cause for you to alter your investment portfolio. Nonetheless, we are journeying toward the American cultural imaginary while already being within it. That gives us hope that we can consume and respond to what we are imagining. And if we are on the verge of a walkabout, we should be able to provide the songline.

Walkabout in a Lost World

To adapt the famous words of Gertrude Stein, it is amazing how
we are not interested.
   —Clive James, "Hit Men," *New Yorker*, July 7, 1997

A *Village Voice* film critic referred to *Lost World: Jurassic Park* as
turgid. I agree: it is flatulent, leaden, awkward, halting—downright
sesquipedalian, which makes it sound apropos for a film about
dinosaurs but this film is long-winded, a long tale of signifiers signifying
nothing. I followed this viewing with some other swollen gems: *Batman
& Robin, Con Air, Men in Black,* and *Face/Off.* Summer blockbuster
entertainment, hijinks and fast-paced action, all go and no know. I
understand the marketing strategy of the summer "Olympics" of
movies; but I also understand any such strategy has to deal with the
American cultural imaginary. It doesn't go on vacation. None of these
entertainments chooses to run head on into what America may have on
its cultural plate this summer 1997. *Philadelphia, The Crying Game,
JFK, Wall Street,* and *Get on the Bus* are examples of such bold forays
into the American cultural imaginary. Neither is there a quick feel and
then a run for cover as in films like *Jerry McGuire* or *Meet Joe Black,* or
a sustained repression as in a film like *Forrest Gump.* What we miss
entirely with this summer's swollen gems is any zestful parodying of our
present American cultural imaginary or exuberant rewriting of it as in
Pulp Fiction, Fargo, Wild at Heart, Clerks, or *Slackers.* The cultural
imaginary, judging by these summer flicks, is registering zero on the
Richter scale.

    You might say they've done what popular film should do in most
everyone's view: pander to the social order but escape it and bring in the
cultural turmoil for laughs. Limit the range of the cultural imaginary to
"machine dreams," dreams of a Hi-Tech future, and clear-cut distinctions in everything: good and bad, beautiful and ugly, rich and poor,
smart and stupid, deserving and undeserving, sane and insane, innocent
and guilty, and so on. Of course. My expectations in regard to popular

film are no greater. But in spite of expectations of the mass audience and the expectations and strategies of every filmmaker and backer, escape is a near impossibility and the harder we render clear-cut distinctions on screen, the more we are reminded that in the headlines, in our lives, in the past, out on the streets, in everyone's mind—these firm categories blur, crisscross, overlap, blend, and generally go messy on us.

What we have in these films is only mock encounters with the culture, as if none of this really mattered, as if this is all so much time filler, so much distraction. It's as if we were all waiting at the airport for someone to arrive—someone whose plane has been unexpectedly delayed— and meanwhile we are telling each other stories to pass the time. Or, perhaps more appropriately, we're not aware that we're waiting for anyone or anything. The stock market is soaring; inflationary cycles seem to be a thing of the past; we are dumbfounded in the face of the economic indicators. No one seems seriously to think that giving anyone anything for nothing is helpful. Everyone seems to believe that what's good for business globally is good for America. The environment seems to be an issue that prosperity will deal with if and when it really threatens. The Federal Government seems to have reached its proper condition: step away from private lives and local dreams. Politicians seem to know that they can worry a bone publicly as long as it doesn't tamper with the real market order of things. And all other issues, from gender and family values to censorship on the Net and violence on TV can turn a profit on the Gawk & Talk TV shows. Everything, in short, is about settled into place. And everyone knows it.

In the end, though, it adds up the way Prime Minister Chamberlain's words added up after a meeting with Hitler: distracting words, distracting facts and figures. The real attention should have been placed elsewhere. End of parallel. We are living with no great attachment to the realities of our social and cultural setting; it's not a matter of reflection. It's not a matter of thinking about the indicators and saying they must be wrong. It seems as if we can have a viable democracy and no vestige of economic equality. Here is the question we are asking the Chinese: whether a restrictive political environment can promote favorable economic conditions, can global-market enterprise interact very nicely with a nondemocratic regime? But the reality of our own oligarchy and its nice fit with global-market enterprise seems to be a nonissue with us. At the same time, this is a "reality," a ground that no one really wants to stand on.

Our dilemma is this: all faces but those of the discredited shine with a Bill Gates-like enthusiasm and optimism. To argue against this is to join the ranks of the already discredited: old liberals like Mario Cuomo and

Daniel Patrick Moynihan or Teddy Kennedy or Bernard Frank or young ones like Hilary Clinton and Paul Wellstone, odd screwballs like Ralph Nader, Ross Perot, Pat Buchanan, passé unionizers and socialists like John Sweeney and Ron Carey. We are at a moment when a discourse that counters our own seeming prosperity is a discourse that cannot be mounted, cannot be formulated, cannot be told. Nevertheless, we are not accepting at face value this reality of post–Cold War, augmenting prosperity. We don't know how not to pay attention to it; we don't know what to do otherwise. And yet, we are not with it and we cannot chart a course against it.

I call this a walkabout moment for the culture—when, where to, how long, and what's the result I have no idea. I'm not a seer; I'm just there in the audience with you watching the summer '97 lineup. And what it shows me is an American culture going through the paces, biding its time, wary of the confidence of the Bullish market, meeting each day's rise of the Dow with neither skepticism nor belief, observing how each day the newspapers try to jump-start with their headlines a culture that is, according to every indication, already moving. And this mood too is part of the millennial journey: we're on the train that will take us where we want to go. We're sure of that. We're very sure of that. There's no other train and there's nowhere else we'd want to go. And surely there are no stops between here and there. Let's have some movies while we're waiting. And the movies, not surprisingly, reveal how steadily we pay no attention to how sure we are of anything.

It is for this reason that these films start and restart, explode sporadically and then fade into background noise. They're having a hard time getting our attention. What would you expect with an audience that is trying to redirect its attentiveness from what "clearly meets the eye" to what isn't even on the horizon? We're filling the screen with blather and elaborate production values and we're accepting because to be nonaccepting—well, that's to fall into some crankish posture, some naive, hopelessly market-ignorant radicalism. Because no one can swallow the blather nor spit it out, we are caught pathless, in a state of aporia. Walkabout emerges from aporia, cultural as well as personal.

To be lost is to be pathless. Dinosaurs are extinct, lost to the present world, various theories contending as to why: fire (meteor) or ice are the two favorites. Now instead of the dinosaurs being kept in Jurassic Park, they are, in the sequel, roaming free on another nearby island. Let's take a raptor leap of imagination and say this lost world represents our lost world. I mean everyone sitting here in the air-conditioned chilled theater on this hot summer night is lost in a cultural morass too perplexing and volatile to map, a social order driven by polls and headlines and thus too capricious to trust, a market order guided by T-Rexlike rapaciousness. But this world is lost only within the cultural imaginary; on paper, on the computer screen, on the nightly business reports, in the mouths of politicians, this America is right on track, "holding a winning course" to the new millennium. The reality of where we are is caught between the representations of the Dow Jones and the representations of our imaginations, caught between the signage of Madison Avenue and Disney, and the signage of our own dreams, caught between hard facts and hauntings. We are lost first as mental travelers, pathless in our own minds, the deepest, most angst-filled, most bewildering state of being lost. Movement in any direction reappraises itself. In a way, the only thing to do is sit back and watch the screen, because on the screen there are words tied to actions, consequences anticipated and realized, certainties upheld, choices made, paths taken, lives rising out of aporia. The burden of making a move in real-time has been transferred to the Big Screen, the TV screen, and the computer screen where all moves are only "as if" they were real.

These screens, however, only succeed in revealing our absolute readiness and preparedness for walkabout, for picking and starting off in a new direction. In *The Lost World* , for instance, the film begins with a seedy-looking Jeff Goldblum on a subway; he has the look of someone who has been on the street too long, who has bad dreams, who doesn't know what to do with his life. He has the look of a man uncomfortable about where he is, where he's going, uncomfortable with the world around him, uncomfortable about being in this movie. Strange beginning for a film that will soon fill the screen with the latest cinematic breakthrough in dinosaur representation, in a film that will have us wondering more about "how do they do that?" than about Jeff Goldblum's depressed state. Goldblum is our link to the previous film, *Jurassic Park*, the small link that will blow up to the impressive pans of dinosaur world. We go with him into the film, but, surprisingly and revealingly, he imparts no discourse of entrance. He doesn't give us a guiding discourse. Instead, all we get are fits and starts; he acts like he's been wired: a sudden bit of current gets him talking rapid fire. But the passion is wired too. It's not an acting problem; the film doesn't know where to begin or how to continue or how to end. Just as Goldblum gives us volleys of words and then drifts, the film gives us fragmented visuals, one take pasted on another, one idea of what will have effect following another. As there is no connective tissue of ideas, feelings, dreams, or desires, except on the level of a tired and tiresome repetition of what has brought us to this state of being lost, we find no way to escape our growing disinterest in our world.

Wouldn't it surely happen that we would lose connection with a world that only pushes stories of connectedness that we don't believe and yet can't refute? *The Lost World* is not lost to that world, to that dilemma; it arises from it; it films the dilemma; it produces and performs the dilemma. The film is filled with alibis that riddle the culture: that "life will find a way," the closing wisdom, mocks those who sit in the audience who have not found their way around in a society reduced to the meaning and value dimensions of a Monopoly board. Surely market interests will find their way toward profit more easily if there is no governmental intervention and regulation on behalf of other than "market" values, say, environmental values. This "lost" world will be okay as long as no one tries to interrupt the "free play of dinosaur energies," the open competition and battles between these corporate giants. Ironically, the "life" in the audience, the lives of all those not sharing in the rewards of the rising market, of gargantuan returns for a minuscule portion of the world's population, cannot find or summon the means to "find a way." Dinosaurs can; people can't.

We are amazingly uninterested in *Batman & Robin* in the same way its makers and backers are uninterested in it, which is just a way of saying that all that's really going on here is that somebody is milking a cash cow and we know it but we're showing up for the milking anyway. I think we show up because screen "highs," highs produced by a rapid succession of technical, cinematic display that give us one "rush" after another but leave us without a trace of recollection in the morning, hide how amazingly uninterested we've become in our own culture and our own lives. It's a constructed, enforced uninterest that popular films like these summer blockbusters augment the more they rev their production engines up to high digital speeds. Technical bravura cannot hide the impasse we've come to: we distrust the world we've constructed and that has constructed this film but at the same time distrust itself is no place to go, cornered as it is already by the paranoia of the Unabomber, of Tim McVeigh, of the Hale Boppers, of Agent Fox Mulder, of the Roswellites; we cannot adopt our screen addictions as reality nor can we find a reality outside our screen addictions. Wired as it is to the cultural imaginary, popular film can neither *not* display our amazing disinterest nor can it *not* accelerate its technical hijinks and panoply. Grounding stories that weave visual pyrotechnics into a meaningful fabric are in short supply; in fact, they are absent. But if the story fractures itself and pulls the plug on itself, over and over again, starts off in a new direction without a look back, then nothing remains to linger in the mind. Story proves as speedy and elusive as pyrotechnics. Result: you leave the theater bearing quickly disintegrating impressions; the film vaporizes; it's all lost on you;

no impact. The more assaulted you are by images that leave no residuals in your memory banks, the more does the world around you lose its intensity, its effect upon you. You make no grounding connections. Now here's a world you are ready to walk away from.

There are more nonstarts, fragmented bits, wandering stories, vacant looks and gestures in *Batman & Robin* than in *The Lost World*. After all, these films are inspired by DC comics; they have a license to sequence in cartoon frames. How much story do you get in a Batman comic? The visuals are always meant to carry the day. And yet this is a film, not a comic book; imagination fills the spaces between cartoon frames but the film *Batman & Robin* gives us no relief from its action barrage nor does it come in close enough to the lifeworlds of its audience to trigger their imaginations into a supplementing role. The opposite, in fact, is pursued: distance from real lives of viewers because all the paths of connection are enveloped in difficulty. Difficulty for whom? For the filmmakers who want to take the easiest path to selling tickets and evidently believe that path is not through directly engaging the cultural imaginary but through "technical bravura." There's more profit to be made being technically venturesome than there is in venturing into a cultural imaginary that is showing, on this level, all the signs of drifting, of going on walkabout.

This state of drift, of being on the verge of walkabout, may infect one generation and not another, the Baby Boomers and not Generation-X, the Batman and not the Robin. At my showing of *Batman & Robin* the theater is filled with Robins. And Batgirls. They are hooking up differently; you can hear it in their exclamations of "awesome!" as a bit of cinematic wizardry fills the screen. For them, there is a future of more and more complex and awesome technologies that will envelop their lives and bring on excitements and thrills that we can't even imagine now. More of everything and faster and easier too. It could very well be that they are marked as "X" because it is unclear to what extent they will invest themselves in a "show me the money" mentality, or whether the seductions of the Screens, of Hollywood simulacra, of digital cyberspace, of MTV, will keep them out of the real arena and merely jacked into virtualities. Or worse. Wes Craven's film *Scream* shows us two young psychopaths who get the motivation for their mayhem from the nonmotivation of Norman Bates in Hitchcock's *Psycho*. They're killing people because it looks cool on the screen. But finally it's an undecidable issue whether this Generation-X will be drawn to digital virtualities or market hard realities. And there is always Bill Gates as a model for fusion: a hacker who jacked into market success. The fascination with technology is evident and the distance between that and the market forces that propel new technology is not great. For Robin, future hopes and dreams overshadow past traumas, past difficulties that make one cautious in the present and wary of the future. The Batman is like this, so wary of what can happen that he tries to control the present, tries to clip the wings of Robin. Robin, on the other hand, wants full technological license; complete being-in-the-world is power to run the machines. Period.

The lurking dark side of the film lies in this melancholia and impassivity of Batman, more clearly registered in Val Kilmer's Batman in *Batman Forever*. Multimillionaire Bruce Wayne's transformation into Batman is Wayne's abrupt departure from his own life. He goes down to the bat caves beneath the Wayne mansion and there he puts on the identity of Batman. It's a variation on walkabout. The two worlds are incommensurable. What disengages Bruce Wayne from his multimillionaire life, from the life of a "winner," and has him don the dark identity of Batman? I find it more than interesting that while the most popular film of 1997, *Jerry Maguire,* has the whole audience as enthusiastic as Cuba Gooding, Jr., in adopting the philosophy of "show me the money," *Batman & Robin* shows us a man of money living an imaginative existence that has nothing to do with money. And the lurking dark side of the film also lies in Robin's impetuosity and presumption inheriting all the powerful toys that have, for instance, made the film *Batman & Robin* possible. In short, a world that we have constructed that amazingly we seem to be uninterested in, will be inflated by the enthusiasm of the next generation. The disease of "dissociative drift" develops after long and close contact with nominal prosperity for some and nightmares for others, with an American culture that cannot tap its own imaginary for fear it will unsettle the Dow. By the time Robin comes to realize that the world of the Batman is not merely in the allure of its dazzling gimmickry and its daring-do, his only option will be walkabout. It won't be an adventure to go to the bat caves; it will be an escape.

Batman & Robin does only a thin, interrupted riff on the tensions between Batman and Robin. Sure, the clash between the Boomers and the younger generations is there in American culture and if you want to bring both to the film, you cast George Clooney for the soccer moms and Chris O'Donnell and Alicia Silverstone for the young and restless. And the special effects will more easily draw the hacker generation away from the imaginative failure of the film than it will the Boomers. Nevertheless, the film is not going *there;* the film is going away from every part of this, especially its own lack of imagination in spite of its technological innovativeness, and especially its own fear of what bat caves its own audience is in. Spins and alibis fill in for all this: Schwarzenegger as Mr. Freeze who "ices" everything, including people, with his ice gun. He does it all to "rule the world." Uma Thurman's character Poison Ivy wants to kill mammals and replace them with plants. Anyway, they're villains; they're evil. It's as easy to see who the heros and who the villains are on the screen as it is to see who the winners are and the losers are in society. It's too clear to question; it's too easy to believe. There is no path to take away from this impasse.

The emptiness of the film stripped of its action scenes fills the theater; one spectacular fix has us anticipating the next, faster and faster until there's no feeling where we are now in any one scene. All pleasure lies in what's to come and when it comes its pleasure too is deferred. Nobody remembers how the film ends because no one is quite sure when it began. The memory is only of having gone out that night to see something, to be somewhere else.

Con Air and *Face/Off* substitute gun play and violence for superhero spectacle and lost-world dinosaurs. Nicholas Cage is a good guy in *Con Air* who accidentally kills a bad guy. Now he's served his time in prison and is being flown to another prison where he will be released. Problem is this flight is filled with the worst psychopaths and sociopaths America has to offer. And they take over the plane. But Cage singlehandedly, in the *Die Hard* tradition which itself is in the *High Noon* tradition, takes on and vanquishes these villains. It's a gymnastic performance, bullets fly everywhere, explosions shoot bodies upward, everything crashes into everything else in Dolby stereo. And in between we get scenes like psychopathic Steve Buscemi at a make-believe tea party with a four year old in a sand box. She survives and he winds up in Vegas shooting craps. Is he going to show up in a sequel? It's not worth thinking about; it's not worth thinking about how hard the justice system has been on a "good soldier" like Cage who was just defending himself from "civilian" attack. It's also not worth thinking about what makes John Malkovitch and Ving Rhames and all the other "bad guys" so bad, about why this country has to imprison a higher percentage of its population than any other country, why we seem to be producing so many psychopaths and sociopaths. It's not worth thinking about these issues now because they've already been thought about. The "bleeding heart," "society is to blame," "rehabilitation" story only now gets played by "soft liberals," "old hippies," "aged radicals," "nonplayers," "bag ladies," and "lumpen losers." On the other side, we have all the certainty, clarity, and common sense displayed in this film: these guys are innately, intrinsically, essentially bad and those who aren't put to death should be put away for life. We all believe in all of this; we all believe in none of this. We believe it as much as we believe there could be somebody like the hero Cage is in this film who does the things he does and the villain Malkovitch is in this film who does the things he does. David Lynch will cross the two—and call them Jeff and Frank—in his 1985 movie *Blue Velvet*; he'll marry heaven and hell, but now in 1997 that seems to be a lost highway. Leaving us no flight out of here, we wind up prepped for walkabout.

Nicholas Cage appears as the villain, Castor Troy, in the film *Face/Off*, a John Woo directed film, which means choreographed gunplay gets center stage. It's meant to energize a script Woo doesn't have full confidence in, doesn't know how to play out without troubling his audience. Still, this film goes further in showing us that we don't know clearly what's what in regard to "good" and "evil," who's the good guy and who's the bad guy, whose family might have values and whose may not, and what may make us happy and what may make us miserable. John Travolta as FBI agent Sean Archers switches faces with a comatose Cage; Cage awakens and manages to put on Travolta's face, a hi-tech variation of Shakespearean character switches. Now we have whatever Travolta is behind the face of whatever Cage is and vice versa. Travolta is the cop after the terrorist Cage, so it's goodness behind the face of evil, in the case of Travolta, and evil behind the face of goodness, in the case of Cage. But it doesn't exactly turn out that way. Cage's exuberant, playful response to life seeps into Travolta's dead-in-life, rod-up-his-butt interior. It's not so easy to detect what Travolta adds to Cage. The revealing scene is between Cage behind the face of Travolta having a "dad and daughter" talk with Dominique Swain playing a rebel-without-a-pause daughter. At the very moment when you think Cage, who likes to pat the asses of young girls, is about to sexually attack her, he sits back, looks at her, and sees what she needs and not what he wants. He winds up giving her a knife for protection. Somebody, not Cage, is going to come on too strong with her. Cage has already shown this capacity to care about other people; a terrorist who's planted a biological bomb is full of an engaging *élan vital*, while the good cop is frozen within his pursuit of evil.

It's not the face per se which changes the character but rather other people responding to that face. Travolta is plunged into Cage's life and Cage is plunged into Travolta. The contexts of different lives elicits different responses. Maybe if Cage stays long enough in the family life of Travolta, he'll drop his terrorist activities; maybe if Travolta stays long enough in the terrorist life of Cage, he'll drop his inflexible, inhuman dedication. Cage's face gives Travolta a chance to break away from the revenge drama he is caught within it; Travolta's face gives Cage a chance to break away from the terrorist drama he is in. Whether the seeds of different selves lie already within us and are simply waiting for the opportunity to emerge, or whether different settings reshape our characters is undecidable here. When the film is not showing us the clear action of gunplay, it shows us that no one is really what they appear to be, and that staying who you are is not as good as taking on an opposite identity. But notions of relative value and relative identity don't just sneak in between the gunplay; the gunplay shoots down the significance of those thoughts. Why? Because the whole culture has already blocked off any thinking about what a constructive view of self and reality may do to the present order of things, an order grounded on market dispensations. There's already a sign up that says "This is a lot of liberal hooey that will lead us to moral and social collapse." You know who you are and you've chosen to be what you've become. Now, let's choreograph some gun play that will make things perfectly clear, including a clear and definite outcome.

In this fashion, in terms of an imminent walkabout, the whole film seems to urge us toward "taking off" from these lives we are presently living, these social and cultural conditions we are presently living within, these meanings and values that produce these identities and this society and culture. A cataclysmic change awaits us if we can just "take off" from the lives we are living now.

Journeying into Slow Time

> *Cybernetics transforms language into an exchange of news. The*
> *arts become regulated-regulating instruments of information.*
> —Heidegger, "The End of Philosophy
> and the Task of Thinking"

There is something awry in Tarantino's *Jackie Brown*, something askew; disjointed, and I am the one experiencing this disjointure so I have obviously walked into this movie with some sense of "jointure." The parts should fit this way; the joints made here at this point, the assemblage and the assembler, bricolage and bricoleur should all fit into my anticipated sense of jointure. It's not hard to figure that my expectations are grounded in Tarantino's previously written and directed film *Pulp Fiction*. Since that film debuted in 1995 I have been further weaned away from a filmic modernist order of things, whether it be a tight, coherent script brought to view under magisterial control of a Hitchcockian director, or the inner/outer perambulations of a *directeur/auteur*, or the rushes of the avant-garde away from "whatever we've got" and toward new aesthetic revelations.

David Lynch, after a long furlough, has returned with *Lost Highway*, which comes in and goes out of my local Midwest mall theater in a flash, and the Coen brothers have done *Fargo*, a film that slowly attracts an enthusiastic audience and sets Frances McDormand up for a best actress award. But it's *Boogie Nights* that has most closely followed up on the postmodern frenzy of *Pulp Fiction*. Tarantino's own followup, *Jackie Brown*, seems more of a precursor of *Pulp Fiction*, rather like the unpublished novels done before but published after a novelist makes his or her big launch. Maybe its Pam Grier in the eponymous role of Jackie Brown who makes this more of a '70s film than a '90s, maybe even a '60s film. There is something about the black tailored business suit and the white open collared shirt Jackie buys and wears, the VW van with the beads and the loud music that De Niro and Bridget Fonda drive, the motif of the Delphonics' R&B music, living rooms with a '70s JC Penney catalogue look, TV Mod Squad-like shots of interior malls and parking lots, the sloppy louginess of Fonda with TV and bong—it all takes us back into an imagining of what was. *Pulp Fiction* on the other hand possessed an ambience of hip coolness not yet seen but soon to be emulated on screen and in real life. That film ran before us, ahead of us, while *Jackie Brown* is running behind us.

Time is out of joint here; askew; what is awry here has to do with time. And Jackie Brown, while seeming to be the essential link with this non-'90s vibe, takes me on a journey to time out of joint, slow time, the times of the everyday, the movement and pace of just getting into the flow of everydayness, of time not back then or time not yet, but being in time now.

The passage goes like this:

Jackie walks into the film to the soundtrack "Crossing 110 Street" and she drives out of the film accompanied by the same soundtrack. She's a black woman, no longer young because it's no longer the '70s, but still attractive. But she's still down, she's still making a barely sustainable $16,000 a year salary with benefits that she admits don't amount to much. The fire is still there, the toughness, the fearlessness, the capacity to take the blows and keep intact. Right up until she sticks a gun in Samuel L. Jackson's groin, we think she's just a victim. We think that because we've seen her apprehended by the cops, bullied and cowed, subdued and submissive, locked up, led around (in short) by the nose, the "fine" black woman of twenty years before at the edge of nowhere, slipping back into nonentity. "You haven't exactly done a lot with your life, have you, Jackie?" one of the cops asks her—a blow she takes without countering. Because she doesn't counterpunch there in the opening scenes of the film, we are ready to count her out. This is one of those people who won't assume personal responsibility, who won't get into the ring and compete; maybe she's a preordained loser, maybe what *The Bell Curve* predicted regarding mental competency and the capacity to compete in a globally competitive environment is here realized in the person of Jackie Brown. But we learn something different; we learn that Jackie knows how to pace herself, her energies don't overspill, are not wasted at the wrong moments. She knows when and how to counterpunch without letting the battles of life suck the life out of "getting off" on everyday life.

I begin to see what is countering the plot here, a plot Tarantino inherits from Elmore Leonard and develops in a continuously overlaying fashion, denoting space for us with captions as in the *X-Files* until we lose our place in this postmodern mapping of the world. And then he overlays time in the crucial scene: first we see the money exchange through Jackie's eyes, aware for a second that she is observing someone observing out of the frame, then through the eyes of De Niro and Fonda, who observe Jackie but also observe a third observer, Max Cherry, who casts another layer upon the same scene. But since Tarantino has set up the scene as a surveillanced scene—everything here is being done under police observation—we are never quite sure who is the final and ultimate observer, whose observation will finally dominate the scene and reveal all there is that has to be revealed. You might say that this movement of observational points takes us back to a postmodern point: it is Tarantino the director who has the vantage point, who has set up the commanding point of surveillance with his camera. Jackie, DeNiro, Fonda, Max Cherry, and Michael Keaton are all subject to Tarantino's gaze. Or the gaze of the lens. Who is orchestrating this reality and where is that person positioned? Is there anything left out of this gaze? And why wouldn't there be if the final surveilling vantage point is just someone positioned somewhere, at some time? It's Quentin's order of things.

Finally. Or, rather, there is no finality because we travel back to ourselves positioned in that theater observing, following closely the aftereffects of the addition of each new layering of plot revealed through different perspectives revealed through a multilayering of time. And we are not prepared to see ourselves as final arbiters, although there was a time when we naively and optimistically assumed the role. Tarantino does all he can to make our journey to truth and meaning difficult, paralleling as closely as he can the continuous layering of time, space, perspective, and chance that everyday life offers us at the very moment he is imposing a plot and we are attempting to derive meaning from both that plot and the way it is imposed upon us.

If plot, no matter how labyrinthine and multiplexed, is itself just a layering upon everyday life, an imposition, and Tarantino makes us aware of this, then he must actually be trying not to focus on plot, he must be filming away from plot. In order to do this, paradoxically, he must set the plot up as overwhelming so that we lose our way and literally stop by the roadside and pause. We take time out. We take refuge from the plot. I attend the movie with a friend who does exactly this; the plot becomes such a difficult thing to penetrate, to take command of, that he winds up retreating from the film. His stepping away from the stress of plot leads him to conclude that with more skill, a director could have made things easier to access. The film could have been more observer-friendly, more engagingly and cleverly interactive. A better script would have pared out the excrescences of peripheral scenes, unessential passages, wandering, purposeless dialogue. To detour from a prevailing roadmap is not a popular nor profitable venture. Tarantino succeeded in making it a stimulating, entertaining one in *Pulp Fiction*. Whether he can succeed with *Jackie Brown* I have no way of knowing now, just a few days after its release.

But the baroqueness of the plot announces its own bogusness to me and rather than pronounce the whole film bogus and its director a bogus genius, I take my pause and note that the film is chock full of Tarantino's own pauses. Time has a stop, or, I remember that time must have a stop if we are ever able to take a good look around, summon everything to the scene, and sum it up. But that's a modernist hope and not a post-modernist one. What does Tarantino—or where does Tarantino take us when he pauses from his gleeful, devilish compounding and complexing of plot? Where are the "crucial" scenes away from the crucial scenes that the plot has erected? Or, is the whole question of what is crucial also caught within a relative frame, varying in accord with the perspective of the observer, positioned as crucial by the positioning of the camera?

I observe that where Tarantino takes us is into the slow time of everyday life, the everyday motions, the repeated phrases and questions, the chance meetings, the interplay, if you will, of living our lives and sometimes reaching toward some formulation of knowing what and how we are experiencing the world. Just as we all don't emplot our experiences in a multilayered script of knowing, we don't bring every gesture and word and thought and event of the everyday into some frame of meaningful grasp. Some say that is what a good film should do if it aspires to the level of art. I think this is something humans do— bring to order and meaning the disparateness of the flow of existence by distinguishing the essential from the superficial, the pertaining from the transient—and we transfer to the realm of art. Or politics, or economic advisors, or priests and psychiatrists. Once again, if this is a way we know what we are as humans, we will not only shape ourselves within this way of knowing but we will evaluate and judge within this way of knowing. Whether one takes this modernist path or detours into a post-modernist one in which all hierarchy is cultural implantation, the fact remains that we spend most of our lives not knowing what we experience.

There's another way of putting this: we bring to a condition of knowing and knowledge only a fraction of what we experience. And plot, whether it appears in our goals-and-objectives statements at work or in a film, can surround the territory of our experiencing but it cannot contain it. And Tarantino, as in *Pulp Fiction*, is true to this recognition in *Jackie Brown*. If we ask the question: Does Tarantino push the envelope beyond *Pulp Fiction?* my answer would be yes, here, in this attempted passage from plot to periphery, from experience brought to meaning, to the flow of everyday experience that the camera normally bypasses, or, if not, winds up on the cutting-room floor. Put it this way: if we reedit *Jackie Brown* so as to run all the "not essential to the progress of plot or the establishment of theme" into one continuous film, perhaps about twenty minutes worth in this film, we would have precisely what a director like Hitchcock, for instance, would never set his camera up to capture, or, would be precisely what his direction would seek to direct *out*.

Let's get to the layer I am talking about. Where is it to be found? It's not easy even to find the Hitchcockian level here but let's say it's where Jackie Brown is since the film bears her name and Tarantino focuses the camera on her almost claustrophobically. But most of the time her actions are not advancing plot but are rather in between plot progression. She's on her way to the next shoot and her being on her way gets the major shoot time. Her prominence is displaced by Ordell Robbie, played by Samuel L. Jackson, who seems to be at the hub of things at the same time Jackie seems to be. The camera quite early on takes to following Ordell who talks his henchman Beaumont into the trunk of his car, drives him to an empty lot and kills him. But Ordell's kinetic evil is displaced by the stolid Louis Gara, played by De Niro, whose gaze filled with absence, his silent take on what goes on around him, keys us to the blank moments, the periphery of action, the silences in between Ordell's steady stream of street rap. And his just plain "being there" is hyphenated by Bridget Fonda's Melanie, Ordell's "surfer girl," reclined always, tending a bong, passing the time with a TV screen. Max Cherry, the bail bondsman who has spent nineteen years "bonding" people, a practice that involves setting them free and then stunning them with a stun gun and bringing them back, seems to have the fullest, wisest perspective on things. Ultimately, we are seeing through his eyes. Or are we? Every center drifts into periphery of yet another center; every consequentiality drifts into inconsequentiality. Where we are going itself drifts into nobody going anywhere.

Ordell is in Max Cherry's office arranging for a bail bond for Beaumont and De Niro moves around in the outer office, in the background. "You okay in there?" Max Cherry calls out to him, breaking the flow of conversation with Ordell. "Can I have some coffee?" De Niro calls back. And then minutes later De Niro comes in and says he's going to wait in the car and Ordell gives him instructions to use the black key to turn off the alarm and not to touch Ordell's radio levels. The camera will in a short while follow De Niro out to the car, watch him opening it, and then return to the conversation. Why go out to the car with De Niro? Why watch him opening the car door? The camera will follow a character to what has no consequence, to a dead end, to a moment that hangs disconnected. Except that out of such moments life is made. The camera comes in tight on Max putting his car in gear, on Jackie rolling a window down, on Jackie kneeling in front of her record collection, looking for milk, pouring coffee, on De Niro sitting there watching Simone lip sync to the Supremes, Jackie turning on her answering machine and listening to Max supply her with number after number where he can be reached, two Federal Agents arguing over whether a bag is pink or white, watching Michael Keaton marking bill after bill with a green marker, Ordell and Max driving along listening to the Delphonics at the very moment when Hitchcock would be paring everything down in the name of suspense. Meaningless flux. Important or not? I guess I would argue that the power here lies in the orchestration of a presence the plot is urging on us and the absence of both plot and urgency—both matters focused on without directorial or guiding discrimination.

There are a number of modernist directors who make the meaningless flux of everyday life their subjects, who film scriptless with handheld cameras to capture the rawness of reality, life without the artificial intrusions of the artist. Ironically, the artistry of such ventures—take Cassavetes's work for instance, or Andy Warhol's—overwhelms the film so that we can never stop asking what the meaning here may be, what the aesthetic behind the product may be. There is a certain "realness" to the documentary style of *Kids* or *Hoop Dreams* or TV's "Real World," which ostensibly captures the passage of real life without editing. But for "Real World" to seem like the real world it must rely on a montage of blackout scenes which keep us mindful of camera and director at all times. *Kids* winds up as emplotted as a soap opera but one which forgets it has an audience and tries our patience as a result.

Tarantino doesn't forget his audience or the popular nature of popular film because his aesthetic collapses the serious and elite with the popular. And he doesn't display an aesthetic intent to capture raw, naive, untouched reality, or life as it is when we don't plot it. Rather, the lacunae of unthought experience perforate the maziness of plot, swell the screen beyond the dimensions of the "well-made" film into the messiness of unemplotted life. If reality is there to be pulped, to be fictionalized, it is also there as unfictionalized, unpulped moments. However, since we have no way of apprehending an unpulped reality without pulping it, that is, without narrating it—and yet such reality must exist not only as our pulping matter but to give us the notion of pulping at all—Tarantino must reach for such moments at the moment of pulping. They have to have context, in other words; rather like a subatomic physicist setting in motion some subatomic particle not to record it but to see in its wake the existence of something there but only visible or recordable by such means. The flux of everyday life brought to no meaning and yet registering a predominant impact upon us eludes direct confrontation with a camera set up to record an image to be observed by others, the very nature of its selectivity and the act of observation moving us from experience to knowing.

So direct exposure of the banal everyday immediately demands an aesthetic of knowing and so our mission is sabotaged. Only obliquely can we film; only by focusing on the twisted path of plot pretending to lead to our knowing, can unemplotted life become conceivable to us. We get the feel of it, if you will, almost as a result of being tired out by our attempts to know what is going on, to keep up. Tarantino goes to the everyday banal flux of meaningless time by means of a camera focused on an elaborate pulping of experience. In between the seams and tears of plot regalia something pops through, something evoked, something we can't quite think about, something that "gets us off."

What a great dilemma when you come to think about it! Here I am thinking about a film which leads me to appreciate the presence and power of what remains unthought: the everydayness, the slow time, the empty time, the fleeing and transient, the ordinary flow of everything experienced. And here I am focused on this at the moment we are all being rushed into a globalized networking of fast, accessible, proliferating information where technology is bringing to a manipulable level everything anyone can make a profit on, and science promises a unified grasp of everything as well as future choice in regard to our own genetic makeup.

Such vast emplotment envisioned and waiting in the wings, so portentous and overpowering that even Tarantino's plots seem timid. Maybe we thought the journey was to be taken at the mixed and variant speeds of *Pulp Fiction*. But here in *Jackie Brown* time is narrated for a different sort of journey.

Long Day's Journey to Boogie Nights

November 1997

> *But it's* Boogie Nights *that has most closely followed up the post-modern frenzy of* Pulp Fiction.

> Anderson hasn't done what he might have, which is to make a movie about the power of eroticism as obsession. After all, this is supposed to be the "'real' story of the porn world."
> —David Denby, "Rude Mechanicals,"
> *New York*, Oct. 20, 1997

> Moral criteria have been replaced by stylistic ones.
> —Stanley Kauffmann, "The Rake's Progress,"
> *New Republic*, Nov. 10, 1997

> Everyone's blessed with one special thing.
> —Eddie Adams to his girlfriend in *Boogie Nights*

> I suppose it sounds strange to call *Boogie Nights* yet another drama of family values.
> —Sarah Kerr, "The Happy Pornographers,"
> *Slate*, Oct. 10, 1997

> Sex and its outer variations is one of those topics we aren't particularly grownup about; we have a tendency to act as if it were beneath serious consideration.
> —Daphne Merkin, "The Skin Game,"
> *The New Yorker*, Oct. 13, 1997

Long day's journey to the end of the night—a mix of Eugene O'Neill who is about dysfunctional family life and Louis Ferdinand Celine who is all about sex. The darkness of O'Neill's play plays squarely at the heart of twentieth-century modernism's angst, its frightened and brooding ruminations on consciousness of . . . of what? The folks sitting across from you at table, the faces in the news, the body your body is entering, the warp and woof of Time and Nature, and always finally the consciousness doing the connecting. Celine's novel seeks to pervert the solemnity of such an angst-filled mood but life becomes a disjointed journey. Headline reads: "Madman at the Wheel Driving Away from Dark Modernism's Heart."

Acts or installments—two sides to the same coin. Celine installs a jest and a fart in between O'Neill's dark journey. In Celine's French nights, there are bodies; Rabelais has drawn their contours, their odors, their movements. In American culture, sex is beneath serious consideration because it has only and always been consciousness and mind that have been on a serious journey to Truth and Reality. The more unsuccessful the journey gets, the more serious it gets. The whole journey a dark, nighttime journey. Put your sexual organs out of sight and begin intercourse.

I take one of the two seats at the very rear of the theater so that I can not only observe a movie which I expect to be a "big canvas" movie, a movie trying to swing wide and catch "a whole way of life," but the audience. I want to see the audience defend itself against a movie about the porn industry. And I don't mean that everyone in this audience has taken Catherine MacKinnon and Andrea Dworkin's side against porn. I mean that a film about sex workers has to remind us that we are taking life's journey in these particular bodies, and that as a culture we are indeed not particularly grownup about the body's sexual acts. Therefore, if we are not particularly grownup about sexuality, or, more precisely, we have not grown up in a culture that is particularly grownup about sexuality, we will have to prove how mature we are by "thinking" about sexuality. For instance, David Denby "thinks" about it this way: Paul Thomas Anderson, the director of *Boogie Nights*, has missed the opportunity to do a movie about the power of eroticism as obsession. In other words, you can't do a movie about the porn-flick industry without actually doing a move about the ill-effects of erotic "obsession." There is no normal curiosity when it comes to sex and the body. We are immediately in pathological waters. Let's move this sort of thinking to another film, *The English Patient*. Has the director of that movie missed the opportunity to do a movie about the power of structuring and imposing *meaning* as obsession? No, precisely because there is no sense in calling what we inevitably do as humans an "obsession." We make meaning out of experience. And there is no sense in saying that every movie about human behavior, intentions, or consciousness should make its subject the power of all of these to become obsessions. I admit that

Anderson's movie is different because it makes sexuality its subject, but he does not make it a subject that he wishes to thematize or theorize. And why should he? It seems clear that because we are not so grownup about sexuality and want our consciousness to organize it as if it were a part of consciousness, we need to have a constant reminder that the star of *Boogie Nights* is an unusually large penis; the penis propels the action; it's at the center of the plot, of character interaction; the *mise-en-scène* is accomplished with this star in mind. Now the only place where you're going to find the story of a big penis, or any penis, is in the porn industry (*pace* Alberto Moravia).

Where do you go these days when you don't want to find the Mind but the Body, when you want to see what kind of life we lead as bodies on the way to the grave? Thoughts don't turn to dust but the body does. Thoughts evaporate before death; they vanish at every moment. It's the body that takes us down the road; it's what we journey in. No, it's where we are situated as our consciousness of the world spins stories of who we are and where we are heading. Look at it this way: When we are absolutely sure that we know the world and ourselves as spiritual pilgrims working out our own salvation in this vale of tears, or when we are absolutely sure that we know the world and ourselves as rational investigators of the world and ourselves as we gradually put together The Big Picture of how everything works—we don't expect every film and every book, every painting and every song to make our obsession—and the power it has over us—with this particular way of knowing the world its subject matter. No, only when a way of being-in-the-world—call it erotic—is explicitly marked as not a legitimate way of knowing the world, only then must it do nothing but focus on its own pathological existence.

Eroticism is caught in an endless round of defense—which always sounds unintelligent to our knowing ears—or, more effectively, in a self-examination that should always wind up exposing its own obsessiveness. What is dangerous to our fulfillment of any of our authorized quests—purity of soul or impassivity of mind—must be always delineated and treated as such. Eroticism cannot and should not escape its ascribed pathology. In other words, sexuality should always be exposed as a diminishment of our human nature, a threat to the sovereignty of mind. But in *Boogie Nights* it is not sexuality that is exposed via the porn-flick industry but Eddie's big penis. And for that transgression we can enjoy the style and mastery of the film, the stylistics of brilliant filmmaking but we cannot for a moment accept the replacement of morality with stylistics. We cannot forget for a moment that behind the stylistics of clever filmmaking lies the destructive power of our erotic obsessions.

Pornography, in the words of Hugh Grant's prissy Reverend in the film *Sirens*, can only put destructive images in your head, scenes of sexuality that corrupt. Corrupt what? The privileged cultural stories we are already in, that we have already adopted. In the Reverend's case, Christianity. But that film focuses on Brits in the early part of the century. Now in 1997 we are culturally mesmerized by family values, by the replacement of moral criteria for our actions with the stylistics of the hyperreal.

Does sex play well in the hyperreal? Are there pornographers on the Net? Are we legislating against the same? Does popular music and popular film push the envelope of our sexual explorations? Do tabloids titillate? I don't want and didn't expect this film to be an analogue of what we should be thinking about when we think of sexuality. I'm as comfortable with this film's penis premise as I am with thousands of films grounded in nonerotic ways of living in the world which don't restrict their focus to a defense and apologia for those nonerotic ways of living in the world.

So let us say that American culture in this century has been on a rocky road to a grownup view of sexuality. And that *Boogie Nights* focuses on 1977 to 1984, a time when apparently some Americans "boogied" in the predawn of AIDS. Production notes on the film available on the Net note the authenticity of the historical retrieval here: "The film . . . captures an authentic snapshot of Los Angeles during the late 1970s and early 1980s—an era when disco and drugs were in vogue, fashion was in flux and the party never seemed to stop." Sarah Kerr in another Net review contrasts *then* and *now*: "*Boogie Nights* follows Dirk from 1977, when promiscuity was still socially acceptable and porn actors still dreamed of being recognized as legitimate artists, through 1984, by which time a combination of Reagan-era values and the rise of low-quality video has brought the industry crashing back to earth" (*Slate*, Oct. 10). You know once you have an "authentic snapshot" of an "era" and can make comments about the past like "when promiscuity was still socially acceptable," you can do two wonderful things that the Enlightenment promised. You can treat the present moment and its perspective as capable of dominating what really went on in the past and you can add to the roadmap that shows clearly where we were and where we are now. Implicit in being able to chart clearly where we were and where we are now is our ability to know where we are going.

If all of American culture is on a journey from some time and place, for example, when discos and drugs were in vogue and promiscuity was still socially acceptable, to a time when discos and drugs are not in vogue and promiscuity is no longer socially acceptable, then the journey is a good journey, a journey in which we are making progress, we are getting better, we are moving ahead. But all this rests on the power of the present to extract its own filtering lens, look back at an "era" in the past, mark its coordinates alongside other such ventures, and add that "authentic snapshot" to all the other authentic snapshots. These pretenses come out of an illusionary way of looking at the world, one that promises authenticity and the power that emerges from that, one that promises a clear mapping from *then* to *now*, one that will reveal through that mapping that we are on a journey to bigger and better things.

So this is the second entrapment awaiting a filming of our boogie nights: The first is that a film about a high-school dropout working as a dishwasher who makes it big as a porn star should go wide thematically and expose the power erotic obsessions have over American culture, and the second is that a film covering an "era" should give us an "authentic snapshot" of that era to add to our historical scrapbook. You break out of the first by doing what I have already done: wondering why you can't show sexuality, either as part of personal life or as an industry, without automatically making it a gawkshow topos, without analyzing it as if it were a deviance, an aberration in the normal course of human existence. You break out of the second simply by adopting a postmodern view of the past: The stories the present spins and films about the past tell us more about the present than they do of the past. The "snapshot" of the past, if you will, meets the present's discernment of "authenticity." The past can only be authentic within the protocols of authenticity that the present erects. Nine times out of ten the present revisits the past because it needs something there to bolster and repair something in the present "order of things." And neither is that "something" in the past a fixed and determinate something but rather something that can be adapted; nor is the present "something" solid but rather something that, with the help of the past, can be molded to meet present needs. It is always a matter of selection and interpretation rather than discovery and explanation.

Boogie Nights is thus resisted or blocked off by two strategies of critical response: It misses the opportunity to portray a pathography of sexuality and its authenticity lies in its snapshot of a past era. But what if we get beyond what it should be, what it lacks, what is absent, and consider how it actually does put sexuality before us? And what if we don't look back to an irretrievable past but remain in the present and observe the connections between American culture at this moment and this film's filming of sexuality? I'm saying that a film done by a twenty-six-year-old producer and director about an era he recalls very specifically when he was a six year old should not be looked at as an "authentic snapshot" of *then* but rather as a provocative snapshot of *now*. I was 34 in 1977 and I lived in Los Angeles from 1981 to 1983 and all I've got snapshotwise in my memory banks is a Los Angeles filtered through the past ten years in the Midwest and an "era" back then filtered through the post-Reagan years. Anything I've got to say about *back then* should absolutely be taken as comments on *right now*.

That may be a hard view to accept because it winds up confounding our "the past is prologue" and "if we don't learn from history we're doomed to repeat it" views. It takes us on a whole other kind of journey, not only socially and culturally but personally. The past *is* prologue in some places and at some times, but in other places and at other times, it's a replacement for the present, or an analogue of the present, or a dream of the future that the present has, a dream of restoration. And when and why and how it is any of these depends upon how the present writes, unwrites, or overwrites the past. The past, in other words, whether prologue, analogue, or futurelogue, is up for grabs in the present. And what we learn from history is a lesson conducted by the present and therefore what we learn is in motion. If time and place never change, we could conceivably be doomed to repeat the past, but as they are in motion in relation to each other as well as to us, the perceivers, we never ever do repeat the past. Of course, we may tell ourselves a story that says we are or have repeated the past, but that, once again, is nothing more than the present moment reshaping the past to meet the needs of our truism: "If we don't learn from history, we're doomed to repeat it."

Our steady, political revisiting in the '90s of the countercultural '60s is an enactment of this truism. We have to get that period right, including Vietnam, or we're doomed to repeat it in the next millennium. And of course, within a conservative social and political view, repeating the '60s is like once again making the same wrong turn we did thirty years ago and going down those same "bad" roads, taking that same frightening journey (to all those folks who came out strong in 1980 to vote for Ronny Reagan) once again. Could it be that the journey Paul Thomas Anderson is taking us on in *Boogie Nights* has a lot to do with fears and fantasies, desires and frustrations, yearnings and hopes, seductions and repression of *now* and not *then*? Let's look at the film as having to do with now and overlook the charge that it doesn't take advantage of its subject. Let's also fail to appreciate its historical verisimilitude.

Two big fears of the present are expressed in my opening epigraphs: Moral criteria are evaporating into stylistics (for stylistics read simulacra and the hyperreal) and family values can lose all value if the family isn't a traditional one. Jack Horner, skin-flick filmmaker, is a surrogate father, and Amber Waves, his live-in leading lady, is a surrogate mother. Neither surrogates, however, typify anything that American society has ever deemed "traditional." When "families" morph like this, into one porn producer and one porn actress, or two lesbians, or two homosexuals, or one heterosexual and one bisexual and so on, then there is, traditionally speaking, no family involved here nor can there be any expectation of there being any family values transmitted.

At the repressed heart of the family matter here is human sexuality. Families are born out of a need to preserve the species; human infants cannot survive unassisted. While biology demands the egg of the female and the sperm of the male, we can now freeze both so that a gay couple can purchase what's needed, have a baby and thus have a family. But biology doesn't demand that a husband and a wife need to rear a child; two women or two men will do. Or, one woman, or, even just one man. Everything else is social/cultural/personal preference. And while doubtlessly a society that values families in very definite ways can push transgressors toward "dysfunctionality," there is no essential reason why nontraditional "families" can't acculturate, can't transmit love and security, can't transmit ways of valuing while at the same time being valuable themselves.

What Anderson does in this film is challenge a mom-and-dad, traditional family with a weird one. The weird one wins, in spite of the fact that it can't escape a social order that exacts daily its pound of flesh. Deviation from the norm is not ever something that the deviant can be allowed to forget or put aside; the same passion is at play when a critic demands that Anderson not skirt the connections of porn-eroticism-power-obsession but "deal with it." Why does society only value a certain kind of family life and deem all others aberrant? Obviously because society is seen by the majority to benefit from a heterosexual family. The male, who might tend to be "nomadic" is tied to one spot. Taxation and billing and accountability ensue. There is value in this sedentary family; besides providing a reliable address where shopping bills and tax notices can be sent, social norms and protocols can be transmitted. What we call "values" at this moment are those attributes of human behavior which foster the sort of social stability that the market needs in order to do business. And so far, what we have seen is that when there's a breakdown in the traditional family structure, disaffectedness and dysfunctionality break out. And criminality is not far behind, the sort of criminality that gets the Haves worried.

Family values have to be made like bricks to shore up the holes in the social order. Without the early inculcation of a social conscience, a fear and respect for the resident order of things, no one is safe—not the underclass where most violence and crime take place, but the entrepreneurial "winners" who have to fear someone breaking through their gates and surveillance systems and quickly turning a "win-win" lifestyle into tragic loss.

But there is a second question that *Boogie Nights* raises: What if a society really doesn't value child rearing, initiation or apprenticeship of the young into that society, or value the family as an other-than for-profit organization? What if market values are really only interested in the bottom line, which is how to herd the young into the already existing niches of about 1 percent astronomical winners, 20 percent meritocratic winners (professional, symbolic analyst, equestrian class) and 80 percent already losers or losing more each year than winning, Allowing Pat Robertson to preach family values comes at no cost, although the Christian fundamentalization of the Republican Party made too public in the 1992 presidential campaign was costly to that party. Because market values only value results, the real focus here is on what to do with the "disaffected," the potentially rebellious, the potentially criminal and violent, those who decide to go beyond canceled credit cards and have no hope of passing a credit check. What if, despite the termination of their consuming status, they still want to consume? What if crime and violence have all to do with overstimulated consumption libidos? What if the marketing force of turbo-charged capitalism operates like free cigarettes, or free Coke, or free coke, until you're hooked and then will do anything to keep consuming? What if we're seducing our young into a consuming lifestyle that only a small percentage will be able to maintain?

Bottom-line and a results-oriented view have necessarily to focus more on restraint, incarceration, punishment, and the tactics of fear than on nebulous notions of conscience development produced by Ozzie and Harriet-type family life. Where, after all, is the corporate manual for "child rearing"? Within a market-driven social order, families don't receive a fraction of the dispensations corporations receive. The "mom" and "housewife" that up until midcentury were at the hardworking hub of family life didn't even get "costed" in GNP and then GDP. Families struggling to send children to university didn't (up until this year) receive any tax relief. And financial aid for university students became in the Reagan years just another opportunity for profiteers to step in the middle and get a brokerage commission. In other words, Jeffersonian democracy and its call for the education of the many had descended to the level of "business for brokers" as usual. If a profit can't be made for the few positioned always to make a profit "for financial services," then our sense of democracy at this moment doesn't seem to be fulfilled.

And, finally, because it makes more sense bottom linewise to hire graduates whose education one has not been taxed to pay for, corporate interest in public education in America is reduced to a simple formula: Privatize it so we aren't taxed for services we don't need. Comparable to the sudden presence of large numbers of women in the workforce in the last twenty-five years is the presence of graduates from other countries who read and write English (sometimes better than our own graduates), understand global-market financing and free-market philosophy, and know as much or more about cyberspace than we do.

What it all comes down to is that in a country ruled by market values there is little or no incentive to take a high road to child rearing and the apprenticeship of the young into society. And the low road—demonize the disaffected in the eyes of not only the equestrian class but also in their own eyes, and get them off the streets when they commit a crime—has had such great success since Reagan that there is no incentive to drop it and take the high road.

Is any or all of this in a film that should have been about exposing the dangerous powers of eroticism and the degradations of pornography? Sure, it's an apprenticeship film; it's the apprenticeship of Eddie Adams, a seventeen-year-old high-school dropout living in a working-class L.A. sprawl stripmall housing tract calling itself a city, who's busing tables and washing dishes at a club in the San Fernando Valley that he has to take a bus to get to. The scene not to lose track of comes early: Eddie returns home after being with his girlfriend who's been delighted with Eddie's "performance" and then he gets another chance to perform after work at Jack Horner's house. This time it's with "Rollergirl," another member of the Disaffected Family Jack has "raised."

"Everyone's blessed with one special thing," Eddie has told his girl friend and the words resound in our ears. How far can a big dick take the kid in a market order of things? What's the entrepreneurial worth of thirteen phallic inches? Tune in. Rollergirl also has one special thing; in fact, it's the thing one critic at least has found fault with: For a disaffected teen she seems far too happy as she responds to Jack's request for her to get it on with Eddie in front of him. She puts on her "theme" music—Melanie's "Brand New Key"—zips off her one-piece roller costume, and jumps naked—except for the roller skates—on Eddie. Her special thing is her sexual joy, the kind of joy Blake wrote about in the *Songs of Innocence*. We see her in class trying to get her high school diploma, and later on in the film we see her being treated rough by a former schoolmate who thinks she's trash and that's the way to treat trash. We know then that it can't be easy to take that off just as she takes off her clothes and make love with enthusiasm and joy. But she can do it.

You can't think of Eddie's mom joyfully throwing herself naked on his dad. So Rollergirl does have a special gift, one that defies our expectation that she should act in a disaffected way in regard to sex. In this defiance she is like director Anderson who doesn't fulfill our expectations regarding how he should be dealing with porn and porn makers.

Filled with the sense that *he* has some special worth in the order of things, Eddie returns home to face a mom who doesn't think he's anything more than a loser. And his girlfriend is just a slut. How long does he think he can go on as a dishwasher at an after-hours disco club in the San Fernando Valley? When Eddie fights back and defends himself, she drives her economics home: Nothing in that room is his. They're supporting him; he's not making it on his own; he has no future; he has no credentials; he has no résumé, in short. But Eddie is like any young artist or genius at the chrysalis stage: He knows he's going to be somebody. He's going to take his one special thing somewhere. You can be sure that mom's salvo against Eddie has been launched in Dad's direction more than once. Maybe she knows what a loser looks like because Dad has already shown her. Maybe, too, Eddie has inherited his one special thing from Dad but Dad kept it in his pants. He wasn't going to ground his life story in his penis. I think we get a hint of this suppressed Dad-penis in one of two scenes that's he in. In the first he's just showing up for breakfast, says a quiet good morning to young Eddie and then attempts to buss his wife on the cheek but she pushes him off. "Don't be trying to kiss me unshaven," she tells him, cowering him in a moment of tenderness in front of his son, heir to this sorry throne. In the second scene, the camera switches to the father listening, angsting, dying inside, but saying nothing. He has no power; he's the head of the family that the religious right is trying to resurrect, but he's without authority. I mean he's the head of an organization that doesn't even get costed in on GDP. The suppressed Dad-penis doesn't make a move to intercede but just listens in another room to his wife telling Eddie what a loser he is.

So Eddie runs maybe from a family in which the penis is repressed and suppressed to the arms of a surrogate Mom who is more than willing to show her sexual organs and a surrogate Dad who is more than willing to film that showing for public viewing. This is neither a family that shows to us where the absence of Ralph Reed-sized "family values" will lead, nor is this a family that shows us what a family free of such hypocrisy looks like. Rather, this is a family forged in the crack between the two; this is a family rebounding from values and meanings it doesn't live by; this is a family fighting to nurture itself in a nonnourishing society; this is where people who don't know where to go, go. All of which makes this a film about a clash between where our social order of things is going and where those who aren't going there, go. Jack's family offers an implicit critique of that social order, for what it leaves out and for what it encloses via seduction and repression. Every one of Jack's family is disaffected in different ways but always in ways that point to deficits in the social order. Eddie's disaffected via not only family life, which has no market value in a social order driven by market value, but also simply by being part of America's "next generation" in an America in which the next generation also has little market value. Rollergirl is also disaffected by way of family life and looks to Amber Waves as a surrogate mom, who is anxious for a surrogate daughter since she has lost legal rights to see her own son. Cocaine helps both of them jump from real-family predicament to surrogate-family harmony.

These disaffected run into the not disaffected but the clash exposes the fluidity of these signifiers. What is really at stake here is a clash between mainstream, socially accepted narratives of being-in-the-world and pornographic, or illicit, ones. At one point, in order to preserve his sense of being a filmmaker and not a purveyor of artless mailorder video, Jack Horner decides to shoot some sex scenes in the back of his car with Rollergirl and random folk they pick off the street. Let's shoot the scene again ourselves and this time not focus on how porny, trashy, low-life this shoot is and focus on the guy they pick up at random. He's a clean-cut, all-American guy and he remembers Rollergirl from school. In fact, he looks an awful lot like the guy in class who turns around and looking at Rollergirl sitting in the back runs his thumb in and out of his mouth. She's the girl in class who gives blow-jobs, and not just in the back of a car but on film for everybody to see. Now, here she is in the back of a car. So all-American young guy treats her like the trash he knows and his culture knows and the social order says she is. Now as he pushes himself on her like she's a piece of meat, Jack directs him toward a better approach. "Make love to her. She's sweet and beautiful. Show her how much you care." But this guy has a strictly polarized view of sex: There's his mother and the woman he'll one day marry and then there are whores and trash like Rollergirl.

You can easily see where he's headed: One morning he'll wake up and try to give his wife a peck on the cheek and she'll tell him to back off. What's implicit in that kind of treatment in the morning is that kind of treatment at night. Wives don't know how to have sex with men whose heads are divided into sexual domains. The penis slips out of sight and eventually doesn't get shown. Maybe the wife dreams of men who show big penises; maybe she rents one of Jack Horner's porno films. Maybe the all-American kid, now a husband not getting any, buys a whore as needed, and assaults her like he's raping her, like he's treating Rollergirl now. Why the violence in the sexuality? Is it because he's culturally been brought up in a society that polarizes sexuality too? A society that doesn't know how to be grownup about human sexuality?

Well, Jack throws him out of the car and spars with the kid a bit and then knocks him down but it's Rollergirl, now angry herself, who kicks at him over and over with her roller skates until Jack has to stop her. You know why she's gone angry and violent: The kid's representing a society that says she's trash, that her joy in sex is nothing more than promiscuity, degeneracy, immorality, that her one special thing is not special at all. It is in fact only a sign of her debasement, her exclusion from the 700 Club, from the contract with the American family that Ralph Reed has forged. I don't know where you are in regard to this scene, but dysfunctionality, like everything else, is relative, and relative to the all-American guy lying groaning on the ground, Rollergirl seems healthy to me. Should she assume personal responsibility? Sure, but to what degree, and who's going to know where to draw the line between what's hers and what belongs to the American social order of the present and the American cultural imaginary? In that cultural imaginary, we imagine our own sexuality on the same level that Clinton "feels our pain." Clinton comes to mind because I can't help feeling that he very well could have been the all-American kid in the backseat with Rollergirl, and, a generation before him, Jack Kennedy might have been back there with her. Men split between the good wife and the Rollergirl in the back seat, between a notion of sex as one to show and one to blow.

If sex between men and women is wrapped up in weird cultural stories, it still doesn't enter the weirdness of the stories that same-sex sex is wrapped up in. We get two shots of this in *Boogie Nights*: one funny/pathetic one between Dirk and Scotty J., the sound man, and one between Dirk and a guy who picks him up and then, along with his buddies, beats him up. In the first scene, Scotty J. takes Dirk to see his new car and doesn't he want to have a ride and then he's got his arms around Dirk declaring his love. Dirk pushes him off, tries to let Scotty J. down gently but firmly. Scotty J. winds up banging his head against the steering wheel, cursing himself for being so stupid. He has no way of handling his feelings and he's clearly not been helped by the culture whose primetime transmitted stories about homosexuality make it a dark perversion, repressed, suppressed, hidden. That sort of cultural pathology incites the homophobia that Dirk runs into later on. These homophobes cruise the streets looking to entrap "queers." Dirk thinks he's back to being paid so somebody can watch him masturbate; it's not a homosexual thing for him. It's a money thing. But he gets viciously beaten because what he's done makes him a "queer" in the eyes of the homophobes. What is it that they fear that makes them think they have to entrap queers and beat the hell out of them? Are they part of a moral police force or are they the sorry products of a culture that transmits a perverse sexual imaginary?

The film also plays the market/porn connection in unexpected ways. Eroticism has enough power to launch a pornography industry that grosses more than legitimate film. Anderson should focus his lens on this, critics say. But he doesn't. Rather, he focuses on Jack Horner's face as the mafiosolike Floyd Gondolli tells him that porno filmmaking isn't on its way to crossing over into mainstream culture; it's on its way out. Videotape and mailorder are where the profits now are. The new technology has surpassed the old; Jack's dreams of making a really great porn film, of perfecting his art, of showing the legitimate industry that he can direct, have gone into mothballs. We get a chance to see what Jack thinks is great film as he reviews the day's filming of a porno James Bond type film starring Dirk as Brock Landers and his sidekick, Reed Rothchild, as Chest Rockwell. We see enough of this "great" film to realize that Jack Horner is in Ed Wood land when it comes to estimating his own artistry. Like Ed Wood, what he has a talent for is living on the margin as if he were living on Main Street, U.S.A. In other words, he takes subcultural dysfunctionalities and difference onto Main Street with a casual élan. Jack's comfortable at home, in his world. He's a grownup living a grownup's life out there in the San Fernando Valley, surrounded by an American culture that wants to see less ease in the life of a porn filmmaker and wants to see Anderson the filmmaker show us why.

Although Jack cuts off discussion with Gondolli about facing up to the new technology and marketing strategy, telling Gondolli that they may or may not continue the conversation, we see later on in the film that Jack has had to give in. We see him strolling through his warehouse of porno videos, checking the mailorder side of his new business, checking with his camera man about the quality of a new videotaping. "It's good," he's told, "it's as good as you can expect from videotaping." It's not filmmaking; it's many steps below filmmaking, but Jack has either to keep up with the changes in the industry or go out of business. He has to stay competitive even if it means a loss in quality. Quality, we are led to believe, is something in the eyes of the beholder. Recall Jack's praise of the porno James Bond films he's made. There will come a time when all that a viewer of porn will see will be mailorder videotapes and the superior qualities of porno films will have to be taken on faith. In a society haunted by suspicions that neither its food nor its air nor its water nor any of its earthly resources are qualitatively what they once were, haunted by suspicions that the very quality of their hi-tech lives brings them less "quality time" than before, this feisty reluctance on Jack's part to hold the line and not give in to market pressures surely resonates with us.

The last bit of dysfunctionality that expands outward from this demimonde into the wider world of our American cultural imaginary has to do with Amber Waves as mom showing up at a closed hearing in which a judge will decide whether she has visiting rights in regard to her son. The case is settled quickly: "When is the last time you were arrested and for what?" the judge asks Amber. Next scene she is outside the room, crying tears that only a mother who has just been told she cannot ever see her son can cry. What to make of this? Her divorced husband has accused her of not being a fit mother because she stars in porno films and lives with a porno filmmaker. This is not a proper environment to bring a child into. We nod in assent. But is there more at stake here? I mean, can you show on film in 1997 a legal battle between divorced parents over child visitation and not evoke the culture wars? On one side, we have "a mom's place is in the home" and on the other side "a woman has a right to work and be a mom in the same way that a man has the right to work and be a dad." The conflict develops a perplexing question, Can you free a woman of half the cultural baggage attaching her to motherhood and at the same time connect a man with the other half? Overworked working moms want to know.

Is Amber a bad mother, an unfit mother? Has her sex life destroyed all goodness in her? Is a woman's "badness" more tied to sexuality than a man's? Would a man's financial success in the porn industry besmirch his fatherly credentials? Usually when a mom turns "bad" and "runs off" to a "nightmare of depravity" lifestyle, she becomes the mom who died. In Elia Kazan's *East of Eden*, James Dean finds out that his mom isn't dead but living over in the next town where she runs a whorehouse. Raymond Massey, his dad, is a righteous, Bible-quoting zealot who knows exactly where the line is drawn between good and evil. Dean figures he himself must be on the evil side, like his mom. He struggles over the easy dichotomy that his father raises. I think we continue to struggle over the cultural lines we draw in regard to women, especially in regard to those who run from the light of perpetual goodness into boogie nights.

The journey that we need to make is not forward toward an ever-expanding GDP because there is no indication, nor has there ever been, that prosperity for the few prompts us all to move away from an arbitrary center of values and meanings and stretch laterally into what now can only appear as the lives and homes of the disaffected. American cultural memory need only call up the saga of antebellum "dysfunctional"

"Negro" life—childish, superstitious, fearful, lazy, licentious, animalistic, loving their boogie nights, and so on—to apprehend how a "stable order of things" corrupts and distorts—and then vilifies through stereotypes—all that its own order excludes. And then hides that exclusion and its consequences in the darkest recesses of the cultural imaginary. In this light, *Boogie Nights* is a long day's journey out of *that* night.

I don't know whether Dirk Diggler is right when he says everybody is blessed with one special thing. Even if we transpose as I do Dirk's one special thing beyond a big penis to the cleanness and clearness of his imaginative grasp of sexuality and thus take his comment as both hilarious and serious, I think it's a classic case of undecidability. Our present cultural imaginary can't conceive this notion because it's already bound up imaginatively in a "winners and losers" scenario. And if this is the case in regard to our cultural imaginary, there is no chance that the social order will accommodate such a belief. If indeed everyone is blessed with one special thing, there are only certain things we are at present allowed to take with us on our life's journey. Given this situation there are multitudes seeking roadways not already blocked off, making fast U-turns and concocting wild and strange detours that will hopefully lead them to where they want to go.

And, yes, in the theater I was in the final scene unzipping of the hidden superpenis caught the audience by surprise. It wasn't the kind of audience that had read reviews already and knew what to expect. It was a "Saturday night let's go to any movie" crowd. For a couple of nano seconds the whole theater wasn't breathing but trying to find a way to respond to what they were seeing. Then a couple of Frat boys in the front row let out some piercing "Whoas!" and the freeze cracked. A student reviewer in the university daily said that the film was a bomb and if you wanted a real porn film, go out and rent one. Put on your dark glasses, work your way to the back of the video rental to the X-rated room, slip in, don't make eye contact with anyone, commit the sin, get a grip, and check it out. This film was socially and culturally scheduled to be on the bad, porn side, a lot of titillation and then a Pat Robertsonlike moral rebuke. It was supposed to be an exposé of the life of sex workers in a moral climate of "assume personal responsibility." There was to be no detours or short cuts into the heartland of rectitude and righteousness. The one special thing about this film is that it doesn't respect that covenant but journeys into the repressed darkness of the American cultural imaginary at this moment.

Side Trip: In Some Dreams You Travel . . .

In some dreams you travel and in other dreams you journey. In your traveling dreams, you are going over old ground, or find yourself on old grounds but you don't know why you're there or where you're going. Something in the past calls you back to it; you go there but don't know what you're really doing there; you're not in control of the sequence of what's happening; it's somehow like your past but it's threatening you. You run out on it. You wake up. It's like a last-minute, dramatic escape. You return to the present unsettled because you know that you can travel to a place in your own mind that is strange to you.

If these were thoughts, you could think them through. But these are not thoughts; these are experiences you didn't experience. Or is it that there was once a world and a time when you did experience them but now you have no way to them? No memory of them? No understanding of them? Depending upon the distance between what you can experience now and your dream experience, you will find yourself traveling back to this dream site. The greater the distance, the greater the level of incomprehensibility and mystification. You somehow bear the inconceivable within you and, like a child drawn to a dark closet, the more you run from it, the more your mind travels toward it. In these sorts of dreams you travel in a circle and journey no place because you neither know the place nor do you see your mental traveling as part of a journey you have mapped out for yourself in the daylight hours.

The sweet light of consciousness may *seem* to be drawing up the itineraries for our journeys but they begin elsewhere, in dreams of journeying. Rather than draw us into a circle we go round and round and can't seem to break free of as in the traveling dream, the journey dream opens the horizon, plunges our head through a mystifying veil and into a brave new world. The momentum of the dream here is all forward; the dream bursts the boundaries of the present mental landscape, and paths open before us that previously did not exist. We are suddenly following a different mapping of things, aware of the world in a thoroughly transformed way. A marvelous epiphany which fills our being with joy, regales the future in splendor. Blake's watercolor *Glad Day!* captures our mood. We feel that we have awakened to a brand new day full of promise and hope—Scrooge after his night of visitations, Mr. Pickwick on the first sunny day of his adventures. And the past, instead of having some dark, mystifying power over us, is a place we metamorphosize out of. We were Kafkian, hard-backed insects before, but have now sprung forth as beings who have wings and can fly anywhere, everywhere.

You can't journey until you stop traveling in circles, from the present to a past that draws you but mystifies you and then a hasty retreat back to the present. I keep referring to the past because it is what personally—postfifty—draws me. But the future can lead you in circles too. In the film *Welcome to the Dollhouse*, we are welcomed into a family sitcom whose comedy would be too dark for TV but whose situation, nevertheless, appears quintessentially American. Of the three siblings we meet, Mark, the computer nerd brother, is the one traveling to the future but is on no journey in the present. His future goal of getting into one of the three best ivy-league colleges in the country rules his present life and keeps it constrained within what yet has no existence. His is a daydream that he's caught up in, a vision of himself in the future that fills his days. Meanwhile, the possibilities of the present, including emotional ties to his family, do not exist for him. He can make no use of them because he's too busy traveling to his future self. He will definitely get there because he is already there. He will get there with nothing more than what he already is because his knowing his future so exclusively and so undeviatingly blinds him to what there is to be learned on the journey. He gets there empty-handed; and what's there has to be empty too because it is only what he has fantasized it to be. He never worked his way there through the world; he's been running in place, call it the present, call it the past, call it the future. It doesn't matter.

You don't journey to the future by fixing upon a story of the future in the present and sticking with it. Ditto the past. The kind of life I've led has now set me up for round-trip travel to the past, to a past that I dream about but is always revealed to me as different than what I can remember. At the same time, I don't think as much about the future, although I get encouragement to do so almost every day in the mail. As soon as I turned fifty, the AARP sent me a membership application, investment firms write and ask me if I've got my retirement finances planned, and so on. But it's not where I'll be in the future that I dream about but the past, and, as I say, I think it's because I've had the nomadic life of a second-generation Italian American. First generation, my parents, born in New York City, lived most of their lives there and then retired to southern California. I took my degrees and left New York City for my first teaching job, and, I've been moving around ever since, finally winding up in the Midwest, the American heartland, with my older brother in Wyoming, my younger sister in Florida, my parents in California, my oldest daughter in Tucson, my youngest daughter in San Francisco, and the remainder of my family and my wife's back in New York City. Why am I traveling in dream, like taking a daily bus to Brooklyn College every day for years, back to the past? I break free of these dreams in a panic, needing to do something but not knowing what to do. I don't know how those dreams connect to where I am, but the very fact that they don't weighs on me, fills me with a sense of loss, of being long, empty miles from where I started, from my home and family in a time that is no place any longer. It's not only that I don't exactly know where I am but that I don't exactly know where I've been and where I'm going.

Maybe I am just nostalgic for a place and time when I was young, that I am mourning in dream my own aging, reluctant to continue on a journey that has the same bad end for all mortals. My wife is not so nostalgic; she remembers too well the noisy and dirty streets of Bensonhurst, Brooklyn, the lack of civility on buses and trains, the discourteous crowds in every shop and at every event, the worst aspects of living in close neighborhoods, the gossip, the sheer weight of ignorance and close-mindedness that filled our working-class neighborhood. I acknowledge all of that, but the dreams do not abate and I begin to think that I have really been on a journey from one culture to another but that the culture that "framed" me doesn't exist anymore and the Midwestern culture I am in now, I am in only as a stranger.

Bensonhurst, Brooklyn, still exists but that neighborhood of the late '40s, '50s, early and mid-'60s whose adult world was made up of first-generation Italian Americans and their sons and daughters, whose masses at St. Rosalia and later at Regina Pacis were said in *three* languages: Italian, English, and "broken" English, whose shopkeepers addressed you in all three, whose protocols were driven by "*la famiglia*," hardworking stiffs, the "connected," the church, and innumerable stories of the neighborhood and its past—

Side Trip

is itself part of the past now, that adult world buried, and its sons and daughters mostly elsewhere, as close as Staten Island or as far-flung as my own family. And, while I have lived in New England, southern Appalachia, the South, the far West and now the Midwest, England, and Europe, what the culture of any of these adopted places may be has always eluded me, which is just to say, I have always perceived them through not the native lens but a different lens. I've blurred the transmission, which is what we all do, more or less. However, I have or had an easier time picking up the cultural transmissions of Bensonhurst because I was not only receiving but doing the transmitting myself; I was born on that channel, if you will. Now, I'm not the only nomad in America; I run into New Englanders living in the South and Southerners now living in New England and so on. I run into former New Yorkers all over the place, and sometimes even former Brooklynites.

The question that haunts me is, am I traveling here or really journeying? Am I always traveling in my mind back to my youth in Bensonhurst, so occupied with that that I cannot journey to a new place? Or, is it that when I come to a different place in America, it doesn't show me any place-transcending qualities that shape a distinct American culture, as distinct as my Bensonhurst culture? In other words, does American culture lie not in any essential, bedrock qualities but in its differences, in the play of differences from region to region? The culture is not one but many, but the many here are in some sort of interrelationship, not simply one imposed by a common social order and its laws, institutions, and practices, but one involving what Raymond Williams referred to as "a whole way of life." But when I think of cross-cultural ties, I think only of the driving force of global-market values that seem to permeate every way of life and either drag it by the nose or propel it into some kind of furious, blind resistance. Perhaps we come to some sort of whole, not oneness or unity, in our imaginations, but I have observed those also to be shaped within market intent. We conceive and create within market-created desires: a new VCR, a new car, a bigger TV, a more advanced computer, a bigger market share, more stock options, decreased labor costs, less taxes, more "pay as you go" and so on. Perhaps there is an attitude that runs like a thread from region to region, state to state, a way of looking at things, a way of feeling about things that joins all Americans and grounds a peculiarly American culture.

How can I perceive this common attitude with my own attitude? The New England attitude or the Midwestern one and so on are never to me what they are to the "locals" but only in the ways they are different from my "local" attitude. Coming from a working-class, Italian-American background where neighbors hung out on street corners and observed life stroll by, put out folding chairs in the summer in front of apartment buildings and recounted the day's events, gathered together as extended family to celebrate everything that could possibly be celebrated, stopped by uninvited any time of the day "for a visit," celebrated church "feasts" every summer, confronted each other on the streets in the passion of both love and hate, abided rules of decorum that changed drastically if you went a mile south into a Jewish neighborhood, or a mile north into a Scandinavian one, or a mile west into a Puerto Rican one, or a mile east into an Irish one, I have been more impressed by absence than presence in the "other" regions I have lived in.

Am I incapable of actually seeing what is present elsewhere, outside my own provincial, now extinct cultural frame? Am I, once again, capable of making the journey elsewhere? Have I ever journeyed off the Bensonhurst map but only attached myself to a theory which encourages such journeys and such new mappings of self and world? Am I on a journey or merely traveling in circles, with Bensonhurst of the past, my center?

I will settle at this moment for a view in which I have been both journeying and traveling, both breaking the boundaries of my Bensonhurst frame and drawn back into it. I don't know that when push comes to shove in my life, at crucial and desperate moments, I am not traveling back to the old Bensonhurst way of "reality making." The values and meanings I express may be clothed in this or that theorizing—my alibi discourse may be *au courant* and seemingly provincial-free—but it may nevertheless emerge from the patterns of cultural interaction that some may call our "mental baggage." I am referring not to your résumé baggage but the ways in which you stuff the world into you and in turn see yourself as part of the world's stuff. So while I believe I have been on journeys into different frames of real-izing and reality making, my travel dreams show me that I have a sort of mental "home base" that I keep returning to, that claims me, that calls me back to its streets, its stories, its voices. And because these dreams are now more emotionally charged than they ever were, I know that I have not been journeying progressively from a less refined or perspicacious way of attending the world to an increasingly more refined way, but simply marking the world differently. And in that marking, I have left

Side Trip

unmarked what still abides in me as not only worthy of being marked but of being distinguished.

I grieve in these dreams, feel the loss of what is no longer distinguished in my present life. None of this deserves to be forgotten; none of this is over; none of this was replaced by something finer. I only have to close my eyes and think of the world I had there in Brooklyn with my mother and father, sister and brother, grandparents, aunts and uncles, first, second, and third cousins, "goombahs" and "goommas" to realize that I am not able to calculate my journeys to difference as journeys upward, but rather as only lateral, widening journeys. For all those who have had what Freud calls a "normal, untraumatized childhood," such may be the case. But those who cannot bear to remember the past are not therefore propelled either onto a journey forward but only endless travels backward to the damage site, the time of injury. Until that damage is repaired no other journey can be taken. I do not think I am driven to look back but nonetheless I am called to look back. In dreams we are called back in such a way that there is no "back there" or "right now" but all at once, a space where all journeys go on together and we are there alive at the crossroads of everywhere we've been in our minds.

Can the traveling dream that calls us back again and again to where we were also become a journey dream, the way I have implied here, an epiphany dream? I think that our American culture has to have that epiphany before I can. I say that because at the heart of my travels back in dream to Bensonhurst is my anger that the American Dream as narrated back then put me on an Horatio Alger journey, a journey up a ladder, a journey to better places, and I willingly left what I had and went forward. My generation of ethnic Americans shuffled off the coil of ethnic identity and ethnic ways and struck out on a journey into the heartland of American and pure American identity. We've gotten to a place where we are being inexorably integrated into a global-market order of Haves and Have Nots, an order in whose name most of my working-class and working-class hero mentality, my assertion of more important values than market values (everything from *la famiglia* to eminently cost-ineffective work, street-corner idleness and the pleasures of merely circulating), my sense of community and fellowship, of sharing work and pain with your neighbors, of retreating into Nature as a balm for the soul, of stealing beauty and not your neighbor's share of the earth's wealth—has been "creatively destroyed," rendered extinct.

My travel back in time is hard for me because American culture has precipitously set me and my generation on a journey forward when the journey was never one in which we had to face forward and walk ahead. Rather, we should have been encouraged to turn to the right, to the left, behind us, above us, or below us and create in our own minds journeys in all those directions. The spot we were on, that I was on in Bensonhurst, was not to be wiped out and moved beyond but expanded. And temporally we were not out of joint, a checkpoint in time on our way to a more marvelous future, but in the same moment we are in now, a moment of infinite imaginative possibilities, a moment that could open up to multiple ways of realizing. But we think we are moving forward in time, progressing beyond blind moments to more insightful ones, a sort of maximizing-of-net-profit approach applied to temporal reckoning. It's a sad one.

Our personal lives may be filled with both sorts of dreams and at this millennial moment, it is clear that American culture is experiencing both sorts of dreams. Chris Carter's TV show "Millennium" grounds itself on the premise that millennial anticipation breeds monsters, psychopaths rushing the world to their own private Armageddons, minds caught in nightmares unable to stand the mounting pressure of what is sure to come—a fiery end to our world. Millennial anxiety has broken through normal personal and social restraint; those who lived normal lives now struggle to continue that normalcy in the shadow of a future now filled by end-of-the-world narratives. Those who were already on the brink of being swept into private mental maelstroms are now plunged into an outside reality that corroborates their fantasies and strengthens their determination to act them out. Each week, a man appropriately named Black, a member of a secret organization bent on holding back this flood of millennial madness, delves empathetically into the mind of the millennial diseased and is able, but just barely and just for the moment, to find it and stop it. Black rarely smiles; he has the look of a man who knows that the odds are against him, that as the millennium draws nearer, more madness is unleashed, less sanity, less reason, less goodness, less hope is available to stop it. He retreats at the end of each episode to the sanctuary of his own family, wife and child, but his family is not safe from the madness whirling about them. Someone is stalking Black and his family; someone without sane motivation, someone who wants to draw them into an end of the world scenario.

Side Trip

The show, as of this moment, January 1997, has not really caught on. Perhaps it's because fans of Chris Carter expected another "X-Files," or, perhaps it's because it is too unremittingly dark and pessimistic, such a downer that its hero, Black, instead of being, at the most threatening moments, capable of jousting *away* from the darkness like "Spooky" Mulder and Dr. Dana, seems already hopelessly doomed, all the joy of life replaced by this millennial fear. He's our protector but we can't see ourselves, or what we want to see in ourselves, in him. He seems clearly to be already a victim, a casualty. And perhaps the show hasn't caught on because it is showing just the dark side of the approaching millennium when in point of fact American culture is visiting both the dark side and the light side equally. I mean that we are dreaming dark dreams of past, present, and future but at the same time we are envisioning bright journeys for ourselves, dreams in which we and the world around us are transformed or guided by bright and airy beings, like angels.

Voices from the Stars, Voices Behind Comets

I mean that we are dreaming dark dreams of past, present, and future but at the same time we are envisioning bright journeys for ourselves, dreams in which we and the world around us are transformed or guided by bright and airy beings, like angels.

As long as I can remember, I've been searching.
—Jodie Foster as Dr. Ellie Arroway in the film *Contact*

In the end, it's hard to tell whether Jodie Foster's Dr. Ellie Arroway has been a *real* traveler or just a mental traveler. The same question might be asked regarding Marshall Applewhite and his Heaven's Gate followers: Did they *really* travel anyplace or only in their minds? And I wonder whether you first have to travel there in your mind before you can make the journey in real time and real space. Ellie Arroway is only a character in a movie, a movie based on a novel: So you might say, there's nothing real about any of it. And Ti and Do and all their disciples were nothing more than cult fanatics, hopelessly out of touch with reality.

What about mental journeys preceding real journeys? Well, they built Bedlam—now a War Museum—to protect society from people who couldn't distinguish a private mental journey from a real-world journey. Clearly, neither a society nor a culture is ever prepared to accommodate every mental traveler's travels. And clearly there is a glitch between human mental reality and "real" reality that everyone but a solipsist accepts. Some may believe, like the Latter Day Saints, that we are heading toward a divine grasp of the world where what we know and imagine *is* reality. But that's a "latter day" affair; right now in our fallen state we can "imagine" wrongly; we can't find the bridge between what we imagine and what is. Even William Blake, who thought that we didn't have to wait for this to happen, believed that most folks were caught in one- or maybe at best two-fold vision: They couldn't imagine the world or themselves as they really were.

You are in search of something "out there" in line with what your mental imaginings conceive. The intensity of the imaginative grasp etches a very detailed map of exploration. The roads to what you are in search of are all passable; the bridges are all standing; the tunnels are all safe. It's all "Go" and all the lights are green. Strange thing is that if you forge ahead as if having a map in hand and an early morning optimism are all that it takes, you quickly wind up a casualty in what Blake calls "Experience." "What is the price of Experience? Do Men buy it for a song?" Call it the "fallen world," call it an opaque world uninvested with the human imagination. Call it "raw reality," or a "hardball court," or "this vale of tears," or a "tough global-market arena," or a "war zone," or the "hood." The point is that innumerable mental travelers, both living and dead, have concocted a world crammed with different social orders and different cultural ferments. We live in the outcome of our imaginings but that outcome shapes—constrains, sustains, denies, contests—our imaginings. We imagine, therefore, within the boundaries of all human interactions—the human worlding—but what is there and has not been humanly recognized or adopted yet constrains our worlding capacities while at the same time drawing us beyond our social and cultural mediations. There is more on the planet, in the stars, in the universe, Horatio, than in our "worlding," in our weaving of ourselves and our environment.

This sounds like a lease granting us right of way through a bit of property nobody owns and that may not even exist. Let's think about Jodie Foster's Ellie who has been searching for as long as she can remember. Now she's searching for "sounds of extraterrestrial intelligence." She wants to make contact with other life forms "out there." First of all, her "science" is constrained by what the discourse of science makes available to her. She "experiences" science or her experience of science is within science "as presently constructed." Even what she imagines science to be in the next millennium is programmed by her experience of science now. Her "brilliance" as a scientist is an interactive brilliance: Mind meets already existing discourse. That discourse of science, however, has no "science" of extraterrestrial life. What that discourse knows of our own solar system points to the impossibility of life as we know it elsewhere in that system. But what about life beyond our own solar system? What hasn't been brought into human discourse may yet be drawing us to its existence, compelling us to imagine it, to bring it to a level of representation, to go in search of it. Now while Ellie as a scientist is in search of her extraterrestrial life, the ex-priest Palmer Joss is in search of his God. Both may be magnetically drawn to what is there but never seen. In other words, if E.T. and Jehovah didn't exist, we wouldn't be in search of them. Air, quanta, consciousness, and gravity are some of the things that draw us to their reality even though we can't see them. We were not only compelled to imagine their existence but their existence stopped us from acting as if they didn't exist. Something outside our own reality frames may trigger our imaginations.

The rub is this: Worldly context surely triggers our imaginations. Only after the fact can we distinguish imaginings without an object from imaginings that are grounded. We are indeed already in the world and part and parcel of it, but we are not in the world directly but within our stories of the world. If we were wrapped up in everything directly, as it is, then surely we wouldn't be able to imagine something that wasn't in there with us. But as we filter the world, and do so changeably and variously, then we can indeed get lost down one or the other byways of our reality emplotments. Anyone who believes that a dog instructed him to murder certain people is on a lost highway; ditto anyone who drills holes in people's heads to make them zombies. Or someone who thinks the only way to end technology is to mail bombs to scientists. Or anyone who believes in the natural superiority of his race, or his sex; or anyone who thinks that God intended Black people to be slaves; or God denied red people souls; or that Jews, gypsies, homosexuals, and anarchists should be systematically exterminated, or that God invented AIDS to scourge homosexuals. But what about someone who believes that a virgin birth produced a man who walked on water, raised the dead, was killed and came back to life, walked around and then ascended into heaven as the son of God? What about a group of believers who think that the Federal Government is a threat to their freedom and that blowing up a federal building is an heroic act? Or those who believe that there's a spaceship behind the Hale Bopp comet waiting to take them to a higher plane of existence? Or a scientist who believes that there is a good statistical chance that there is life in other galaxies and that some may be technologically sophisticated enough to transmit radio signals to us?

Ellie doesn't sound as screwy among this crowd. But still the valuation here is very shaky, very relative to immediate cultural and social circumstances. Revolutionaries have been blowing up governments for centuries and some of these do become revolutionary heroes. And Christianity is a foundational Western cultural story, despite how poorly it stands up to the Scientific Method. And while the Heaven's Gate group seemed too whacko to elicit a serious response from the government, Roswell's fiftieth anniversary triggered the release of the government's Roswell file. The talk of a coverup, of Area 51 and so on, hasn't exactly been dismissed in fifty years. There certainly isn't any spaceship waiting to pick up the Hale Boppers, but there certainly was a spaceship that landed in Roswell in 1947. Go figure.

There are certainly enough reality narratives in here with us in our world to put anyone on a search for anything. And more stories get introduced every day. They ebb and crest, fade in and out like fads and fashions; the media latches on to anything that comes in duplicate: airplane crashes, sex scandals, street violence, terrorism, satanic rituals, UFO sightings. We are at this present moment riding a sort of double crest, a crisscrossing of wave currents: the coming new millennium and revived chatter about Outer Space: evidence of life in a meteorite from Mars, the Hale Bopp comet and the Heaven's Gate rendezvous, the robot Mars landing, the fiftieth anniversary of Roswell, the Russian spaceship Mir, the global popularity of the TV show "X-Files," big alien blockbuster movies like *Independence Day, Invasion from Mars, Men in Black, and Contact*. Perhaps NASA's return to credibility began with the film *Apollo 13*, a film that once again rekindled our interest in space. And NASA's ability to launch economical explorations, sort of "blue light" specials, in a political atmosphere inimical to "long-term investment" in anything has brought space exploration out of moth balls. Investments in places like the former Yugoslavia, the Mafia-ridden former Soviet Union, or politically hostile China seem more precariousness now than investments in the stars.

The feeling that there may be life inside the planet Mars comparable to the archebacteria that lives deep within the Earth sparks our renewed interest. At least investment in films and TV shows about space can show quick returns. But doubtlessly the increasing presence of the new millennium fuels our interest here: What better way to enter the twenty-first century than with a magnificent discovery of life on another planet! We could pack up all the cares and woe of the last quarter of this century and archive them while optimistically turning to a "brand new product," the new fascination.

The dilemma of the day: What do we do with a democracy that is spectacularly Bullish marketwise but at the close of the twentieth century won't look much different than France before the Revolution? Space exploration, therefore, not only meets market requirements—that it *not* increase taxes on the rich—but also market needs—that it seduce and distract. It keeps us looking up at the stars or further up the road when perhaps at this moment we should be looking at transnational escapades and not intergalactic ones. Aliens may be abducting some of us for unknown purposes—perhaps malign, perhaps benign—but infinitely more of us are being seduced and transported away from our own best interests and the best interests of the planet not by the alien but the too familiar—all the well-known trademarks.

All the complexities of our cultural and societal involvement with the stars—the stories out of which our links with the stars are made—

do not obviate the existence of life on Mars or anywhere else. It doesn't in fact prove that Ellie didn't travel to a distant star system and make contact with alien life. There is no contact with this possibility except through the stories currently making the rounds. And the film runs through a good number of them and in this fashion it is more reflective of life *here* than *there*. We, in the audience, have a millennial disposition toward accepting a really Big Happening, something Super Big and dramatic to end the millennium. Otherwise, we seem to be slouching toward it, our heads hung low, too aware of all the riches, both private and public, both personal and social, we had at the beginning of the last century, too aware that we turned the Frontier into a parking lot alongside a stripmall. And the spectacular performance of the Dow Jones here in 1997 is becoming more and more like e-mail from a prosperous relative whose prosperity you can no longer deceive yourself into thinking is somehow your own. So, I think we want to believe Ellie because she offers us an escape, a journey to yet another new frontier.

The film is not oblivious to our millennial susceptibility. For all the psychological profiling of Ellie—her Mom died in giving birth to her and her father died of a heart attack in her presence when she was eight and her search for "life out there" is really a search for her dead parents— we know she's not unstable, not manic or depressed, not so unbalanced within her own being that she projects inner need into her work. She is passionate and reasonable; she is both self-scrutinizing and resilient. Perhaps the sure intelligence that lies behind Jodie Foster's eyes, the feeling of enthusiastic attachment she evokes, put us on Ellie's side. James Woods's wisecracking, skeptical, and ambitious national security adviser runs through the old stories of alien encounter: They're coming here to enslave or kill us and take over the planet. While that story played well in the Cold War '50s, it sounds paranoic now that we are out of that Cold War mentality. Tom Skerritt is the top national science adviser but he's a "player" first and a scientist second. He's as much on the make careerwise as young Bud Fox in Oliver Stone's *Wall Street*. It is ironic that while he represents the market's candidate for Entrepreneurial Hero, Our Man on the Rise, the film shows him as odious, transparently shady, if you will. Palmer Joss, a sort of "moral adviser" to the president, is supposed to be some sort of New Age moralist opposed to the Ralph Reed-like adviser played by Rob Lowe. The nuances of religious opposition here confuse me but I note the malicious wit behind casting a morally questionable but baby-faced Rob Lowe in the part of baby-faced Christian Coalition leader Ralph Reed. There is intelligence behind Ellie's belief in the possibility of extraterrestrial life but what intelligence lies behind the religious opposition is hard to fathom. Technology is okay, Joss tells Ellie, but the men behind it deify it "at the cost of human truth!" Now he's telling this to Ellie who has given her whole life to the search for Truth and she's willing to use all the tools that humankind have invented to assist her. Science, in her view, is obviously a thoroughly human enterprise that employs the products of human inventiveness. So the concept of another "human truth" that Joss alludes to doesn't ring very clearly to her. Or to us.

The whole of American culture is trying to counter a market-science-technology nexus and the values it promotes with another nexus and other values. The question of the day: What plays well against the "show me the money" philosophy of life? Certainly the spokesmen for religion in this film give us nothing but rhetorical bombast. Now Ellie may think she is doing pure science and is in a pure pursuit of extraterrestrial intelligence, but what the film shows is that anything and everything is filtered through societal and cultural dispositions. And Ellie lives in the America we live in: Science generates technology, which produces new products, which expand markets and increase profits. If we can get to that place in the stars where she's been taken it will mean no more than another new territory to expand our markets after we've saturated China. There must be more to us than our market values, our greed and competitiveness, our transformation of everything into market terms. But expressing the words *human truth* is as empty and absent as showing us Tom Cruise in *Jerry Maguire* drafting a declaration of "human truths" that the film never expresses. It can't because the whole culture at this moment can't. It's not a script fault that Joss mouths empty words; it's a fault of the society and the culture.

The film doesn't just settle for a few characters representing various cultural takes on our newest close encounter. Rather, it expands into the media in the same way TV expands into the headlines. We get clips of "Larry King Live," "Crossfire," "The Tonight Show," "Letterman," "Geraldo," and countless others. And President Clinton is drawn into the spectacle, and rightly so as politics, the pundits and advisers, and the media immediately spin around the event, rushing it into an ongoing cultural drama. The dignity of Ellie's quiet listening, of her dedicated pursuit of the stars, is carnivalized. Did she imagine her trip to Vega? Maybe she did. But surely she didn't imagine the ways in which it would be caught within this carnival of contesting cultural imaginaries. And the film cashes in on them all. You might say the first return on the imagined or real existence of life on Vega is to the investors in *Contact*. They made contact with the American cultural imaginary of the moment.

Hanging on the Last Rung on the Way to the Millennium

Expressing the words human truth *is as empty and absent as showing us* Tom Cruise *in* Jerry Maguire *drafting a declaration of "human truths" that the film never expresses.*

It used to be that being in first class only meant you'd get a better meal but now it means you got a better life.

An immortal message, a timeless beauty, an unsurpassing eloquence, an earthshattering performance are not phrases I would use to describe the film *Jerry Maguire*, nor would I care to argue that the film has some of those qualities here and not there, partially fulfilled, or not at all, or that the film is poorly written, or only adequately directed, or could have been acted better, or couldn't have been acted better. And so on. I'm writing about the film because it seems to me to be exactly where American culture is right now at the very beginning of 1997. It's a pure product of the moment, not in the relevance of its subject matter, but in the note it hits, the vibe it puts out. In a way, its biorhythms are the culture's biorhythms.

And what is its mood? It's a film shot without a firing pin; it shoots blanks all over the place; it miscues, misfires, doesn't fire, fills the screen with blanks. The faster Jerry moves, the more he gets no place and his best scenes are when he collapses, has to sit and take it: His scenes in the car with the big-headed, goggle-eyed four-year-old Ray, and then again, drunk and at the bottom of his own personal well, being visited by the same kid, Ray, getting up from bed and visiting the visitor, who he likes. The kid likes Jerry. He sees that deep down, Jerry is father material, that he will pan out, that he will find a place to rest, a home, a connect point between his energies and desires and his hope that the world can bring those energies and desires to good use, to a noble purpose.

There is so much in this film that is not just Jerry's but American culture's. The whole American culture, haunted by some twenty years of "me-ism," of "winners and losers" rated by an inhumane social Dar-

121

winism, is saddled now with an America for the greedy and the rest, all the great unwashed underclass, be damned, go extinct "creatively" to satisfy the needs of the market. The whole culture needs to experience a moment of epiphany, a sudden cataclysmic, soul-shattering revelation, a sudden ray of light illuminating the road ahead. Out of the dark woods that surrounds us in the midpoint of our journey, we await the moment of epiphany. It must be a moment, as Blake says, that Satan cannot find, in other words, a moment free of market rule and dispensations, of the psychology of net profit, the ambition to get yours and let the rest be damned, of the power of the spin that drives desire into need, fellowship and love into a drive "to get the money, get the money."

Jerry has his breakthrough moment at the very beginning of the film. He visits one of the players he represents in the hospital. This particular player has had four concussions and his young son asks Jerry to urge his father to stop playing ball. In response, Jerry, all smiles and fast talk, spins the kid toward seeing his father as an invincible hero. He won't ever give up playing. He's just too tough, too much a hero, and the like. The son's response catches Jerry off-guard: "Fuck you," the dutiful son says and walks away, only to turn around and give Jerry the finger. The kid sees through Jerry's rap and what he sees is an agent who can only get his commission if his father keeps on playing. The money comes first with Jerry and the kid's father comes second. And the kid sees that. And through the kid's eyes Jerry begins to see that at the age of thirty-five, he's a hustler for a buck and that's all he is.

What strikes me is how tepid this epiphany is. It takes me awhile to realize that Jerry is upset because of this, that he's indeed upset on the ontological level, his being-in-the-world has been unsettled. It was a small scene, quick, rushed, flying by so fast amid a directorial style that has been running quick cut scenes from the very beginning of the film. This one is snuck in, like an extra ace in a deck when you're not looking. I didn't even know an epiphany card was being played. And I'm not blaming directing or acting or writing. In fact, the way I see it now, it's a perfect kind of epiphany—an underplayed, quickie one—for a culture that, quite frankly, is not undergoing any ontological conversions at the moment. In fact, there is a need to underplay this cinematic moral reawakening because it hasn't been scripted in the culture as yet. In other words, if you're trying to take a player on the make, a hustler for commissions in an "all against all" competitive arena, and show him changing direction, giving up the path he is on and heading for another one, taking, indeed, a journey toward a more humane awareness of self and world, then you're trying to represent what at this moment has no existence in American culture. Or, such a tiny—now you see it now you don't existence—that the best you can do is to stage the epiphany peripheral, or suggest it, and then rush on to the aftermath of this. If Jerry has suddenly seen a new day, a glad day, an opening ahead which will pull him out of his own selfishness, his own emptiness, his own benighted sense of winning, then what he has seen can't be brought to the screen because American culture hasn't witnessed it already and doesn't know how to witness it.

At the same time, the film is true to the vibe of the cultural moment: There is some millennial desire in recreating ourselves from the inside out. There is a cultural desire to rise above the logic of "the man with the most toys in the end wins" and "profit not people." "Get the money!" seems less equal to the American Dream now in the last years before the new millennium than it did ten years ago. So the desire to see a hustler, a speed talker, a man with a spin on the make, a man who is winning, a man who knows how to play the game, do an about face and set off in a different direction is a cultural desire that the film attaches itself to. That's why I say the film's heart beats with the culture's. And rather than puff out the moment of conversion to a major dramatic event whose truth and integrity the film could only simulate, this film rushes by the moment and relies on the residuals: What happens in consequence of such a dramatic change from playing to caring.

In a sort of sleight-of-hand way, the film opts for a twenty-five-page mission statement, a text that we don't get a chance to read, that Jerry writes that inspires one young woman in his office but leads all the unconverted players to conclude that Jerry will last only another week in the tough competitive arena. He's gone soft; he's lost his edge; he's giving up wanting to be rich; he's forgotten how to win, how to deal, how to spin. And indeed, in one week's time he is fired, shot out into the cold world of the nonplayer, the loser. Throughout the film, the new journey that Jerry is on is grounded in that absent twenty-five-page text. What could he have said? Of course, if that discourse based on an epiphany were not absent but present, we would have had an epiphany scene of biblical proportions. And the whole American culture would have had it. We would all be reading those twenty-five pages describing the road away from our global-market nightmare and toward a world in which the winning is shared, in which we care more about each other, and we give up the drive for money long enough to see what we can do to complete the lives of others.

We are nowhere near writing and representing that text; in fact we see only the cover of it in this film; what's inside is yet inconceivable. So we have to go back and retrace our connections to American culture at this moment. At the same time there is a desire to rise above the equation of the American Dream with a dream of pursuing *my* happiness and the hell with the other guy, the Dow Jones is recording astronomical rises in the market and optimism is so rampant that Alan Greenspan of the Federal Reserve has tried to put the brakes on such happy, limitless speculation, a caution that only depressed the global market for a day. Popular films like *Michael, Fly Away Home,* and *The Preacher's Wife* are given wings to our market speculative flights, as angels descend among us and invest angelic time in maximizing our fun, our good humor, our love lives. In other words, we are trying to take a fantasy trip here, fly away gayly from the disastrous effects on equality and social justice in our democracy that have been perpetrated by a global-market logic of maximizing the profits of a very few.

Jerry is like the kid who points out the emperor has no clothes, that we are bowing to a ghost mentality, one that will make a phantasm of what this country has struggled to build. Since, however, the Dow's balloon is still rising and the spinmeisters have spun us all into believing that we are sharing in the good fortune of the Fortune 500, extended now to include a global Fortune 500, we just don't know what to make of Jerry Maguire's conversion. America is spinning against any transformative epiphany. And the filmmakers here too are being spun in the opposite direction, against what they want to represent, so we wind up with a nominal reality, a simulacrum of an epiphany, twenty-five pages of absence. And a Jerry Maguire whose own crisis can only be depicted in the language of the Dow balloon floating magnificently upward and ahead to the new millennium.

So Jerry Maguire wonders if he's a "loser," or fears other people think he is a "loser," and we wonder whether his great reawakening is really all about the "fear of being a loser," of doing what a "loser" does and loses his competitive edge, his "will to be rich." Could it be that what Jerry has can't "materialize" because he's suddenly gotten his head full of the kinds of thoughts that separate the winners from the losers: He's talking about caring, about cutting back on the drive to "get it all," on replacing the time-honored notion of an ever-expanding bottom line with the notion of a steady-state, sustainable list of clients. If you can't give quality, personal attention to each of your players then you're overextended and have to contract and thus reduce your commissions, lessen your own "take." Now while the present market logic is all for the "creative destruction" of Nature, egalitarianism, occupational safety and health standards, diversity of species, labor unions, governmental regulations, and entitlements to the underclass, it absolutely forbids the downsizing of profits in order to reach a nontoxifying relationship with the environment, or a just quality of life, both economical and healthwise, for workers.

Jerry Maguire's conversion doesn't make sense according to the rules of market logic, which remains the governing logic of both the film's viewers and makers. There is a moment in the film when Jerry's only convert, now his only employee, rushes to put the mission statement in the hands of Jerry's only clients. She wants them to know that Jerry is working for them in a new way, as an agent who cares, as a man reborn into a whole new world where people come first and commissions last. With document in hand she rushes toward the clients but Jerry stops her and the mission statement goes back into the drawer. She had wanted the clients to feel what she felt, what she feels Jerry has done for her: He has given a noble purpose to her work. She is no longer just an accountant to the greedy but a person inspired to help other people, to become like Jerry: Agents who care, who reach out to others with their hearts. She and Jerry have become guardian agents.

The inspiring mission statement doesn't reach us, and those that find it in their mailboxes see it as the words of a man who is self-destructing, a man who, for whatever reason, can't go the distance. He's in the competitive arena and his legs have given out, he doesn't have the killer instinct, he's doomed to drop to the bottom. Throughout the movie, Jerry's a man hanging on the last rung of the ladder. And maybe the whole American society is, but right now that whole society also sees itself afloat and above any need to be converted to "outworn beliefs and ideologies." If we can't conceive a discourse of transformation, of spiritual reawakening, of moral conversion—except of course for the dangerous and violent underclass—of the moment of epiphany, then we can fantasize winged flights upward into the stratosphere of the Dow Jones.

With so much inconceivability and so much Dow optimism, Jerry Maguire's conversion can do nothing but collapse into the ups and downs of love, marriage, separation, and reconciliation. Jerry becomes not a man revolting against the market order of things, against a "go for the money!" philosophy—and hence a timely hero for the entire American culture—but a man with love problems, a man who has to realize that the woman he's married "makes him complete." A drama originally cast on a cultural stage is now reduced to soap-opera level. Love may conquer all in a Hollywood film but the sheer play of market contingencies has already forced too many Americans "to lose that loving feeling" and seek the protection of guarded communities.

The Princess, The Mother, and the Clothes Designer

Each of us here as divinely as any is here.
—Walt Whitman, "Salut au Monde!"

Am I self-aware enough? I do not want to start writing about the murder of Gianni Versace, the unexpected death of Princess Di, and the expected death of Mother Theresa in a state of Stallone-like un-self-awareness. Can I write about our celebrity culture without advertising it? Can I write about the deaths of these people without profiting from it, without exploiting it? I do not want to be caught up in the vicious circle that Brian Gorman describes: "The media, of course, feeds this out-of-control celebrity culture. Witness the idiotic Pop Cult pundits who sat in front of cameras this week and compared the death of Diana to the assassination of John F. Kennedy. If celebrities come out, we photograph them and if they talk, we quote them. If there's anything the media has to answer for it's the inflated sense of self-importance that has overtaken actors and models and people who are famous just for being famous." Self-awareness also prompts me to see real distance between a media feeding voracious appetites exactly what they want and my unasked-for, probably bewildering and irksome attempt to connect three deaths that in the fall of 1997 have churned up, in differing ways, the waters of American culture.

On our way to short-term profits, symbolic analyst credentials, a café-latte lifestyle, and the millennium, we have suddenly been stopped by a tragic car accident that has taken the life of a de-Highnessed Princess. And it is her presence just weeks before at the funeral of the murdered clothes designer Gianni Versace which suddenly and inexplicably makes that death a sort of augury of Princess Di's death. A photograph shows the Princess consoling a grieving Elton John, who will at the Princess's funeral, launch a song in her memory, "Candle in the Wind," a rewrite of his 1974 tribute to Marilyn Monroe. And because we know primordially that everything like this comes in three's that the third death, the death that completes the triangle, is the death of the eighty-seven-year-old Nobel Peace Prize winner, Mother Theresa. She is

126

mourned, you might say, in the wake of our mourning for the Princess, a Princess who never won a Nobel Peace Prize but whose publicizing of the dangers of land mines may have attracted more attention than the work Mother Theresa did for the poor.

This triad emplotment has no rational base; there is no tissue of logical connection. Nonetheless it is a product of the cultural imaginary, it resides there and functions there. On this terrain, we can take side trips to other tragic deaths like Monroe's, like another Princess, Princess Grace of Monaco, like Elvis's because, here in the American cultural imaginary, tragic celebrity deaths will also be cast in the shadow of Elvis's death. Commentators have already compared the funereal turnout of Princess Di, Monroe, Elvis, and Princess Grace. An editor has been quoted as saying, "This is the most important event since John F. Kennedy was assassinated," a comment which brought a bevy of "I knew John F. Kennedy, and Princess Di was no John F. Kennedy" rejoinders, all of which served nonetheless to connect Princess Di, a princess on another soil, to that Court of Avalon that a youthful Kennedy presidency erected on American imaginary soil. One tragedy sparks recollections of other tragedies in a sort of Wordsworthian fashion: Kurt Cobain's death sparks a recollection of Jim Morrison's death in the countercultural imaginary, which immediately forms a Jimi Hendrix-Janice Joplin triangle, which in turn is encompassed within the larger triangle of JFK, Martin Luther King, and Bobby Kennedy, a triad brought to song by Dion's "Abraham, Martin and John." Abraham? JFK's assassination rekindles Lincoln's, while MLK's murder lies in the shadow of the emancipator Lincoln, that murder deeply troubling the depth and breadth of our notion of emancipation.

There are, I think, some tragic deaths which do not die in our imaginations, personal and cultural, but continue to resonate, perhaps because they bring a life to closure but not what that life meant or had yet to mean within a self or a culture. JFK, for instance, created an ambiance that no amount of scandalous revelations regarding his personal life can tarnish because what is purely personal—his sexual escapades for instance—play out on one stage, and cultural impact, the value and meaning that surrounds his name, play out on another. The promise of a new day dawning, of a goodbye to the darkness of the world wars that Ike still evoked, was in JFK's voice, in his Bostonian speech rhythms, his smile, his gestures, in the same way, at the same time Pope John XXIII—in age and appearance JFK's opposite—symbolized the same promise of a great awakening, a new direction, a new journey not only, as Rod Serling told us week after week, of body but of mind. And our spirits were touched.

My postmodern leanings prompt me to observe how "our spirits are touched" within stories of how "our spirits are touched." Witness for instance how the suicide of Thomas Chatterton, "brilliant fabricator of the purportedly fifteenth-century Rowley poems," in 1770 at the age of seventeen affected John Keats in 1815:

> . . . *Thou art among the stars*
> *Of highest heaven; to the rolling spheres*
> *Thou sweetly singest—nought thy hymning mars*
> *Above the ingrate world and human fears.*
> *On earth the good man base detraction bars*
> *From thy fair name, and waters it with tears!*
> ("Oh Chatterton! How very sad thy fate")

And witness how Keats's own sad death of consumption at the age of twenty-four affected Percy Shelley in his poem "Adonais":

> . . . *till the Future dares*
> *Forget the Past, his fate and fame shall be*
> *An echo and a light unto eternity!*

And Shelley's ashes are buried beneath lines from Ariel's song in Shake-speare's *The Tempest*:

> *Nothing of him that doth fade,*
> *But doth suffer a sea-change*
> *Into something rich and strange.*

The tragedy of those dying young resounds within a thick repertoire of stories; but if elegies bore the images of those dying young forward from past into future, it is surely now the commemorative lyrics of an Elton John or the photographs on the covers of *Time, Newsweek, People Magazine, TV Guide*, and such, the tapes of TV interviews, the work of paparazzi appearing in tabloids in supermarkets, the relentless report-ing on tabloid TV shows such as "Hard Copy" which aggressively work at "touching our spirits" for the sake of profit, for audience share, for market share. Every life and every death which has entered the ether of the Hyperreal now suffers a sea-change into something rich. Period. And the riches are accrued not only by the image makers, by the glitz mak-ers, but by their subjects, who ironically must seek their own objectifi-cation and commodification to achieve the epitome of human subjectiv-ity: transcendent luminary status. This is all quite different from the Romantic tradition of registering tragedy that I have echoed in the lines of Keats and Shelley; the "how" of how our spirits are touched has such stupendous facility now that the manipulation and the seduction has hollowed out that spirit which words, images, and sounds were only meant to evoke and to augment.

I do not lay the blame here at the doorstep of postmodernity for the proliferation of stories, of images, of spectacle, for representations cannot in themselves elide the realities that incite them—the realities they seek to present but can only inevitably bring to presence on the level of the signifier, on the level of representation itself. Whether we hold that reality is self-present and self-evident on the level of the signifier, on the level of words and images, of representations, or whether we do not, the politics of warring accounts of things goes on. And it is within this politics that we have for some reason detached tragedy from the tragic levels previously signified in Western Culture. The elegies of the Romantic poets are no more than charade, hype, carnival, sensationalism, exploitation, commodification. We have consumed the Princess's death as if it were a packaged product on a shelf; the feast lasts as long as our media-generated attention span.

Maybe Gianni Versace's murder is more surely shrouded in mystery than the Princess's but the Princess's death mystifies me more because I don't quite know how her life reaches tragic proportions. Surely a princess dying in a Mercedes going perhaps a 100 mph after dinner at the Ritz in London chaperoned by a "playboy of the Western World" and driven allegedly by a drunk on Prozac is an event I am more likely to see up on the screen than in my experience. Maybe these are misrepresentations of the "true" facts; maybe the speed was moderate, the Ritz not so ritzy, the playboy more serious than playful, the driver not drunk or depressed, the Princess really just like the girl next door. Nevertheless, it all seems inconceivable to me, this princess way of life. Life as I cannot even conceive it collides with Death, a destination we will all reach but does not, for all that inevitability and universality, demystify Death. There is too much inconceivability here for me to see how this death produced the media event of her worldwide mourning. Then it must not be the death itself but the life which touched our spirit, the ending of a life which touched our spirit, the premature ending of a life which touched our spirit. Some of us, as I have said, are so touched that we consider this to be the most tragic event since John F. Kennedy was assassinated. Perhaps the Princess connected on a subliminal level with an entire shifting of cultural tectonic plates, as the Kennedy administration arguably did. When the American cultural imaginary connects Kennedy's assassination with Lincoln's there is a cultural parallel: Both men were on the verge of reconstructing our cultural psyche, were about to take us on a new journey. And those journeys never began but were suddenly aborted. Listen to Walt Whitman sing in "When Lilacs Last in the Dooryard Bloom'd" how a culture mourns the death of Lincoln:

Coffin that passes through lanes and streets,
Through day and night with the great cloud darkening the land,
With the pomp of the inloop'd flags with the cities draped in black,
With the show of the States themselves as of crape-veil'd women standing,
With processions long and winding and the flambeaus of the night,
With the countless torches lit, with the silent sea of faces
         and the unbared heads,
With the waiting depot, the arriving coffin, and the sombre faces,
With dirges through the night, with the thousand voices
         rising strong and solemn,
With all the mournful voices of the dirges pour'd around the coffin,
         where amid these you journey,
With the tolling bells perpetual clang,
Here, coffin that slowly passes,
I give you my sprig of lilac.

Whether or not the Princess's life connects with a journey the British are taking away from their present relationship with their monarchy and toward something that the Princess captured in her own life is a possibility I cannot comment on. Nor can any of us detach a life packaged for us incessantly by the media from a media-free intersection of her life and any cultural imaginary, British or American. She was indeed packaged for transnational consumption. And it is this dilemma—that the life is so powerfully bound up with palatable product, with digestible tidbit, that is culturally significant without significance having anything but a commodity value—that prevents us from knowing if a comparison with JFK's death is apt or, if it is not, why is it not? Hers was a face and a body, a hairstyle and a lifestyle, a dress, hat, and shoes; a look, a gesture, a series of photo-ops that reached us before we could know how she was like us and we were like her. And indeed, the way she always came to us prepackaged was specifically designed for us to see that she was not like us, her life transcended ours, she lived where the rest of us could only dream.

It seems to me that our mourning for her continues within this promotional campaign: Her heart was never ours to connect with because she was first already a simulated queen of our hearts. Only because her life was so thoroughly removed from our own lives, so thoroughly filled with fame and fortune, could we so mourn her loss. In losing her, we lose a life that we have been taught how to feed on in the absence of fame and fortune in our own lives. That her life was filled with sadness, with suicide attempts, with humiliations, and with injustice does not remove her from the luminary ether but rather, as in the fairy tale stories of princesses, such sadness adds luster to her star. She was never, for most of those who mourned for her, more than this packaging. I don't know how you can be objectified for commodity reasons as a figure transcending everyday life and yet hope to retreat to a core subjectivity in private moments. Elvis and Marilyn Monroe are our greatest failures here. Perhaps the Princess was on her way to an uncommodified life, but none of that death scenario gives us a sign of this.

And I am not interested in staying on the level of a personal that begins and ends in mystification. I am only interested in the cultural connection. Why do we Americans now need a queen of our hearts? Why do we need superluminaries to stud the American skies? How have we developed a desire to know all we can about these superluminaries? Why have we become a nation of voyeurs? Why do we have lives that need other, distanced, and vastly different lives to supplement our own? We do not need a Sherlock Holmes to tell us that the paparazzi are not the prime movers here but rather one chain in an elaborate order of things established to fulfill our desire to dwell vicariously in the realm of the rich and famous.

The difference in all this is not the arguable difference between the Princess's death and JFK's, or the difference between our public mourning for her and for Mother Theresa, or the difference between what the media will stoop to print and image now as opposed to 1957. The difference we should be concerned with is in ourselves, in our desires, our appetites for "uncommon" lives and lifestyles. And I don't mean the life of Allen Ginsberg, who also died recently, one of the Beats who in the '50s set up a howl and tried to set all of America "on the road" to different values and meanings. Ginsberg's death summoned memories of Jack Kerouac, his Whitmanian Camerado. They wrote in the Whitman tradition of self-celebration, a self that assumed that "every atom belonging to me as good belongs to you," a celebration not merely for the privileged, for the winners, but for the underprivileged and the losers. I mourned Ginsberg's death because I too lived in the story of traveling together and the invitation Whitman had made so long ago:

> Camerado, I give you my hand!
> I give you my love more precious than money,
> I give you myself before preaching or law;
> Will you give me yourself? Will you come travel with me?
> Shall we stick by each other as long as we live?
> ("Song of the Open Road")

have rushed to condemn the paparazzi and the media. We attend the Princess's funeral in such large numbers and in such deep grief because we have already consumed her life; we have put aside our own for hers; what she is on the level of the sign, within the magic of the code spun for us, has become what we are on the level of the imaginary. Her sudden death is a death to what we have imagined ourselves to be. We mourn for what is left in her absence: Ourselves bereft within a world in which luxury and privilege, wealth and power have demolished the story of "each of us here as divinely as any is here."

There is, however, yet another allegory within which we weave the Princess's death, one in which she became for us a symbol of one struggling to leave a world strangled by the constraints of tradition, privilege, wealth, and power. Like us, she is yearning toward a more equitable, compassionate, liberating, and nourishing world. Her brother, Earl Spencer, marked this identity in his eulogy:

> *All the world over, she was a symbol of selfless humanity, a standard-bearer for the rights of the truly downtrodden, a truly British girl who transcended nationality, someone with a natural nobility who was classless, who proved in the last year that she needed no royal title to continue to generate her particular brand of magic.*

The "classless" Princess? An oxymoron, perhaps, certainly a stretch. But that a palatable allegory of a classless Princess, a People's Princess, could hold ground has a great deal to say about how desperate we are as Americans to regain that sense of "each of us here as divinely as any is here." But how distant we are from achieving that in the present when such a dream of selfless humanity, of reasserting the rights of the downtrodden, of classlessness, could all become associated with this pitiable, Prozac-ed Princess. Because she is not more pitiable in her life than we are in ours, that she both represents how far we are from other and older allegories of democracy, egalitarianism, and social justice as well as being herself that far from the same, the allegory is empowered.

It is indeed a magical thing that the Princess's life and death has taken such a hold on the American cultural imaginary. America, so far along on its journey to what Whitman had sung, can summon no more imagination to make the roots of attachment and interrelationship conceivable than a British Princess's life and death. Our spirits have now been touched too long through the mediation of how we imagine winning and losing. If the Princess's life was held up for our consumption by the unrelenting drive of market forces to make a profit anywhere and anyhow, those same forces had already formed our appetite. She reaches the end of her road, driven by a driver fighting his own depression with a pharmaceutical, chased by paparazzi competing viciously with each other for an "edge," mourned by whole cultures being driven by an allegory of greed and selfishness, of seduction and repression, toward an unimaginable future.

global-market present offers a future that is always nebulous and uncertain in its relation to this Cool Beans generation. If that future is somehow controlled by a free-market free play, a market sort of casino logic in which no one knows which way the Dow Jones will blow or where fortune or disaster will turn up, like cards at Vegas, then there is already a built-in confusion, frustration, bewilderment, and volatility in this generation. If rancor breaks out, there are reasons. Every twenty-something generation is different but this generation is different in a different way—a qualification of course that every twenty-something generation has made. Nevertheless, difference, like anything else, is caught within a certain cultural expressiveness, a certain formatting of what difference is and how it is to be recognized. Shakespeare's rebellious Prince Hal has the same genre of gripe against the "Establishment" as a '60s protestor. But this present Cool Beans generation isn't looking for trouble. It wants to fit into a "winning" role in the global-market order. It wants that order to "show them the money." That order, however, doesn't, as an accountant would say, cost them in. And the Cool Beans generation is beginning to feel that neglect.

What order of things is begging the compliance of youth in the present only to leave them to the absolutely stochastic universe of global-market free play? It may prove unprofitable careerwise to violate the academic order of things, but that order of things itself is polarized between "career stuff and party time." There is no connection between the two because the curriculum as a connecting force between student and social and cultural matters other than markets, jobs, money, and "winning" is being steadily eroded. You might say that the curriculum has "privatized" in the sense that it is rushing to connect itself to the master narrative of "Show me the money!" And at the acceptable "party" moment—when life is not serious or to be contemplated because profit is not involved—all the rancor that youth can feel against such a reductive, uninspiring, mercantilistic reality frame breaks the surface. Youth doesn't yet have the necessary cynicism to fully accept greed and self-interest as the only goods. It takes a lot of Think Tank manifestoes, TV pundits, and economic and political game theory quantifications to bring a social order to this sad state.

The immediate administrative and community counter to this is swift, public, and strong punitive action because what can break the surface once, can do so again. Towns and gowns in the '90s live in the shadow of the explosive student rebellions of the '60s. The message of the conservative '80s and '90s has been "No Repeat."

But nothing repeats in the same way because repetition is what someone observes at some time and in some place. Now that I have done a "play by play" and given my take, I need to retrace the journey I've taken from one to the other. Why is my journey at fifty-four—a bad time a running mate tells me because it's said to be the point in the road when you know you're on the "bell lap" but you don't want to speed up—crisscrossing the journey this new generation is on? Beware my own nostalgia for my own youthful rancor, for a time when I could speed up without fear of seeing the end.

With Gunson, I myself begin a journey that crosses the most important journey any society is on at any time: The journey of its youth from apprenticeship to maturity, what Blake calls Innocence to Experience, a journey of promise fulfilled, of potential into actuality, of what we can imagine and what we can realize, of those who will walk the paths we mark and in turn create paths of their own, of those whose reality we have constructed, a reality the young are thrown into. *Juventus spes mundi*: Youth the Hope of the World. I believe this with all my heart. But I don't think our society does.

What do I know of this generation I see sitting before me every day? From what world does the Gunson Street Riot emerge, an event that could have played out differently within a different context? I think we have to step back further than nonalcohol events, and basketball at night, and more police, and $10,000 rewards, and convictions for baring breasts. Within what cultural imaginary does this present generation live? What journey are *they* on?

"I'm not of Generation-X," one of my traveling companions tells me. "We're the Kurt Cobain generation."

Maybe so, maybe not. It all depends on whether a product line can bring a new generation signifier home. In the realm of fad and fashion, generations come on fast and leave suddenly. I'm at the vanguard of the Boomers, arriving on the scene just when the Allied Forces landed in Sicily—August 24, 1943.

I hung around Greenwich Village in the late '50s and listened to bongos and free verse at the Café Wha? Kerouac's *On the Road* was my *vade mecum*; I talked like Neal Cassady—or tried to. I had a goatee and dressed in black. I thought William Burroughs dressed really cool. Was I Beat? When I subwayed back to Bensonhurst and hung around the neighborhood, tacked on a corner in front of Ernie's Luncheonette, looking myopically at the passersby, smoking Camels and slicking my hair back with VO5, wearing the collar of my red jacket up like James Dean did. Was I a Greaser? Of course that term wasn't coined for the *Rebel without a Cause* rumble set

now are from what you are no longer, from what those outside your special stage in life can be identified as. You need the clothes, you need the look, you need the sound, the movement, all the accessories. Youth today needs to be "fully loaded." There was always that psychological need for youth to be "fully loaded" but now everything needed seems to be available for sale. Product and push have answered psychological need. The spectacle of youth is being screened at your local mall. It's fitting, I suppose, that all the old movie houses have been torn down and multiscreen theaters opened up in huge suburban shopping malls. Spectacle and product are conjoined for easy access; one seduction and consumption segues nicely into another.

You might say that when the psyche is in motion, moving rapidly from change to change, there is greater opportunity to push product than there is than if the psyche is sedentary, stay-at-home, less liable to think that a new look will be a new birth. At the same time, in a culture seriously repressing death while opening itself to all manner of death-repressing seductions—we will all live long and happy lives with our toys—staying young or more precisely simulating youth is a cultural desire. Right now for instance, something called the Macarena sweeps the country like a hoola hoop craze. The music of the young; you could hear it and see it on MTV. But if you were past thirty or forty or fifty and danced this dance, you would be hooking up with youth. The market follows youth not only because the young go through products and services as they rapidly go through dreams and desires of identity but because the aging and the aged employ them as models for what youth is now defined to be. The reality of being furthest removed from dying and death is there to be found in the look, the vibe of the young. And they are the creations of the market. Even when they struggle not to be the pure products of the market, models for consumption, they are commodified, just as the Beats and the Hippies and the whole counter-cultural crowd wound up just so many consumable products, from the pot and hash to the jeans, boots, and hairstyles.

As a sometime adjunct lecturer before rooms filled with twenty-somethings, my courses about the "postmodern" vibe are often, for the sake of understanding what the hell such courses might be, transformed into "critical thinking" courses. In this light, which I don't step out of for practical reasons, I'm teaching undergraduates how to question stereotypes, reject sophistic thinking, distinguish the kernel from the chaff of an argument, bring overgeneralizations to ground, topple fallacious foundations, probe semantics—and so on and so on and so forth. If I can do all this, in other words, I can provide the student with an arsenal to be used against Big Brother, false advertising, smear campaigns, courtroom trickery, the door-to-door salesman's pitch, and the pressures of cold calls at dinner time and direct mailings promising you a million dollars upon receipt of your signature. But in my postmodern view a critical thinker is only armed with critical reason and I just always wonder where that reason comes from and for whom is it critical that you think in this way at this time in this place? And anyway, I don't think global-market values are driving educators to help students resist the seductions and repressions through which the market herds them toward a lifetime of consumption—strictly to "grow" the economy to ever-increasing proportions of course.

No, even if there were such a miraculous outside-the-flux entity such as "critical thinking," it might get some play in small, experimental colleges with big endowments but the bulk of education would continue with its training curriculum—doing what it can to make a nice fit between a recent graduate and whatever the entrepreneurial mood and market strategy might be at the moment of graduation. The fact that we have been in a "downsizing," "outsourcing," "no security, no benefits, no unions, no workers' rights" mood for the past fifteen-to-twenty years has not compelled educators to give up "training" and take up "critique." Rather, educators are advising students to prepare themselves for "several careers," and liberate themselves psychologically from the notion of security or even expectations of being treated in a rational, humane, concerned, healthy, just, and conscionable way. Corporations owe you nothing, unless you happen to be a shareholder. Then you've got all the rights we used to grant American citizenship.

And the choice between training youth to fit into prearranged slots, or more precisely, to consider themselves moveable pieces on the global-market game board, and teaching them to "critically think" is a choice modernity, not postmodernity, puts before us. In the postmodernist's view, if we begin to talk about what critical thinking is, we do so within a present contesting of narratives, a contesting which the metanarrative of the market always wins. Therefore, thinking critically is defined as thinking of ways to gain an edge on your competition, whether in the form of the student sitting next to you or the entrepreneur across an ocean: increase profits, reduce labor costs, hold off regulations and taxes of all

Side Trip

ping impatiently at the side of a monitor when a double click of the mouse failed to bring up a fast screen. You can't read either Wordsworth or Proust by tapping a book cover: They don't know how to respond to the new need.

Of course, we should be prepared for this ontological change: Witness what the Industrial Revolution did to the inner landscape of mind, to the style in which humans lived in the world. Witness the way America has become modern within an "automotive framing of reality." Varied notions of the "Frontier" displaced by highways to Vegas where you can lose money gambling at a place called *The Frontier*. It is not just the physical terrain of modern America which could have been different if there had been no internal combustion engine, but without that invention as the point of reference for human perception of the world, we would not now be seeing the world the way we do, seeing and talking to each other in the way we do, thinking of ourselves and the present moment, what has past, and what is to come, in the way that we do. So therefore it should be no surprise that our move off Highway 66 onto the electronic highways of the Internet would reorient the way we identify ourselves and the world, the way we have our being-in-the-world. We should have been prepared not only for a Generation Gap but a new conceivability of what such a thing could be.

Depending upon when you went online, when you were "wired," you have inculcated a digitalized mediation of the world. If you were born into it, like the first generation of kids brought up on TV, there would be no glitch between linear/mechanical/continuous mediation and electronic: You just know that a lot of things bore you and some things don't. In the boring moments, you can, if allowed, put your headphones on and listen to a CD Walkman where your music moves at the right speed. Or, you can accelerate the movement of time and space by slamming beers or smoking dope. It suits the young more to surround themselves in the fast nonsequiturs of MTV, running *your* music with *their* commercials, than it does to be without images to respond to. The world has to be as replete with fast interactive screens as a pentium chip computer: Hypertexting is a way of being-in-the-world that has cyberspace as its model. It is perhaps a model more ultimately devastating to the physical planet than the internal combustion engine. How so? It generates a way of being-in-the-world that replaces that physical world, its needs, limitations, and crises, with virtualities. The simulations and seductions of cyberspace speed up the rate at which a privileged few in the world are consuming that world. Look at it this way: They are consuming for about at least four-fifths of the world's population who have already been seduced into debt. And because consequences are only marked within a virtualizing of reality, real-world consequences don't compute.

This present youth generation, the "Cool Beans" generation, is therefore not digitalized in an innocent or disinterested way: Virtual space is already owned by the free play of the global market. It is becoming increasingly entrepreneurial space: What is accelerated is the impulse to have, to consume, to buy, to reduce the world to products and services, to profit for someone lurking behind every home page. They are jacked into simulated shopping although the message on the screen is "Real democracy awaits us in cyberspace!" and "Real education through technology!" "Information is the most valuable commodity!" "Hooray for the Third Industrial Revolution!" But the grounding connections remain these: "new technology—new desires—new needs—new products—new purchases—increased profits." The Computer Revolution not only generates a desire for the latest hardware and software, but cyberspace, as I have indicated, generates a new way of desiring because it rewires the way we experience, the way we consume and respond to the world. But the young aren't just wired into the seducing mode and seductions of cyberspace. They must enter cyberspace, which has come to mean they themselves must enter the strategy of seduction in the name of profit. They must enter the market reality frame that is bankrolling the computer revolution. In order to do this, they must repress desires that have no market value. Ironically, at the very moment when most people feel that "surfing the net" means expanding at a geometric rate human knowledge, potential, imagination, community, understanding, democracy, and so on, in a renewed Enlightenment optimism, more doors of perception are being locked and boarded up, more paths to human self-development and mutual aid blocked off than any "ism" ever before has ever succeeded in doing.

So now we can go back and come in tight once again on the Gunson Street Break Dance and Riot:

A week before the riot, unscheduled, I asked about sixty undergraduates to jot down their first hook-up—their first mental response—with a series of words. I started with *wealth* and I got fifty-nine dollar signs except for one guy who wrote "Nick." Nick Welth, a good buddy of his. So I asked them to try again and they told me names of various products, from cars to a house in Lake Tahoe, to all the money Bill Gates had. I then asked them what would Mother Theresa have written? She had just died that week

Hunting Expectations

Will you seek afar off? You surely come back at last,
In things best known to you finding the best or as good as
the best,
In folks nearest to you finding also the sweetest and strongest
and lovingest,
Happiness not in another place, but this place . . . not for
another hour, but this hour . . .
——Walt Whitman, "A Song for Occupations"

Now I get that old Jewish joke: What's the difference between a
garment worker and a poet? A generation.
——James Atlas, "The Whistle of Money,"
The New Yorker, February 1998

The joke is not only old, the optimism is. And the idea that moving from garment worker to poet in one generation is "trading up" is old, over, and adios. In some mythic time in America, it was thought that with enough time, will, talent, and good trade winds, a child of a garment worker could become a poet. Moving upward in America was a doable thing; the thought existed in the American cultural imaginary as foundational, as what indeed inspired one's imagining of one's own future enfolded within the American Dream. It might take time but time was not a problem. What was needed was the will to succeed, the desire to better oneself. The odds? Always against you, but that was the challenge. Talent? Brains? That was somehow connected with ambition, a will to power. Education was a much-admired thing but the chatter in the street was that "experience was the best teacher" and the "egghead" would time and again be bettered by common sense and "worldly wisdom." If you put these things in your pack and set off on your journey upward, you could have the greatest of expectations and yet see them fulfilled. In America.

Charles Dickens's *Great Expectations* abides by and within this myth, although it is nineteenth-century England that provides the context. Dickens's inspiring model was his own meteoric rise to great success from lowly beginnings. It was also a confirmation of his optimism in regard to social mobility. This personal mythos—from murky beginnings rising to fame and fortune—appears again and again in his novels, but always accompanied by a darker probing into the injuries he has sustained on the way to his success. All of this dark probing intensifies in his later novels although he strains to "keep heart." But for all Dickens's connections with "social reform and causes" the heart of darkness for him never moves from his own autobiography to Victorian culture and society. What is dark is always private and personal with Dickens; he has no trouble declaiming his social views on the bully pulpit but can only work *into* but never *through* his personal psychopathology in his fiction.

Alfonso Cuaron directs the film *Great Expectations* into *both* a personal and cultural darkness. Times have changed.

How so? Begin with the garment-worker-to-poet story. Finn Bell, Dickens's Pip, has a talent for drawing, and Joe, who brings him up, is a fisherman who isn't allowed, by government restraints on fishing Florida waters, to fish. Fisherman to artist. But Finn's will to make that journey doesn't come from Joe. He has, in fact, stopped drawing and painting. His will to succeed, to climb upward, has to be rekindled. And it is rekindled when he misinterprets unexpected and anonymous financial support to go to New York as support from Ms. Dinsmoor, the wealthiest woman in town. He believes that once again she has entered his life in order to make him an equal to her niece, Estella. He wants success as a New York artist only for the money; money will bring him into her view, take him out of Joe's lowly world and give him membership in the Borough Club, where he first meets Estella and some of her friends and is pursued outside the club by a club steward.

"Sir, you have a club jacket. This one is yours." And the man helps Finn off with the club jacket and on with his own.

You can see that Finn is embarrassed, the moment out in the street so awkward, so crippling that you know he won't forget it. Dickens has such a specific memory—something to do with someone seeing him washing bottles or following him to his family's digs in the Poor House—that stands in his mind as the moment, the event he must move away from, distance himself from. It may be mythic, surely insignificant in anyone else's eyes. But such a moment propels a life—forward? Discreetly, say—away from that haunting moment.

Wealth and social position are what Finn now wants; the art is a means to get both. The opening of his show in one of the most exclusive galleries in New York is a countermoment to the one outside the Bor-

he had already given up. Her wealth is also a link with Estella so Finn sees himself as being given the chance to have great expectations by wealth—Ms. Dinsmoor—in order to direct him toward wealth, to put him, therefore, in a chain of significance that includes his heart's desire, Estella.

The further link, however, is to the state of the American Dream now: It may be global and it may promise a record-breaking Dow Jones and it may be open to the ever-new designs of technology, but there's all the reason and logic, all the sanity and good-heartedness of Ms. Dinsmoor behind it. Like Finn, we have undoubtedly misinterpreted the signs; our expectations will be fulfilled by the same sort of aberrant contingency that floods Ms. Dinsmoor's mind—only we call it the free play of the global market, an enterprise whose ups and downs—like the here-again/gone-again quality of Ms. Dinsmoor's mind—the Dow Jones so slavishly follows.

What lurks beneath this designer's dream? This product of money and mania? What do great expectations held within such a world run into? I think they run into Robert De Niro's Lustig, an escaped convict who rises up out of the water and grabs the boy Finn and promises to kill him and his family horribly if Finn doesn't bring him food and a chain cutter. In other words, expectations held within a world ruled by the good-hearted Joe, or the guileless Finn himself, do not fail to meet opposition. There is more in the world than what Joe has led Finn to believe. However limited that "good-hearted order of things" (which Dickens himself tried to keep faith with) may be, it does not itself breed monsters from the deep. The convict Lustig erupts, like Blake's pestilence, from standing waters. We cannot forget that in this poor coastal town, Ms. Dinsmoor is the wealthiest citizen, and her manor house is in the same state as her mind—collapse. Such a dispensation of wealth and privilege speaks ill of the social order fostering it; that sort of world will breed rebellion, crime, monsters.

The world that Finn aspires to, the world of wealth and social standing, the world that Estella occupies, is, at best, crippled, stone-cold dead at heart, like Estella, but its very wealth and social prominence privileges its values and meanings, the very foundation of that privileged state—money. The possession of, the expectation of having, the accumulation of, the investment of, the inheriting of, the losing of, the failure to have—these are the desires and fears that fill the world Finn wants to belong to.

The convict appears from the dark side of this state of affairs; if there is a highly lauded Fortune 500 world, there is also an Underworld. There will always be thieves for sure but we now live in a world in which a "show me the money" attitude puts questions of "how done?" and "where from?" in an outworn and bygone ethical context. Money possessed is its own explanation and justification; money is meaning; money is value. So part of the present expectations regarding fulfilling the American Dream is this attitude that nothing is more important than the money itself; it is an end that justifies *any* means. That attitude runs head on into the Law, especially laws which protect property and, of course, the owner of property. What those in Estella's world do is make their privileged positions exclusionary and well protected from those who would take what they had—including their lives—if the Law didn't pursue and punish them.

We are in a "tough on crime and criminals" posture now because there is such a startling gap between the world that Finn comes from and where Ms. Dinsmoor lives. Thoroughly seduced by a "show me the money" global campaign and filled with great expectations that great wealth will reward an "entrepreneurial spirit," the folks in Finn's world are staggered by the resistance that a "moneyed order" has created. Staggered first, and then angered; drawn, if you will, to the dark side, where Lustig comes from. We live now in a world that spawns monsters; but their criminality is like the last desperate effort of an endangered species—the Have Nots—who, in turn, are endangering the lives of everyone, including themselves.

Finn has beguiling moments on beautiful sunlit days with Estella, but Lustig comes to see him at night, hoods prowling outside, waiting for him. The sunlit beauty of Estella has a dark soul; the dark, unsettling visage and manner of Lustig conceals a goodness beginning to flourish within. His actions on Finn's behalf have redeemed him. Bald and savagely frightening years before, Lustig returns bearded and long-haired, different and yet the same in his very difference from the world Finn aspires to. And in Finn's company, Lustig is chased by the hoods and then stabbed to death.

Violence and murder ask for Finn's attention; crime has provided Finn his great expectations; the convict Lustig has been his benefactor. Money made by foul means has paid Finn's way; great expectations rise out of darkness. Otherwise, there would be none. And yet, Finn forms a bond with the convict; he sees in him the good-heartedness of Joe, the unselfishness that has no market value, the desire to do a charitable thing for a fellow human, for no gain but the heart's. In contrast to the way Ms. Dinsmoor has used her money to make a monster of Estella, Lustig has sought to do a good deed with his.

Who the criminal is, and what criminal behavior and acts are, fail to meet our normal expectations. And why not when we ponder that our

paint may come up with a product that sells but that genius doesn't create a technology that can be globalized or transnationalized nor is the genius here, after all, something that lesser talents can employ through new formulas and principles and templates. The essence of genius lies in its uniqueness; the goal of technology is redundancy.

The interest can be broken down along class lines also: Working-class kids are not encouraged to become painters, poets, or composers but are led to business and technology, to the numbers of accounting, to the numbers of engineering, to the sciences which make numbers their "language" and the careers, like medicine, which depend on both. And our Third Revolution, our so-called Computer Revolution, is grounded in Boolean algorithm. To program is to compute. And one computes numbers. Even the "human sciences" like economics, sociology, and psychology emulate the quantification preferences of the sciences; cognitive science grounding AI research indeed attempts to quantify consciousness. The path here is too slippery to take but it begins with a translation of "consciousness" into the brain as "biochip" circuitry affected by chemical intervention.

What we finally wind up with is a tremendous appreciation for a certain kind of intelligence—scientific/mathematical—and a stupendous inattentiveness to other kinds of intelligence. This is all in the domain of and on the level of "formal, institutional" discourse; it's on the *Bell Curve* controversy level. It's what's said when educational institutions outline a connection between curriculum and marketplace, skills and jobs, knowledge needed for success, the path to take when seeking to go from garment worker to "winner." Contemporaneously, there is another discourse, an informal one, a street-wise one, the anecdotal discourse that parallels the formal one. And it goes like this: Genius can be manipulated by shrewdness, a savvy hardball player uses genius to suit his or her own needs, genius works for Rupert Murdoch and Bill Gates, for Donald Trump and Michael Eisner. Gordon Gekko in *Wall Street* knows how to "network," Robert DeNiro in *Wag the Dog* taps the genius of producer Dustin Hoffman, and every Think Tank economic guru advises the big players at the top of investment firms, banks, the Federal Government, the media, the universities.

There's a story that says Bill Gates had his start by buying someone else's creation and patenting it. There are innumerable stories of great talent and genius being swindled by their managers, their accountants, their handlers. Elvis had the talent but Colonel Tom Parker had the slyness to profit from it. We live in such mythologies; there is no hope in trying to establish how much truth and how much fabrication comprise them. The weave, whatever it is, is powerful, and the sense that the way big money is made has nothing to do with a genius for complex equations, or any sort of genius at all except the genius for making money, is what I would call a perennial part of the American cultural imaginary. If you peruse a book like *Corporate Lives*, interviews with successful players, you cannot extract a uniform program to success. You cannot make a list of courses to be taken, abilities to hone, moves to make, books to read, models to study, expectations to have. The way to where they are is not clear; you can spot the play of Chance—of birth, appearance, opportunity—you can also note the "wise moves," but only in hindsight. And the "savvy moves" are braided in Chance while Power already possessed blurs the discovery of a beginning, a moment before success. Their lives, in hindsight, may look like they are progressing steadily toward the present; there seems to be connectedness, method, discrimination. But is that a story of progress, of "I Did It My Way" imposed upon a life of fracture, of absences, of gaps and unseen jumps, and Chance interventions, or is that "The Way It Was"?

I bring these matters up because *Good Will Hunting* not only sets up mathematical genius as poor, orphaned, and unknown, but also our dilemma in regard to recognizing the relationship between a successful life and a successful career. If the link between making money and what the genius for making money is remains opaque and shrouded in our imaginations, the link between a fulfilling, successful life and the genius it takes to have one is just as shrouded. I propose that the first is not clear to us because we must spin ourselves into believing that in our casino-market world, success is a thing we can will, that we can assume personal responsibility for, that we can "want to make money" and fulfill that want, while the very nature of the casino market really takes that volition from us. But what percentage of life is Chance? What about the moments when genius can flourish?

Look at the South Boston world Will Hunting is in. Every morning Will's good buddy, Chuckie, comes by to pick him up. They travel from the Irish ghetto of "Southie" to MIT where Will has a janitorial job. At night, Will and his buddies cruise around, drink beer, talk about the "babes," and lead the kind of young working-class life that is already chosen—accident of birth—for many. Few are called beyond this life, although Will will be. The closest thing to this lifestyle shows up on TV in shows like "Cops" where no one owns a shirt and the police are always kind. A film like *American Hero* with Jeff Bridges is truer to working-class life; TV finds this working-class life too lackluster, too much just hanging around and not enough crime and drugs. TV confuses Will and his buddies with gangbangers, which they are not, and the whole working class on TV is transformed into a stupid, violent, seething, criminal, drug-

has two objections to traveling down that road to success that the "best and the brightest" are supposed to automatically take because being bright they naturally perceive what's best. And what's best is taking the medal-winning road to prominence, to power, to possessions. But Will is drawn to other logics. Start with the "logic of love." Love is a sort of counternarrative to the necessity of rising from Southie life to professional life. Love doesn't exclude upward mobility, doesn't detour us from "being all that we can be" and developing a strong, varied portfolio of investments along the way. But it is an irrational force, something that Will can feel that has nothing to do with his extraordinary ability with numbers. The numbers genius is something that he has, that he can do, that just flows. But love sets up a sort of complex equation in another part of his being. We say love is in the heart and numbers are in the brain. But what this imagery merely connotes is our sense that what we feel may be divided from what we can think. Will may have a love for mathematics just as Gordon Gekko and Don Corleone may have a love of money and power. But reason and logic can be summoned to fulfill those loves; the love that Will develops for Skylar, the lively Harvard premed student, doesn't draw upon his mathematical genius, but his troubled lifeworld certainly looms large.

Now, that troubled lifeworld has to work itself out to an unknown degree in order for Will to have a healthy and not a stunted connection with the world around him. He is doomed to lived experiences that constantly play back to suppressed anger, and, most significantly in his case, to an absence of love or the capacity to love. So from the lovestory angle, Will has to travel a different road to success than the one our "show me the money"/"winner take all" American cultural imaginary is presently fostering. He is drawn to two opposing stories: In one, getting "all the money" will have no affect upon Will's capacity to respond to anything, to his own self-esteem. Mathematical medals do not affect ontological being, especially if that being-in-the-world is ensnared within an embittered, self-destructive frame. The quality of being, in other words, has as little connection with wealth and power as does Will's mathematical genius with his love for Skylar. In the other—the "genius climbs upward" story—his love for Skylar can be subsumed, or will shape itself according to his worldly success. That success will gloss over both the difference that loving is, its unworldliness, its irrationalism, its obliviousness to profit, as well as his traumatized lifeworld. Damaged psyches can play with their winnings as well as healthy ones; love can be bought in the street. There you have the two rivaling narratives that Will faces. And he opts for love first. Love is not a by-product of market strategies, nor can it be left aside until market values find a place for it.

The other objection Will has to traveling down the road, or up the ladder to the success Professor Lambeau says he will have, has to do with the connection between the quality of life and what one chooses to do in life.

Right now, there is an almost airtight link between money and quality of life. The quality of Will's buddies lives will be demonstrably less than the quality of the Harvard prig they meet in the pub. And Chuckie, Will's best friend, accepts this axiom and pushes it on Will. He wants Will to use his genius to get out of the no-future jobs and life they're in and follow the road to success. In response to Chuckie's plea for him to climb the ladder out of the Southie life, Will says he sees nothing wrong with the life they're leading. It suits him. When Professor Lambeau holds out to him the felicities of a don's life, Will says he doesn't see anything appealing in explaining the same thing over and over again for the rest of his life. And when Professor Lambeau seeks Will in the MIT janitors' office, he plays the part of the academic don to the hilt, something that doesn't exactly endear him to the maintenance guy he's talking to. "Asshole," the janitor says when Professor Lambeau leaves. That sketch of the increasing "failure to communicate" between classes follows the scene between Chuckie and the Harvard prig in the pub. When Will then tells Chuckie that the life he's living is okay with him, there's a certain amount of working-class pride here. Heros have and can come from the working class. There is also a readiness on the audience's part to agree with Will's preference for Chuckie and his buddies rather than the haughty Professor Lambeau and the snobbish Harvard student. You leave Southie, in other words, and you wind up with a bunch of wimps, snobs, and assholes.

Class, however, is a suppressed and repressed signifier in the American cultural imaginary. Therefore, we don't see "solidarity" and a call for solidarity and working-class pride behind Will's refusal to climb the ladder. We may feel the moment but it gets swept away by more prevalent understandings in the cultural imaginary. Why the hell is Will not going through that door that's been opened for him? Through the window of opportunity. Maybe it's resentment and rage that give Will this view, perverse I think in the eyes of most Americans his age. Perverse because here's Will with a genius for something everybody wants—a genius for higher mathematics which grounds research and development which grounds technology which grounds both private and governmental enterprises—and he refuses to make use of it. Watching Will throw away his chances has to be particularly antagonizing here in the '90s; only the *expectation* that the film might be all about how he eventually "sees the light" and pursues success keeps this audience from walking out.

Resurrect a '60s audience in America and the expectation would be that he would get in that old beatup car that his buddies give him and "head west just to see what was there." But his buddies give him the car so he can make a different kind of journey, a journey "out," a journey "upward," a journey to success. The film's ending straddles the expectations of the two eras: the old car going down the road heading toward Skylar, toward love, and maybe a beginning toward a medal-winning career. But clearly love comes first. We are to understand that resentment and rage have been countered by love, that he can be loved, that he can love. He gets "out" of Southie not because now his resentment and rage keep him from perversely staying there, but because he is free to pursue love. Math may lead to fame and fortune but love is what makes us and stays with us.

"Rosebud," the dying Charles Foster Kane murmurs and it turns out to be a logo on a childhood sled, a sled he played with when his mother loved him, before she sent him to live with a bank guardian, a love he had before he made his millions, earned his fame. Will chooses to take the nomadic journey to love, nomadic because it has no plan really, there are no coordinates to this journey, there is no math to apply.

The intriguing question remains: Is there a qualitative difference—not in terms of talent, intelligence, looks, money, prestige, possessions but in terms of love, peace, imagination, wisdom, generosity, friendship, kindness, joy, sentiment—in life at the top and life in the middle and life at the bottom? Or, are these difficult-to-quantify attainments relative to the person? That is, is there one road to individual human fulfillment, or many? Do the nonquantifiable, nonpurchasable qualities mean less than the quantifiable, purchasable ones? Does having the latter necessarily generate the former? Or, perhaps, do all those things that can't show up in a shopping catalog eventually lose their significance once one has purchased everything in every shopping catalog?

This is an academic question in the sense that any individual is already infected with the priorities of the cultural imaginary he or she lives within. The way in which we "understand" something has a great deal to do with what we think has to "stand under" something in order for us to realize it. Those "stands" or undergirdings are social and cultural; from family, religion, and education to corporation, these are constructed and already standing. You might say individual understanding leans on them and thus comes into being. And when we "real-ize" we make something real within an already existing "frame of understanding." So both realization and understanding are at once always social and cultural and never purely individual. A person can turn his or her back on the prevalent "show me the money" fever of the present moment but only always as an act in which he or she is turning from those values. One is living "against" or "counter to" something, which hardly provides a brave new world of being but rather only always living in the shadow of what cannot be distanced.

It is possible to "understand things" like "peace," "love," and "joy" within the extremes of a Buddhist cultural imaginary and a global-market one. It is possible to realize the goal of life is money and power and be at a loss to realize it in any other way. Or, to "real-ize" it only the way a Medieval ascetic might, or a charismatic Christian, or the way Kundun, the Dali Lama does. While all understandings and realizations refuse other understandings and realizations, none can bask in legitimate, self-evident supremacy. Therefore I would say that though Chuckie seems right to urge Will upward and onward and Will seems perverse in wanting to stay in a dead-end job, we have only culturally imagined the valuations here. There is no way of knowing what journey Will should "really" be on and setting up a crossfire between money and love, between working for NASA and being a janitor at MIT, doesn't help much. Will isn't necessarily going to find peace, happiness, and love in his life if he turns his back on his genius; and that genius isn't necessarily going to take him there either.

It seems that the important thing is to spring off from particular readymade understandings and the dualisms they set up toward other readymade understandings. The personal is in that without obviating the presence of an always already social/cultural. Put blankly, the journey to be taken is toward experiences lying on the outer side of one's knowledge. If you seek far off, Whitman tells us, for happiness, you will "surely come back at last." That journeying far off is perhaps the journey of "great expectations," the "show me the money" journey that Finn takes for a time and that Chuckie urges Will to take. But when you come to your senses and get off that road, what do you "surely come back" to at last? The journey Whitman urges us to take in "Song of the Open Road" is indeed a journey to someplace but not knowable:

> "They go! They go! I know that they go, but I know not
> where they go,
> But I know that they go toward the best—toward
> something great."

When Will heads toward Skylar at the end, his mathematical genius can give him no knowledge of what to expect, and I take that to mean that he is journeying toward life and not toward what the market values in life; toward life and not any formula for success in life, either mathematical or magical.

Side Trip: *Passeggiata*

We arrive in Amsterdam in mid-May and rail to Utrecht, paying a point-to-point fee rather than use our rail passes for such a short trip, about a half hour. It's easier this year than last year when the rail at Schiphol was being worked on and we had to go out and take a bus to another rail station and then rail to Utrecht. From Utrecht we take a bus out to the countryside, to the hostel in Bunnik, a converted country estate with a wonderful manor house. Erik the cook there is a friend of mine and we talk food, cook food, and eat and drink far into the summer nights.

I'm sitting at a round table in front of the bar room, looking across the darkened lawn at the manor house, lights from rooms beaconing across the lawn almost to where I am sitting. A pint of Dutch beer in front of me; Erik, Kim, and some of the students at the same table. I don't know what we talk about but we laugh a lot. In my mind I am in one of those Dutch paintings of the sixteenth century where the red-faced and thickwaisted sit outside a country inn, surrounded by geese and dogs, smoking long-stemmed pipes and eying with pleasure the flagons in their hands. If it's not a painting I'm in, it's a Washington Irving tale, probably Rip Van Winkle, or maybe Disney's version of Irving's "The Legend of Sleepy Hollow."

Jaap, an earnest young history prof at the University of Utrecht, wants to free Holland of such stereotypes but at the same time he probably would admit that Duke Wayne fills his imaginings of the American West and Scorcese and Coppola his sense of Italian Americans like myself and the New York City we come from. Maybe he even has some pictures in his head regarding my American students? He saw them in such films as *Reality Bites* or *Less Than Zero* or *Clerks* or *Swingers*? And my students? Maybe their heads are in "The Real World," a TV show they watch to find out what they're like.

Which pictures in the head are correct?

I find European women more sexy than American women. I've thought about why after being asked numerous times why—by American women—do I think this way. Let me switch from sex to food here because there's something comparable going on. Americans need innumerable cooking gurus to show us how to cook. We need a Martha Stewart for instance. She probably puts something on the table that looks as appropriate and neat and tidy as she looks. But I wonder about the taste. I wonder if she can develop the real flavors the way my Sicilian grandmother could and the way my own mother can and my own wife can. With anything. My grandmother, for instance, didn't measure, food process, KitchenAid, power can-opener, nuke, convect, catalog, browse the Web, think Kraft-made cheese or gassed tomatoes were real cheese or tomatoes, substitute chemicals for sugar, or *faux* butter for butter, and on and on. But she was a magical cook. She had direct access to the Ideal in food. I once attended a bring-your-dish soiree in the Midwest and a woman showed up with a Sicilian *caponata*. She called it a Cake Poe Netter. She had all the ingredients, including the right cured olives, salted and not pickled capers, and a homemade tomato sauce. How did it taste? It tasted like the colored illustration of it that was in her Southern Eye-talian cookbook.

Nominal reality. Simulacra. But I couldn't tell her that when she asked me for my opinion. All I could say was that she was on her way to making a really great *caponata* some day. But it wasn't going to happen. She'd go on to a French cookbook and cook up an illustration of a *coq au vin or cassoulet* and then maybe do what most American restaurants have done—go on to "Fusion cuisine." That's when every European cuisine is mixed with a Southern California flare, not forgetting a little sour cream and red grape garnish with a splash of arugula for the *cognoscenti*.

American women are the same way with sexiness; it fills the pages and covers of the slick magazines they read; countless articles on expanding the orgasm, dressing to make men beg, exercising for sex, and so on. Sexiness is a marketable product, the next thing on your shopping list. And American women serve it up the way Martha Stewart serves up a meal. Can you get food that has a taste to it in Europe? A loaf of bread? A bottle of wine? A real cheese and not a chemical surrogate? Milk and butter whose taste matters more than the packaging? Can you see women in Holland, Belgium, France, Italy, Spain, Portugal, Ireland, and elsewhere who make you think of real sex and not a video of sex, not a cover of a magazine, not the apparition of that fleshy, aromatic, health-exuding, mobile thing I call sexiness? Is this a picture in *my* head? Doubtlessly. I can't be spanning the gap between picture and reality. Am I ever passing through from one to the other? When am I actually traveling? When am I on a real journey?

After Bunnik, we travel to Brugge, Belgium, and then back to Utrecht, this time staying in the city itself, at Eveline's. You need a Dickens or a Balzac or a Gogol or Kafka to describe Eveline's. Or maybe just a Theodore Dreiser or Sinclair Lewis or one of those American Naturalists—or better yet a Zola—who could run a probe on that carnival of life I call Eveline's.

Wasn't it ironic that I meet some French jazz musicians there whose latest gig is at a circus, playing accompaniment to a bunch of clowns, mimes, acrobats, and jugglers? I think all of those were staying at Eveline's, including three Ukranians and one Russian, none of whom spoke English, but who "helped" Eveline with her "guests." White South African women commandeered the breakfast table before daybreak I think and held their ground until White Australian women, husbands in tow, battled for dominance. Some of the least observant of my students wandered into the breakfast fracas and were never heard of until much later in the day. The former Soviet students served no one in particular but always with a frown and a "I'm sick of you" look on their faces. Requests in English elicited surly Ukranian or Russian responses. Moon, my Surinamese friend who had been a full-time porter of the place the year before, now had a full-time job elsewhere and was just living at Eveline's so the hotel was now out of his control. He returned tired and defenseless about seven each evening and left before dawn. He took me aside the first day and slipped me the key to the laundry room, swearing me to secrecy and security. The key was never to get into the hands of the Russians. It was belated but I was finally actively involved in the Cold War that no longer existed.

"They will let all their friends wash their clothes," Moon tells me. How many traveling former Soviets are there in town I wonder?

"Russia is on the move," one of the jazz musicians tells me in French but he may have been saying something else, maybe something in English. The jazz musicians—Christian who likes to talk, the small one with big eyes who sleeps in the van, and the French Sprocket who plays bass—sing their English with a jazz beat. They improvise English conversations or more precisely montage it, snip-

Side Trip

pets from lyrics from Cole Porter to Van Morrison. Big Eyes and French Sprocket do the rhythm section and Christian riffs a conversation. I think it very appropriate for Eveline's—this impromptu jazz improvising in place of normal hotel conversation here and there. It's an improvised, impromptu place and Eveline is in it and of it but not at the center of it or on the top floor or at the head of the table or in charge in any way. I think she has the presence of the archetypal innkeeper and if she had gone along with Chaucer's pilgrims there would be tales told but every one would intersect the other, the Miller's into the Pardoner's, the Wife of Bath's into the Knight's, all into each other. To a jazz beat and the lisping narrating style of Christian, the soup spoons in Big Eye's hands, the basso of the French Sprocket.

Those of us who hack at the French language and who go to the circus at Christian's invitation get an invite to a chateau in late June where there will be some kind of jazz festival. The chateau is owned by Christian's wife's family. I want to go but my father and brother await me in Patti, Sicily, at that same time. Maybe next year. I will postpone that trip to the chateau until next year.

The Sicily trip has already been postponed once. In 1996 Elaine was to meet with me in Rome and then we—myself and my daughters Amelia and Brenda—were to travel down to Sicily together. Relatives that we had there were expecting us. But Elaine is operated on for breast cancer and the trip is off. Brenda and Amelia want to return home at once to see their mother but she has me promise her that I won't allow them to do that. There is nothing for them to do for her at home; she is recuperating; she has friends. She wants more time to rest, away from us. "I won't know probably for years if I've licked this thing or not," she tells me. "Right now, I'm fine. Don't frighten the girls and have them rush home." I promise. I won't frighten them; we'll come home when the program is over. We'll all travel to Sicily some other year. Some other time.

Christian's invitation won't stop us now. Amelia is not with us but living and working in Tucson and Brenda won't be traveling to Europe until later in the summer.

From Eveline's we go off to Grindewald, a small town in the Swiss Alps. When we return to Holland, we go to Leiden, but are off the first weekend to London. From London back to Leiden and then from Leiden to Paris where the World Cup games are just beginning. Elaine arrives in Amsterdam and is in Leiden just a day before we rail to Paris. After Paris, we rail to Milan, where we stay only one day, and then on to Venice, which Elaine loves and we stay for three days. We go on to Florence and then the next day to Rome. From Rome, we rail to Sicily, where the Sicilian version of the Dutch Eveline's awaits us.

The stage is set: My father and my brother, Pete, have already been sharing for too long a bedroom in our cousin Diego's house. At our arrival, my father and my brother are barely speaking to each other. My Sicilian relatives are caught in a sort of tranquility/volatility dualism. Diego, the oldest brother of five and the one who bears the "professorial" title his father had and his father before him, prefers things to be "*molto tranquilo.*" His wife, however, is *molto volatilo*, a small dynamo working at the heart of her and supplying her with enough energy to light the city of Boston. She drives her Fiat up and down the hillside town of Patti as if the roads were fire hot and she had her bare feet pressing to them. She downshifts on a 180-degree turn, braking just slightly before the turn, snapping Elaine, Pete, and myself seated in the back seat from one side to the other, our necks heading for the glass, our heads for the streets and walls. My father sits in the front seat, without a seat belt. I don't think the imminence of peril registers totally on him so enwrapped is he in remembering his youth at this or that particular locale that Rita is speeding by.

"This is where I used to live," he tells us. "Was," I say, because Rita has already shot up the hill and passed it. She has no time to stop for his memories. "You drive this car as fast as it will go," my father tells her one day after she has made one of her blind sharp turns and this time has gone face to face with another Sicilian driving in the same *molto pazze* style. Rita swerves the wheel just enough to miss collision. No braking, no outward sign that given a nanosecond either way the five of us would have been eating the metal of the other car. Driving conditions only reach Rita when she is behind someone not going eighty miles an hour up an alley-size street with switchback turns every forty feet. Then she curses them mightily. They are holding back her progress.

What a pressing sense of progress this Sicilian has when the rest of the world continues to see Sicily itself as a place not at all interested in progress. Northern Italy wants to divest itself of any *mezzo giorno* connection, especially a Sicily feudalistically run by the Mafia. The North wants to race at breakneck speed into the new global-market order while the South wants to take a long nap from one till five. How then to explain the rate of speed of my cousin Rita? The time/space frame she is in is like the personal equivalent of *Star Trek* warp drive.

"If I had a Ferrari," she tells us in response to my father's comment,"I could go as fast as I want to go."

Later on, her husband Diego will take us on a tour of Palermo, which he thinks is the most beautiful city, second to Rome, that he has ever seen. He points out Mafia strongholds as if they are civic centers. For me the city is dark, dirty, and sinister, even on a blazingly hot summer day, and I have all the wonders of Italian and Arabic architectural synthesis before me. The first time Diego sets up to park, a teenager appears out of nowhere and guides him into the spot. And then promises that he will watch the car so that nothing happens to it while we are gone. Diego smiles and nods. This is just amusing, his manner indicates. We have come for the splendors of the architecture, the sculpture, the paintings, the fountains. But I am from New York City and I know that the kid is putting the bite on us. If we want the car to be as we left it, we had better give him something. Extortion greets us like the very heat bouncing off the pavement.

If Sicily can get rid of this Mafia curse, then investors from all over will come in and real development of the island can take place. I decide then and there to make a proposal to the Northern politicians: Buy my cousin Rita a Ferrari, send her to Palermo, put her up for about a month, or, maybe just three weeks, and just let her drive around Palermo the way she's always dreamed of driving around. At her speed. She may take out some innocent citizens but chances are she would decimate the mafioso population in record time. I keep wondering if there are road accident statistics in her hometown of Patti. I look around for the maimed, the crippled, for the people on crutches but as there are literally no sidewalks in this hillside town, but only medieval passageways now being used by my cousin Rita as raceways, I do not expect to find the wounded. I do not expect to find pedestrians.

Elaine and I go out for a *passeggiata* one night, accompanied by Piero, Brenda's twenty-something boyfriend, who knows how to walk around without getting killed. Nevertheless, we make a few wrong body moves and are almost run down. By the time we get to the Piazza Marconi at the center of the town, our nerves are frazzled and even inside *La Standa*, the *supermercato*, we are jumping to the right and left even though folks are only pushing shopping carts and my cousin Rita is nowhere in sight.

I never see Diego ride with Rita and I wonder if he would advise her to drive more tranquilly. From what I can follow of the conversations between Diego and his son Paulo, Paulo is anxious to find his entrepreneurial opening, hoping, he tells me, for a big change when the Euro comes into play and the EU builds up steam, taking Sicily and him along with it. Diego isn't entrepreneurial; he is seigniorial. He wants Paulo to get a university degree, become professorial, seigniorial, stay out of the sun, live a quiet, calm, life stylized by generations before him. *Molto tranquillo* is what he recommends to Paulo as a lifestyle. The crap shoot of the global market, of finding a niche in a volatile setting of global finance and investment, is not anything Diego can understand. But Paulo yearns for such volatility for in that mix and mess of global variables he hopes to make his fortune. Claudio, the younger son, is yet not that young—twenty-four—and though he smiles constantly, he refuses to learn any English or attend at all when English is spoken. "*Io non capisco,*" he tells me. "*Io non comprendo. Io non parlata Inglese.*" Still smiling. But Claudio is lit up nonetheless. Once, while we are speeding through Patti Marina, Claudio comes up alongside on his Vespa. We shout at him, he waves, we wave and he's gone. Another time as we walk along the beach, we see Claudio in the distance with two other companions on Vespas. The second time he shows up late for pranza his mother reprimands him. He doesn't live in the family house but with his maternal grandmother, who they say wants the company. And when he meets me for the first time he asks in Italian if I am a "hippie." He has seen *Easy Rider.*

He is in fact an easygoing rebel. There is no question about him going to university; he is the second-son free spirit who can break the mold of tranquil seigniorial life. History has written a place for the second son on this island. He has no idea of where he is going and cares less for what the future holds. He can live his whole life living carefree in this town on the bay of Patti among his friends. His volatility fits an historical pattern; he is like Fellini's *I Vitteloni;* maybe a little later in his life he will dash off and do something really volatile and then, like the biblical prodigal son, return home. There is an ancestral precedent for Claudio. He is the second son, not made either to be tranquil nor sedentary.

So Diego is the sedentary center of a family explosively volatile in every direction and in every possible way. A calm center setting itself up amid a volcanic overflow; a contesting of calm, deliberative dominance and impassioned drives from earth to the fiery center of the sun.

At some point I begin to realize that when I look at and hear my own eighty-four-year-old father at close range—and we see each other close there in Sicily, both visitors to our ancestral home—that both his emotion and imagination are here taxed. He has had little chance in his life to follow Shelley's advice and "exercise" both. His sentiment and compassion are called upon here but he is having trouble responding. He has no memory if memory is what Dickens had, what Wordsworth sought, or what kept Proust alive. He's always been uninterested in the details of things past and has scant experience with the natural beauties that sustain other lives, and even less an eye for human creations that put the color and music and the joy into our lives. And without all that, now at eighty-four, my father's left a little thin, paper thin, in all the ways we are human that have nothing to do with earning a living. Tending his stocks and his money market and his portfolio without the aid of a broker, none of whom does he trust, has taken its toll, consumed his focus. He only hears loud voices that repeat what they say and only when he turns his good ear toward the speaker, so his selective hearing has a physical base. I, as yet, have no such excuse for mine. It seems to me that my father pays little or no attention because his experience has already told him that this or that speaker can tell him nothing of significance. So he is alone with the thoughts he has managed to hold on to up till now. I suspect this in him because I already suspect this as mounting in my own life. I suspect that for my father nothing new has intruded for decades. All the old pictures serve. The mental journey has somehow been foreclosed. I don't know how to respond. I hear my own family tell the same story about me. Old connections are getting in the way of seeing or hearing anything new.

But then my father always surprises me: There are times when he knows exactly what I am saying. He surprises me and rails, like Keats once did, against the moods of his own mind. Several years ago when I called my father on his birthday he thanked me for the good wishes and told me he hoped on going further down the road just to give my brother and I a report on what to expect.

Maybe I deceive myself when I say I am on a journey. Where my father is at now may be my destination. I don't know what to think of the road ahead. Criticizing him is just railing against my own fate. Hyperconscious narrating doesn't free me. This family journey back to our roots is depressing me.

My father rails at my older brother, Pete, whom he doesn't respect perhaps because he knows my older brother's financial "picture." Mine makes him no more respectful but since I write books he extends me more patience than he does Pete. But he also extends me some doubt because if I knew anything about anything that really mattered, my financial picture would be a whole lot better than it is. My older brother, in turn, rails against the low esteem my father has for him. He shouts for respect, compassion, love. My father doesn't hook up; he doesn't understand the rage. He'll walk away if my brother continues. I have only one bad scene with my father: I respond with a lot of venom and then walk off but when I return it is clear that my rejoinder had blown across the Bay of Patti and had never entered my father's ears. I lost my temper and said something there was no use in saying but he never heard it. So much the better. How can you rail at your eighty-four-year-old father?

My father is the son of Sicilian immigrants who took him to Sicily for a visit but the visit lasted fourteen years and my father didn't return to the United States until he was seventeen. He returned with all the immigrant stories of America in his head: For the smart, shrewd, ambitious, clever man, there were fortunes to be made in America. Now at eighty-four my father returns to Sicily where he wasn't born but where the earliest and I suspect most lasting pictures in his head were developed. He is returning, perhaps for the last time, with his two sons, to see if there is anything of his youth that he left behind there. I don't know what a man with little sentiment can hope to find in the place where he was young. There were donkey carts when he was here last; no Ritas driving at breakneck speed.

When we arrive on the island of Lipari and my father is greeted by his first cousin, Gaetano, also eighty-four, he greets him like he greets all the old people in Oceana, the WASPish retirement community in Southern California where my mother and father live. And when they get a chance to talk, my father only has chatter about recent things that have happened. I see the effects of Oceana in him—the superficial courtesies of being on golf courses too long with those my father has always seen as "real Americans." I have to turn the talk again and again to the past, trying to prime Gaetano's memory of what his father, who died at the age of ninety-two, might have told him about my grandfather. I am anxious to know about my father's father, who was killed in the first world war in 1917. My father was only three when his father, Pietro, was killed. But my father has no questions to ask this cousin whose memory may hold stories his own father may have told him of his dead brother. Would not a brother who lives to be ninety-two tell stories of his dead younger brother?

But telling stories and asking other people to tell stories are things my father doesn't do. He can talk but he talks around revealing anything personal and shies away from conversations in which others reveal the personal. Elaine says this is not a trait she has seen among Italians; but my father is a Sicilian and Sicilians synthesize Arabic and Western in the same way the architecture of Palermo does. He has returned to Sicily with his sons not to hear stories or elicit stories of the past but to do something he has not the breadth or depth to do. He filibusters the journey, talking around the heart of the thing, the return to where he was young, where either he had the heart and passion of the young boyfriend of Brenda's, Piero, and took it to America where he lost it on his savings and investment career, or he never was like Piero and started out with any eye for success, for winning, kept his eye on the winning course.

Maybe America was the place where he developed a mercantile edge, lost the connection between heart and mind. This journey back to Sicily is a painful journey for him but he didn't expect it. It's catching him by surprise. He has to spend all his time talking around and away from what Sicily wants to show him.

Strange that he never meets Piero. I remember when he first hears Piero's name, he says "Like my own father's name." No, I say, Piero not Pietro. Same thing in Sicilian he tells me. It's not the same thing. But in his mind it was the same thing. Stranger then that Piero, close to the age that my father's own father was at the time of his death, and my father never meet. Piero shows up on his Vespa with an armload of beautiful flowers for Elaine; he shows up at our hotel when we leave with a bag full of the lushest black figs, so sweet that you know at once what Homer is raving about. He shows up at the rail station with the half of a shell that when you put to your ear, sings the songs of the sirens that lured Odysseus on the Aeolian Islands, the islands of enchantment, the islands my father's relatives now live on. Piero has the other half so that when Brenda, my youngest daughter, puts her shell to her ear she will hear what Piero has in his heart, what he is telling her from across the oceans and the largest sea in Europe.

If my father confused his father Pietro with Piero, the young Sicilian man who is wooing my daughter, he may have feared that meeting. So much youthful romantic spirit, so much unconcern for what should be saved and what should be invested in. And so

Side Trip

much tragic emptiness, marking the fluctuations of the Dow Jones, no flowers blooming, no siren song in deaf ears. Is this the culmination of the immigrant's journey to America? What sadness such a meeting of these would be and who would be most disappointed?

Side Trip

Death Ahead

Even in Texas, it seemed, it was not yet a crime to flee a private corporation.
—Eric Bates, "Private Prisons," *The Nation*, Jan. 5, 1998

With that jury [O.J. criminal trial jury] what did it matter?
—William Tucker, "Unbroken Windows: The Good News on Crime," *American Spectator*, March 1998

By privatizing prisons, government essentially auctions off inmates—many of them young Black men—to the highest bidder.
—Bates

The Southern states, which have carried out the vast majority of executions in the past twenty years . . . pay token amounts to an inexhaustible supply of incompetent, uncaring, hack lawyers to provide only perfunctory representation to those facing death. It is this poor quality of representation that facilitates executions.
—Stephen B. Bright, letter to *The Nation*, March 2, 1998

I am a participant who advocates for the condemned, but a participant nonetheless. Was I serving to legitimate the system by helping to provide sanitized executions, executions with the aura of legalism and therefore the appearance of fairness?
—Michael Mello, *Dead Wrong*, 1997

Twenty percent of the population in this country is ready to impose swift justice on the other eighty percent, either imprisoning them in private prisons or executing them. It's a simple matter to come to determinate verdict within a "mutual admiration society," what I call a commonly shared view of reality and its truths, what's right and what's wrong, what's justice and what's not, whose life is trash and whose is "top-of-the-line."

Why shouldn't the Fortune 500 and their servers think that the death penalty was not only a good idea "for the country" but also an

idea with "right reason" on its side? Give me one reason why someone
with a lot to lose—beyond just *his* or *her* own life—wouldn't want the
death penalty for everything from trespassing and theft to murder? I
mean if property is happiness and the death penalty is an effective deter-
rent, why not do all you can to deter someone from deterring you and
your pursuit of happiness? Why would market values allow for something to get in the way of you and profit? As long as you're not the one
fighting for your life in some Southern courtroom represented by a
lawyer who is racist, ignorant, drunk, and asleep, why not secure your
winnings by playing hardball with criminals? After all, you made your
millions by playing "hardball" with your competitors. Why shouldn't
winning ways in the market work with something so important as keeping the criminals away from you and your own?

I therefore predict that trespassing and invasion of private property
will get you five to ten in five to ten years. And computer terrorism—the
death penalty. Why? Because like Willie Sutton said, "inside computers
is where the money is." Anybody who can break into a system to
implant a virus—purely for the sake of giving the system a hard time—
can break into investment accounts and transfer funds—maybe downward. Back to the people. The twenty-first-century Robin Hood is a
hacker. Popular film is already screening this.

When *The American Spectator* argues for the impeccable sovereignty of new technology in proving beyond a doubt that someone is
innocent or guilty, it makes one allowance. Such indisputable scientific
evidence would be wasted on the first O.J. jury. Nothing rational could
matter to "that jury." Science and technology cannot penetrate irrationality's defenses. Obviously, "that jury" doesn't belong to *The American Spectator* Equestrian class, that mutual admiration society in which
everyone admires each other's "winning-in-the-world" ways. O.J. was a
winner too, one of them, but it was the jury and its decision that generated *American Spectator* wrath. Their verdict cast aspersions on the dispensation of justice in America. And since that signifier—"justice"—
now comes to meaning in a climate in which justice is best served by a
"hanging judge" and not by soft-hearted liberals, any tarnishing of the
"wheels of justice" is itself a hanging offense. Imagine how frustrating it
is to want to render swift and righteous judgment and the means to
achieve this glorious end—the American trial by a jury of your peers—
isn't up to speed. I mean if it was up to speed, the O.J. jury would have
been reprimanded, countermanded, and remandered.

But doubt had already riddled the justice system. The O.J. jury's
crime was to imply by its verdict that behind all the rational arguments
of the prosecution, behind all the scientific evidence they presented, lay

"White supremacy," "White power," "White wealth," and "White justice." The speed at which they came to verdict, the aura of disdaining inattentiveness they showed throughout the trial, and the verdict itself expressed a disdain for the entire justice system. Everything here only appeared to be fair; but in actuality they knew that such trappings of fairness, impartiality, reasoning, evidence, and justice itself were what White America used to convince themselves and the world and posterity that their treatment of Black America was fair, impartial, reasoned, and all the rest. The jury saw through or behind that discourse of fairness and justice, not to a specific LA police conspiracy, but a conspiracy of wealth and power to shape a self-protective "justice" system, a system defending what the Haves had gained from what the Have Nots might do.

By paying no attention to the elaborate "prosecution" of O.J.—dismissing it in two hours—the jury was guilty of a foundational disrespect for an order of things which was already set up not only to keep everyone in their place but to protect one from the other. All this reasoning, the jury seemed to be saying, was "your kind of reasoning" and you can see the fruits of that all around you. Thus, the verdict wasn't personal; the jury wasn't really thinking of O.J. After all, O.J. was one of the Haves; he didn't live in South Central or hang out with the "brothers." He had enough money to buy a Dream Team and with that Dream Team buy himself justice.

Did he in fact buy himself justice? Yes and no. Yes, if you accept the notion that Johnnie Cochran awakened in the jury an already there sense of an unfair American justice system when it comes to Blacks and O.J.'s money brought Cochran on the scene. No, if you accept the notion that this jury would have come to the same verdict if O.J.'s lawyer was drunk, a racist, and asleep. The verdict was not personal, not really connected to O.J. This seems fantastically absurd. But is it? The verdict wasn't personal because if you follow through on everything this jury did, you come to one conclusion: They didn't think that *this* system was ready to be making personal decisions, rendering verdicts that would dispose of a person's life. And they didn't think that because a postmodern problematizing of truth and reality was undermining the social order and all its institutions. They thought that because they already knew that an unbelievably high percentage of Black men between the ages of eighteen and thirty-five were already in the penal system, either on trial, serving time, on parole, or running from a warrant. Now either young Black men are preternaturally or naturally criminal or they were living in a country that was nudging them toward crime. And the institutions of that kind of country are the first suspects that have to be rounded up in any criminal investigation. The country then stands accused in the eyes of this jury; the justice system it creates is not in a position to stand in judgment of anyone.

Doctors don't tell patients they have cancer if they think their diagnostic tools have been tampered with. Teachers don't tell students they're dumb if the teachers don't think they have reliable ways to determine that. Or, more appropriately here, if the tests are set up with a view of "smartness" only 20 percent of the population holds, it would be an injustice to impose that upon the other 80 percent. Of course if that 20 percent has the first call, has the necessary votes, has all the influence, then what they decide intelligence is, or what justice is, holds sway. But this O.J. jury wasn't swayed by that because they couldn't be reached. And I don't mean what *The American Spectator* implies by their insulting, racist remark—that reason could not reach them. I mean they couldn't be reached on the job, which is where most people are brought to heel. No one was holding the purse strings here. And there were no managers to manage the jury's dissent, to constrain their contrariness, to stifle their rebellion. The jury was unreachable although after the verdict, the equestrian and managerial classes stepped forward to vilify them, to publicly humiliate them. But it was to no avail; the verdict was in. That verdict could not be stopped; market needs could not reach it. However, it stands in the American cultural imaginary in the same place our defeat in Vietnam has stood: It burns and rankles and will someday be redressed. The Gulf War was dramatized by CNN as such a "return to Bataan," such an opportunity to redeem a national image, monumentalize it once again in the American cultural imaginary. How will the O.J. jury's insult to American justice be avenged and our image of how spectacularly just and fair we are be reasserted?

That jury was free to vote its conscience and it did. Now that order of things that they summarily rejected wants to preclude that ever happening again by tightening their control of the justice system. First you demonize, vilify, ridicule that jury and then you start a "national debate" over "improving the justice system," which I read as "making sure the courts keep the rich safe and outside prison and the poor safely inside prison." I want not to believe this outrageous statement but what else can prevail in a country that has dug a new Grand Canyon between rich and poor, advocates survival of the fittest as a natural law not to be tampered with, and now obviously fears the consequences of both?

Behind justice there is an impersonal reasoning that the O.J. jury could not rise to—this is a reasoning fast invading the country. My counterreasoning? Simply that the reasoning that prevails is the one that suits and supports a resident order of things. What that reason construes as "justice" abides as long as that magic circle of mutual reinforcement abides—an order of things produces a reason that maintains that order of things and this reason in turn produces notions of justice, fairness, and rightness which in turn produces an order of things.

> *We continue to demonstrate no human is wise enough to decide who should die.*
>
> —Michael Mello

> *The buzzsaw that criminals and their attorneys have run into is biotechnology, the most rapidly advancing science on the planet.*
> —William Tucker, *The American Spectator*

> *Congress created twenty federally funded programs in 1988 to supply legal help for prisoners awaiting death. In the fall 1995 session of Congress, all funding was cut.*
> —Colman McCarthy, "Murder, Inc."
> *The Nation*, Dec. 29, 1997

> *Corrections Corporation ranks among the top five performing companies on the New York Stock Exchange over the past three years. The value of its shares has soared from $50 million when it went public in 1986 to more than $3.5 billion at its peak last October . . . C.C.A has richly confirmed the title of a recent stock analysis by Paine Webber: "Crime pays."*
> —Eric Bates, "Private Prisons," *The Nation*, Jan. 5, 1998

Okay, we've been on trial in America and we haven't been as lucky as O.J. We're Black or Brown and we've got a state-appointed lawyer, no Dream Team. What's our crime? We went "entrepreneurial" and sold drugs; or we started in pursuit of happiness down the only open road—drugs; or, we went Uptown and stole a luxury sports van so we could have money to buy drugs; or, we got into the competitive arena with an encroaching dealer of drugs and shot him; or, we broke into a pharmacy and stole drugs; or, we . . . drugs. And now we're in prison. And this prison is not run by the feds or the state but by the Acme Prison Corporation. The Corrections Corporation of America is a "top performer" on the New York Stock Exchange; the prison "market," like the health "market" is booming. It's an American entrepreneurial success story. "Private prisons essentially mirror the cost-cutting practices of health maintenance organizations: Companies receive a guaranteed fee for each prisoner, regardless of the actual costs. Every dime they don't spend on food or medical care or training for guards is a dime they can pocket" (Bates, 14). What do the wise investment prognosticators that show up

on Louis Rukeyser have to say about the future of private prison investment? Why, it's Bullish! "There are now eighteen million Americans
behind bars—more than twice as many as a decade ago—and the 'get
tough' stance has sapped public resources." And, as every budding
entrepreneur brought up and educated in Reagan's '80s and now walking around with a head full of Market Truths knows—"the government
can't do anything very well" [Thomas Beasley, cofounder of C.C.A.
quoted in Bates].

The movement here is inescapable but circular once again: The
supremacy of market criteria and values produces a society in which
winners are enfranchised and entitled and losers are a potential problem
which produces the growing split between Haves and Have Nots which
produces a concerted effort by the Haves to anesthetize those Have Nots
unaware of their worsening plight with Bread and Circuses and incar-
cerate the rest which produces the proper stable investment climate and
continued prosperity for shareholders which produces renewed faith in
the supremacy of. . . . And if Bread and Circuses and prisons produce
healthy profits along the way, why that's absolutely Bullish too!

How much of this would the O.J. jury have known? Unknowable.
How aware might they have been of facts like these reported by The
Sentencing Project in Washington, D.C.:

1. *One in three African American males, ages 20–29, are in prison or under
   supervision.*

2. *In California, 40 percent of African American males in their twenties are in
   prison or under supervision.*

3. *In the District of Columbia, 42 percent of African American males, ages
   18–35, are in prison or under supervision.*

4. *In Baltimore, Maryland, 56 percent of African American males, ages
   18–35, are in prison or under supervision.*

5. *Between 1986 and 1991, the number of African American women in state
   prisons for drug offenses has increased 828 percent.*

6. *African Americans and Hispanics represent about 90 percent of drug
   offenders sentenced to state prison.*

—Keith Watters, "Law without Justice"

Although African Americans make up 12 percent of the American
population, they make up 74 percent of all drug prison sentences. You
only have to be found in possession of five grams of crack to wind up
with a mandatory five-year prison sentence. But possession of cocaine
powder is five hundred grams for the mandatory five-year prison sen-

tence. Not only is cocaine powder an "upscale" drug and crack a "bargain basement" drug but police don't "clean sweep" the "upscale" neighborhoods. But African American communities are open territory for police, reporters, and TV cameras. You could say it's because this is where the drugs are and yet 52 percent of crack users are White and 75 percent of cocaine powder users are White. Let's put it this way: If Bill Gates or Rupert Murdoch or John Malone or Donald Trump or others who can absolutely afford private lives are snorting coke daily, the cops are not going to be "clean sweeping" their domains. Keith Watters of the National Bar Association notes this form of discrimination against African Americans: "Grossly disproportionate arrests from targeting of African American communities through discretionary law enforcement strategies, techniques and resources."

It's easier to target folks who don't have a battery of lawyers and lots of cash to make their case. It's also risky for cops to be hauling in a city's "benefactors" and "social luminaries," friends of the mayor and the governor you might say. But logistically, it's a lot harder to get to where Gates may be sharing a bowl than to get to where a dozen Black men are hanging out on a public corner in a neighborhood in which the police never feel they need show up hat in hand. Have Nots are just more accessible; they occupy more of the public space because they can't afford private space. Think of hunting snarks: You can find the most snarks in a thick forest or in caves or underground but you go after the ones you can find in a big, open parking lot because you can easily get them in your sights.

But deeper than this logistics level is what I myself have been pushing here: The "Disaffected" are destined to become more disaffected; the threat to our present market order of things does not lie in Bill Gates's compound or in the Trump Tower. It lies in these Have Not neighborhoods. Drugs may mellow a Warren Buffett out after a hard day of financial hardball; nobody on the AAA social register need worry about where their next snort will come from. They won't subway to a wealthy neighborhood and steal a car, knock someone over the head, kidnap a prominent citizen. They won't terrorize the resident order of things, that order of things that has already put them in towers, made them prominent, made them winners. They have no reason to be disaffected; they are intensely interested in everything, including upholding that order of things that does all right by them. This is not the case with the Have Nots, and the situation is destined to be much worse on the road ahead, in spite of what Bill Gates tells us.

Clean sweeps of "bad" neighborhoods will get the losers off the streets and into prisons where shareholders can make a profit off of them. It's what's called a "win-win" situation.

What about personal responsibility? Why can't someone from a bad neighborhood choose to be "good," choose in fact to be entrepreneurial? Choose to say NO! to drugs, and then go out and start a business? And if none of the lenders will help them go entrepreneurial, then why can't they start with the best job they can get, go back to school, work on their résumé, save like crazy, go on to a better job, get more schooling, save even more, go entrepreneurial again. And so on. Compete and win. Such ambition should not be impeded by minimum wage, unemployment benefits, welfare payments, medical coverage, aid to dependent children, social security contributions, federal taxes, public education, capital gain taxes, any form of entitlement, and any sense that society had woven a safety net for them in case they fell. Why would they fall, except through their own fault? Chance? Entrepreneurs make their own luck. Level playing field? Everyone is born equal under the law and has the same opportunities. Brains and talent? Here's where the winners show their winning ways. Entitlement? The winners are entitled to their winnings without having to pay for the loser's expenses.

A very rosy scenario. And why not? It's written by the winners. Now when life intrudes in this self-serving fabrication, what happens? Well, the kid in a home without a Pentium chip computer, or even without a copy of *Reader's Digest* gets a chance finally to compete with a shareholder's kid. And when that Mac job at minimum wage (which if Dick Armey has his way will be a job at Brazil wages) doesn't produce enough to buy the Big Mac special and pay the rent, then another Mac job is added to that one. Now our emerging competitor is officially one of the "working poor," working two jobs and just about paying the bills. With the time left over, he or she takes some "career improvement classes" at the local community college, where he or she can use all that stored up erudition and those fine literacy skills already gleaned from public schools supported by the tax dollars of their own impoverished neighborhoods. You know the type of school: taught by those who had the same sort of education from the same sort of impoverished neighborhoods, and filled with all the computer technology those neighborhoods can afford, and attended to by kids who don't come home to the Brady Bunch household. With that sort of life you look for what brings relief: Sex is number one because it doesn't have to cost anything. Not until kids are born and the parents can't afford to marry; or marriage is seen as an obstacle that can be avoided. It's sex, after all, that gives the pleasure, a pleasure you can share with the Bill Gateses of the country. After that comes drugs. Drugs bring relief; crack is not that expensive. You can handle it on minimum wage, with a little grifting here and there. And if you see the connection between being entrepreneurial and drug dealing, then you've found your path to winning in America. You might say you've got two paths: Get high and feel just like you're winning and most importantly forget that you're losing; or sell drugs like cars and hamburgers are sold.

So you're on the road to prison because you're living in a society that has an eye out for the disaffected. If they don't pick you up on a drug charge, you're liable to deteriorate further, become more desperate, more disaffected, more dangerous. What pushes the Have Nots toward drugs is not ever totally dissolved by drugs; the disaffected are into drugs because it's a relief from lives that go no place, that don't materialize, that see no light, that can't think of the future, that can't think of themselves as significant, that have only a being-in-the-world that haunts them, that terrorizes them, that they fear. If there is a lurking psychopathology that triggers one's actions, Prozac and its breed will merely cover up the problem, or some observable symptoms of the problem. The Have Nots take drugs not because they have no will power or have addictive personalities or because they are born escapists but because they can find no other way out of lives in which every path but the one drugs opens up is closed off.

Drug arrests put people away before they get a chance to do a crime that hurts others, especially those people who fear they would be the targets of this quintile of the population. Drug legalization would keep them on the street longer and thus increase their chances of committing the really scary crimes, from the Haves' point of view: theft, kidnaping, destruction of property. And drugs, like prisons, also turn a profit. No one really believes that the international drug market is managed by local users. Big global-market players backed by brainy system analysts, computer nerds, legal eagles, top investment counselors, and accountants ply the drug trade the way they do everything from computer chips to Nikes. Drugs are another win-win situation for the Haves: They keep the Have Nots subdued, make them vulnerable to arrest, and they produce ready cash at crucial cash-flow-problem moments. And every good global-market player has those moments. Joe Kennedy made his fortune on bootleg Canadian whiskey; that road is now a drug road and there's a lot of traffic.

Too bad. You're not only in prison but you're on Death Row.

In a book called *A Primer to Postmodernity*, I gave my postmodern take on capital punishment and I don't want to go over that ground. Put blankly, while the social order inclines variously to the reasonableness of capital punishment, and the cultural ferment puts this issue to the boil variously, we humans never vary in our capacity to establish precise correspondence between word and world, between what anyone says went on and what really may have gone on. We can't do it well enough to erase "reasonable doubt." We "doubt" within a changing game of what reason is and what's reasonable; social orders are notorious for creating "reasonable" laws, practices, and institutions that lead to things like slavery, apartheid, holocausts, diaspora, and surgical bombings of civilians. The rules of the game, thankfully, change. A jury could not find reasonable doubt in the Sacco and Vanzetti case, although subsequently countless people have. A jury could find reasonable doubt in the O.J. trial, although at the same time countless people could not. The whole concept of "reasonable doubt" no longer does what an Enlightenment view of things hoped it would do. You can just as doubtfully come to a point where you say you have reason to doubt that the reasons here presented lead to any determinate conclusion as you can come to a point where you can say that the reasons here presented do lead to a determinate conclusion. In other words, determinacy is always doubtful for humans because human reasoning is temporalized, contextualized, narrated, situated, relative to changing personal, social, and cultural mediating frames. Thus, in the postmodern view, you don't have "reasonable doubt" but rather you doubt reason so you can neither have "reasonable doubt" nor "doubtless reason."

I think the Rodney King tape revealed something clearer than whether or not police brutality was involved: It showed us that were we all from Missouri and had to be shown, we still would be interpreting what we see from various perspectives. Of course, it remains to be seen whether technology is just presenting us with more stuff that has to be interpreted; we have seen O.J.'s Dream Team as easily take a DNA report as a glove as something to be interpreted within a particular narration. "Smoking guns" have been presented as evidence and defendants have gotten off; recall the first Menendez brothers' trial. They killed but they weren't murderers. They didn't dispute the blood evidence; nor did the Dream Team dispute the FBI lab reports except to say that they were what they were because they just might have been tampered with and they might have been tampered with because there might have been some sort of LAPD conspiracy against O.J. going on. In this way, technology's definitiveness collapses into narration. But the hope that William Tucker reports in *The American Spectator* is that very soon no perpetrator will be able to leave a crime scene without also leaving behind incontrovertible DNA evidence. A speck of anything will do; the suspect can be matched to the speck, provided that there is a suspect. In a thoroughly modern world, people murder for a reason and they therefore murder people they have a reason to murder. Those reasons form a trail from them to the victim, a trail Sherlock can follow. In a world in which the semblance of reason has not been destroyed by postmodernity, regardless of how often the attack is made, but destroyed by a global-market imperialism that confuses reasoning with profiting, there seems to be no reason not to pursue profit whenever and wherever you can. Crime, after all, pays for the underclass as well as the overclass. Stranger murders, murders committed by total strangers who see no profit in leaving behind a potential witness, leave fewer suspects than Sherlock Holmes found available. So the whole premise that DNA testing will bring certainty to our justice system has promise as long as the police can apprehend the right suspect. Rounding up the usual suspects, those habitual low-lifes that one wants to put away, may not prove profitable. Indeed, DNA testing may wind up preventing a social order from getting as many of its undesirables off the street as it would wish. The difficulties of planting a speck of something at a crime scene would be infinitely less than planting drugs or a weapon or a fingerprint. Let's say John Gotti had continued to come to trial and be found innocent; a hair from his head, a bit of saliva, a bit of skin flake, and so on would give the prosecution its win. Everyone knew he was "dirty," as the police say. It seems to me that herein lies the deficit side of "total justice through technology": Even if a Have/Have Not social order wasn't gearing up to maintain its gross inequality by demonizing and then imprisoning the turbulent underclass, all that late modernist angst would be returning as no one would go to bed at night without worrying about having a DNA speck of theirs turning up in the wrong place. And, what is all this technology doing when it's not being used in trials? Do we face a future of genetic discrimination? Of being identified by DNA and thereby placed in neat niches, as in the film *Gattaca?*

I've wandered away from death. You were on death row. The jury decided there was no "reasonable doubt." You're hoping to delay execution long enough to test my theory that a different time will create a different context, all of which may create a different "reasoning world" for a different jury out of which—behold!—there is now "reasonable doubt" and you're free.

Good luck.

Let's say though that you turned to God sometime after you were convicted of murder in the first and sentenced to death. All the cynics out there expect you to "find God" and then ask for a stay of execution on the grounds that you are not the person you were then. How does a social order handle an issue like this? How does it handle an issue like assisted suicide? How did it handle the issue of abortion? How is it handling the issue of smokers' rights? How is it handling Clinton's sex life?

These are all very different and yet they all have something in common: The question that in each case comes up is, what's the dividing line between the strictly personal and the social? If a death-row convict repents and is "born again," is this like a haircolor change or growing a beard or getting a law degree or marrying? I mean is it just personal? Does it matter that the person whose life the state takes was a sinner because of the crime and is now "born again"? Maybe the person didn't think they were sinning when they committed their crime. Maybe they had no sense of sin. Maybe they were like Raskolnikov who commits murder precisely to show that there is no sin in the act. On the other hand, the state is putting to death someone different from the person who committed the crime. The whole experience has awakened the death-row convict's moral sense; he or she has passed through the dark night of the soul and now emerges as a person fully aware of the sacredness of human life. This person now wants to join Mother Theresa's order and do only good in the world. This person is now an asset to human society; a saint, not a sinner. What sense is there now to execute the redeemed? It seems that the crime of taking another's life is not merely a personal matter and so personal acts cannot redeem it. The crime has passed from personal to social. What the social order will do depends upon how it is constructing this order at any particular time.

What about assisted suicide? Is Kervorkian doing a right thing or a wrong thing? If I call Dr. K in and ask him to off me, is this totally a personal decision? Have I come to a totally personal appraisal of my situation or is it already wrapped up in social and cultural stories? Have I seen the way people with such and such an illness die on the screen? Consider my sense of "Not Being Able To Go On." Do I have a fixed sense of this? Where does it come from? How do I see the other side of "Not Being Able To Go On"? What if I can't go on but Chance intrudes and I do go on. Am I going on and how am I going on? Has my sense now of "NBATGO" changed? I thought "I would just die" but afterward, when I didn't die, I see how easily it is for me to go on living. Pain and suffering are surely real but the way we deal with them, the way we meet them, narrate them, plot them, respond to them are all shaped by how we are personally, socially, and culturally situated. Someone will say that time will only make things worse. Ahead is only deterioration, humiliation, pain, agony, defeat, death. But who has the right to say that but you? And if you are saying that to yourself, how much of that self-appraisal has to do with the particular lifeworld frame you are in? Consider this: You are hypnotized or you get a concussion. You don't recall who you are. Dr. K shows up right on time. He tells you that you're not able to go on and he's there to assist you so you won't have to go on.

But you're not you so you don't recall why you can't go on; he shows you your medical charts. All the numbers, all the lab reports, all the X-rays. But when you woke up that morning it was a lovely spring morning and you saw a robin in the branches of a tree just beginning to bud a marvelous shade of lime green. You ran into an old friend the day before whom you hadn't seen in a long time and you went to dinner and talked and laughed about old times. It was wonderful to laugh like that. You've felt pain but you don't know what it means yet; where it's heading. You narrate your medical charts toward spring. You, the concussed You, thinks you'll go on a bit longer. Everything factual has remained the same; only you have changed. There was nothing really permanent and indelible in the "You" who could be the only one who could tell you that you couldn't go on.

The personal here is inextricably social and cultural and thus your decision to commit suicide must be temporalized socially and culturally. The society and culture that frames your "You" also frames the assisted suicide debate, temporalizing that debate as well as your own narration of your need to die. Your dying is a social and cultural matter, our societal and cultural support of assisted suicide fluctuating within the changing order of both, a fluctuation that your "You" is also a part of. As in capital punishment, legislation in support may alter to legislation against. And You who can't go on may be caught in the same narrative of "legislation against" and feel that you can go on.

Mythologizing the Journey

Myth is a type of speech.
                    —Roland Barthes, *Mythologies*

Knowledge kills action; action requires the veils of illusion.
                    —Nietzsche, *The Birth of Tragedy* 7

*Crick argues that as humans we long "for presence, for feature,
for purpose, for content," and thus we believe in myths "in order
to convince ourselves that reality is not an empty vessel."*
                    —p. 30 of Graham Swift's *Waterland*

The merest coincidence, the sheer play of Chance, brings before me
just weeks into 1998 the mythological mapping of our journey. I see
three films within as many days: *The Postman*, *Wag the Dog*, and *Snow
White*. Seeing these films leads me into a whole meditation on how we
enframe imaginatively our being-in-the-world, and I want to follow that
meditation as background to discussing these films.

What these drastically different films led me to think about is the
whole matter of what we fill our lives with, how we structure our movements in time, visualize ourselves in space, superimpose our dreams and
ideologies, the Keatsian moods of our minds, upon a planet rotating on
its axis while at the same time revolving around the Sun. We create a
world out of the cold, silent turning of spheres within a vast, expanding
ether we call the Universe. Our "worlding" this cold frame into human
dimensions begins with Nature, which we have envisioned as a kind of
benign, comforting, picturesque retreat for soulful contemplation as well
as soulful recuperation. Nature has also been narrated as the exact
opposite, as red in tooth and claw, as a daemonic domain we can never
be at peace with, that we must oppose vigilantly and continuously in
order not to be crushed by it. In between, we tell a story of an indiffer-
ent Nature, a Nature that has no intent, neither good nor bad, but is
merely context to the human drama we unfold within it, or, outside it,

191

depending upon the story of Nature/human relationship we tell ourselves. Nature here goes on in its cyclic way, somehow composed of living creatures ruled by their instincts, instincts respondent to the "forces"
of Nature itself, as well as composed of ourselves, whose cerebral cortex has replaced instinctual response and therefore leaves us orphaned
from the bosom of Nature itself. Or, in an existentialist view, orphaned
by the cosmos itself.

Of all living creatures on the face of the earth, we humans do not
resonate completely or precisely within the rhythms of Nature; we have
made from within those rhythms our own paths, or are continually trying to forge those paths. Ironically, we have wound up here at the
threshold of the new millennium as a threat to the Nature which was
at this millennium's beginning, a threat to us. At the beginning of the
last century of this millennium, we had shifted to threat mode as our
brains, cut free of mere instinctual responses, invented the machines we
dragged into Nature's garden and then employed according to the scenarios of what we thought had to be done, what needed to be done,
what our survival depended upon, what progress was defined to be. We
produced the myths of how to produce, we produced the myths by
which to deal not only with Nature, but with ourselves, as individuals
and in society. And sometimes we called them the myths of Nature herself, anthropomorphizing Nature, giving her a human face: *her* face;
and stories of Deity beyond Nature, *His* face. What Nature is, and
beyond Wordsworth's Nature, the infinitude of the Universe in its dark
coldness, its emptiness oblivious to time and space itself, and yet not
empty but filled with random accelerations, hot flashes of meteors and
comets, strong stabilities like our own solar system—what all this is
outside our mythologies of what it is, is unfathomable, unreachable.
May I say this is so because we are already a part of this confusion of
being and emptiness. We cannot get outside one or the other in order
to "fathom them"; we are already what we would "reach" for. But with
our newly resident brain power we have driven ourselves far from living in that connectedness; we are driven to tell stories of what our connection is, or ought to be, or was.

We are the only creatures on the face of the earth who go on a journey from birth to death because we are the only ones who think we are
on a journey and thus we think about it. What is this journey like and
where are we going? And who am I who is going on this journey? And
what will happen to me? And who will I meet? In our human view, every
other creature is in place, journeyless, from beginning to end, they are
creatures in the present, for the present, for and in a place that they have
no dreams of making a different place, another place. We live in a time

now when we are casting an eye upon our mythologizing of our personal and societal life journeys. Call it the postmodern moment.

What was it like before? Maybe the story goes like this: A man and a woman pick up their tools at the crack of dawn and head for the fields, where they will work all day, and in the evening after cooking and eating, they will go to a revival tent and listen to a story of sin, repentance, and salvation. And at night in bed they will fall into each other's arms and make love, the reward of the day, the pleasure and joy without a price tag. They can afford this pleasure and maybe for them this night, this pleasure will be greater than any rich man or woman can have. Regardless how simple, how hard, how mindless, how pitiable this daily life may be, it is always taken to be life itself being lived by those living it. Life is a journey already that they are on and they fill it day by day according to their lot; given sudden riches, they would fill it differently. What they do and what may affect them from the outside are the shapers of the journey, they make up what life is. Never for a moment do they think that both what they do given the conditions of their life and what comes into their lives from the outside—Chance, societal forces, Nature's forces, God's hand, Fate, Karma, Destiny, or whatever—are nothing more than various mythologies of how we journey in life, narrative designs from ancient to born yesterday, that concoct and trigger our personal and cultural imaginaries.

Once you cross the postmodern border, you can't go out into the fields at morning and think this is you living your life, another page in your book of life, another step down the road of life, but rather you are moving within a way of living in the world that results from your knowing and believing in the world in a certain way. And you reflect on what those certain ways might be at that moment in your life. And this leads inevitably to your thinking about other ways of being there and about what is left out of your being there in your particular way at that particular moment. You begin, in short, to reflect on how you are mythologizing the world, but not just the personal you but the "you" that is you because you were born into a certain society within a certain culture at a certain time, all of which has been in motion in ungraspable, undeterminable ways.

The social order, for instance, is committed to redundancy, or at least to a stability whose response to Chance and cultural pressures appears essentially unchallenged, flexible, accommodating, reasonable, civilized—but essentially unchanging. The cultural ferment, on the other hand, is the site where what has not yet been brought within the social order is going through endless, sometimes turbulent, sorting out. When that turbulence gets too great for a social order to respond to, a revolt occurs. But it can't occur until the cultural ferment shapes itself within a revolutionary mythology, and that requires the kind of coherence, continuity, stability, unity that the social order claims. In other words, the cultural ferment must cease being a reservoir of contesting voices, battling dissident ideologies, but must itself become a "social order," a Bizarro one, a dark-side social order.

Revolutions replace one social order with another: A social order of restricting and constraining protocols is not replaced by a cultural pluralism or heterogeneity. It follows that you can institutionalize Enlightenment mythology because it argues for a rational grounding of any order of things but you cannot institutionalize postmodern mythology because if it grounds anything it is the proliferation of multiple, contesting, contradictory orders of things. And it does so because it questions the means of establishing a common, pervading ground.

Mythologies put up front alibis or ideologies. The pervading ideologies backing a particular social order always make it appear that they are "in the very nature of things." "Ideologies," James Rule writes, in the spirit of Althusser, "offer us plausible descriptions of the world and purport to explain why it is as it is—while, simultaneously, surreptitiously exhorting us. If we take them seriously, we cannot help favoring certain courses of action, certain social arrangements, over others. At their most powerful, ideologies are vague and subtle enough to make the image of the world that they convey seem almost unexceptionable. Yet they are relentlessly partisan" ["Markets, in Their Place," *Dissent*, winter 1998, 29]. Rule affirms that market ideology is the intellectual "totem" of the last decade of the twentieth century: "What the Rights of Man were to the French Revolution—or what Manifest Destiny or the quest for the Kingdom of God on Earth were to their times—the market is to our own."

The extraordinary power the market has assumed at this moment has reached nothing less than the magnetism and magnitude of mythology. The very dominance of this mythology provokes its own psychologizing, ironically, not unlike that applied to the way the market itself works. I refer to the fact that such overwhelming domination in a context where any domination is only self-defined and self-legitimizing stands on no firmer ground than its own mythic spin. The two marked drops in the Dow Jones at the end of 1997 evoked similar analysis: The Dow had been breaking records for growth for no other reason than investment was going on within a climate where growth was breaking records. A sudden realization that "only imagination or will was making it so," had produced the same effect that the thought that one's dick can go soft in the midst of copulation does. Stepping back into the mood of unending free-market growth got the market hard again and the Dow rose accordingly. The matter is as crude and rude as I have put it here. Perhaps Manifest Destiny was an equally crude mythology but clearly the Rights of Man and the Kingdom of God, in Heaven or on Earth, had and have a good deal more sophistication.

It is the very crudity of the market mythology that has one looking about for its deconstructor. But if you consider the postmodern moment within which this mythology is holding sway, you look about for self-reflections on the nature of mythologizing itself. What also would seem to precipitate a scrutiny of our resident mythological real-izing is the millennium looming just down the road. Or up the road. Or down below. Or off on a cul de sac. Whither is our market mythology taking us? Or, more precisely, where has it already taken a very small percentage of the world's population while the rest stand and serve or cannot stand at all? Thus, the climate is right, the moment is right, and the market mythology lies before us like the emperor without clothes.

The chat about Kevin Costner's *The Postman* was all bad even before the film was released: shades of *Waterworld*. But I hook up positively: The films seem to share a similar fascination with the world just down the road apiece. And to my mind, however one wishes to argue the aesthetics of the film (which to me as a postmodernist are arguable only in relation to how and to what degree a film rankles or strokes the prevailing values and protocols in sway at the moment of release), a film done in 1998 which begins with an intriguing time—2013—in a somewhat less intriguing place—Utah—after the collapse of the United States of America is a millennial movie. It is a movie created in the shadow of the millennium, before the millennium but courageously projecting beyond or into the next millennium. Not too far beyond, just thirteen years, which is a shrewd number of years because it is not so far into the future that the way we are now cannot still be recognized, not so far into the future that both filmmakers and audience are sprung free of the exigencies of the present. So all this change that we see here in the empty flats of Utah has taken only fifteen years. But there is not a whole lot of change to see because the camera is focused on Utah's open vacuity and not New York City's congested riot. Utah here is like the waters of *Waterworld*, a sort of blank screen upon which to project the future, to play out a mythology of the future not distracted or detoured by the need to see in detail what has become of all the things our market imperialism has collected. While water, as in the Bible, is a "liquid form of Nothing," Utah exists in the popular imagination as a flat vacancy, although water is not nothing nor is Utah flat and vacant.

Whereas an environmental catastrophe had led to a flooding of the land and created the dystopia of the future that the film *Waterworld* portrays, political turmoil in *The Postman* has led to the destruction of the Federal Government and a feudal state in which walled towns pay tribute to a roving warlord, a former computer salesman with a gift for demagoguery and brutality. What many fear will be the fate of the former Soviet Union—a chaos of feuding tribe/nations brought under the heel of a ruthless demagogue—is in this film presented as the fate of America. Of all the shards of a unified America that Costner could have chosen, he chooses the postal service to resuscitate, the sight of the uniform of the mail carrier worn by Costner on the back of a bold steed, proves in the end a sufficient catalyst to the reemergence of . . . of what? I suppose that American revolutionary spirit that we now only apprehend through the mythology of the American Revolution itself—Founding Fathers to Boston Tea Partiers to Paul Revere's Ride, Tom Paine's revolutionary common sense, Washington boldly crossing the Delaware, Patrick Henry's fiery speeches, Nathan Hale's "I regret that I have only one life to give to my country," et cetera.

One wonders why Costner could not have seen what I and everyone else in the theater saw each and every time we saw a trailer for *The Postman*. The trailer is excellent but ends on a laughable note, presaging the response the full film will get. The voiceover at the end of the trailer cautions us that we fail to recognize the value of our postman now but there will come a time when the sight of that uniform will stir patriotic feelings in all of us. Actually, we'll all go pro-Federal Government at the very moment when conservative cries for "devolution" and militia recruitment in preparation to take on the Federal Government in combat have reached their highest pitch. It seems clear that this anti-Federal Government feeling of the present leads to the feudalism just fifteen miles down the road. Just as in *Waterworld,* Costner once again projects a staunch liberal's view of a dystopic future caused by the antidemocratic mythology of market conservatives, for it is they who fear the regulating and taxing and punishing power of the Federal Government. And he projects this view at the moment when the market mythology is in sway. I am not surprised that all manner of aesthetic criticisms emerge regarding the film. At the same time, the film is certainly open to negative reviews, somewhat because of Costner's failure to displace himself as a dominating point of observation. Rather than a postmodern subject, we have a full Romantic Ego, and the megalomania of that ego seems closely connected to Costner's directing and starring in the film. In other words, he is not only too fascinated with the force of his own observations, himself as a mythologizer, but he reveals himself to be a less than compelling observer and a rather simple-minded mythologizer. Now, this doesn't play well at a postmodern moment either and critics have seized upon this to jettison the movie. And although those who were in the audience with me seemed to enjoy the movie greatly, it did not remain long in our mall multiplex. One would have to apply Chaos Theory to figure out how and why some films capture an audience regardless of how strenuously critics lambast a movie. In this particular case, *The Postman* could not surmount the ridicule.

Perhaps Costner was too lost in his own image of himself and his capacity to create great mythologies to sense that a postman could never symbolize the last remaining spark of the American spirit, could ever transcend the image of postal workers as disaffected losers who periodically go berserk and kill their fellow postal workers. In what way does the American Dream lurk in the hearts of these disaffected Federal employees who are over and over again held up to ridicule by private enterprise when it argues that the Feds can't do anything right? "Take a look at the post office if you want to see governmental incompetency" is the common conservative appeal. For whatever reason, I think the poor reception this film receives stems from this fundamental misreading of the American cultural imaginary at this moment. We may be less anti-Federal Government because the Tim McVeigh and Terry Nichols' trials are in the headlines and we see the dangers of extreme attacks upon the Feds, but we are hardly in a "the postman-is-the-hero-of-the-future" mode.

Don't ask me who Costner should have chosen as a reviving spirit of American solidarity but the postman comes pretty close to being a "Saturday Night Live" send-up, or worse, a daydream of the future in the mind of Homer Simpson.

So Costner comes up with another myth cast just beyond the threshold of the coming millennium but this film differs from *Waterworld* in that it belabors its own mythologizing. The film is ploddingly intent on showing us how the spirt of mythologizing is still alive and well. Indeed, *The Postman* is a product of mythologizing and a guide to the process thereof. Beyond the millennium a dystopia awaits us for sure but it is not any more related to "the empty vessel" of reality, no more calibrates that reality to human intent and design than does utopia. We are always engaged in spinning ourselves, of giving presence to the absence of our spinning orb. From the notion of time—which imparts sequence, movement, linearity upon this absence—to the notion of space—which brings our earthly context into human proportions—we are implanting upon the vast ethers a livable script. Now Costner obviously sees a need to implant a script upon the near future since he has made two costly films that attempt to do just this. He wants to convince us that not only the nightmare scenario of the future we are writing for ourselves can be rewritten, but that we have not in this postmodern age lost our capacity to fill the empty vessel of reality with our human presence. And we can do that through our mythmaking, even a myth about as uninspired a mythic hero as a postman. Negative response at the box office however, proves that while mythmaking may still have its fans, postmen don't have quite the presence needed to take on the role of mythic hero fifteen years from now.

In the last scene of the movie, we are at the unveiling of the statue of the postman on horseback, stretching out to take a letter from the hand of a small boy, a boy now an adult in the crowd who remarks, "Why, that's me as a boy!" If we didn't know we were witnessing American history not yet transpired from a point after it has transpired, we know it now. The film has taken the long road to this inspiring moment when we pay homage to our national heroes, when the young learn at the knees of their elders the stories of our American struggle, breathe in deeply the mythologies of our American nationalist spirit. But after the long Bizarro journey of this film, and its oddest of heroes, the postman, played by a reluctant mountebank played by a director/actor who seems caught up in his own self-mythologizing as "the man who made *Dances with Wolves*," we are not filled with patriotic zeal and pride but rather with an aftertaste of the hokey, of something oddball having been brought to the screen. The fact that the actor who plays the part of the mythologized young boy is also Costner's son intensifies this sense that here cultural and personal mythologizing mix as Costner's own heir is projected into a mythological future as a mythic being. Future time is cast into that statue of postman and young boy, immortality delivered along with the mail.

And the whole question of outlandish filmmaking, of bizarre pastiche and blind self-parodying, of florid, misshapen mythmaking at this very moment is intriguing. If you combine a classic Hollywood Romantic Ego, a postmodern "fractalizing" of temporal and spatial linearities—that is a postmodernizing of the "mental landscape" and the means to map it—and, finally, the paradoxical presence of the coming millennium as a "real" demarcation separating us from what we are not and what we are to be—I think that adds up to what you get in Costner's *The Postman*. In short, you get fanciful linearities of plot and character, some sort of thaumaturgic mental dream-works of Costner/Postman, historical bric-a-brac as *mise-en-scène*, a Breughel-like round of activity that round-like, repeats itself but never advances. We are to sense that something not wholly rational but mythical is going on, but myth is both supramundane and prodigious in human eyes, something Costner cannot achieve here, something he cannot pull off. And it comes as no surprise, as our entire cultural imaginary backs away from both the art and substance of mythmaking.

Wag the Dog, on the other hand, registers exactly where we are now: so aware and inured of the reign of spectacle over reality that we are in that we can laugh at a cynical, parodic send-up of what our democracy has become and what dupes as citizens we have become. What a sad fate has befallen this great democracy when the spinmeisters, the purveyors of simulacra and the forgers of the hyperreal wag the American body-politic! The great pity of this fallen state relies upon some former time when the opposite occurred, when the lawmakers and our leaders in Washington used word and image to convey "the state of the union" as it really was, when spectacle corresponded to the "reality that was," when signification, in effect, was tied sharply to what "really happened" or otherwise would stand forth in everyone's eyes as hype. Alas! What happened to those times? Thus, the film is parodic but also performative: It urges us to put an end to a "tail wagging the dog" politics and back to a "dog wags the tail" politics. Since our present "Big Bird" Bill Clinton is at this moment trying to break free of the Paula Jones sex scandal, it's pretty clear that the action we are being urged to perform is to dump Bill, the president we've got now who may need spinmeisters to cover up what he's really up to.

Ideas of what Clinton is really up to have themselves reached the level of spectacle as "underground" videotapes documenting Bill and Hillary's "real activities" from Whitewater and drug smuggling to the murder of Vince Foster. When you want to show people the "reality" of the Clintons's "depravity and deceit" you hire a filmmaker who comes up with a script and then tapes it. The idea of these "exposures" is that *in this case* the spectacle corresponds precisely to the reality, but *in that case* of spectacle coming from "the other side," there is absolutely no correspondence. *In that case,* there are only free-floating signifiers, words and images fabricated and concocted by individuals contracted to do one thing: Replace what is "really real" but damaging to Big Bird with simulacra that replaces the "real" and bolsters Big Bird's rating in the polls. The presidential spinmeisters are therefore working the post-structuralist/Baudrillardian vein in the reality mines, while the Exposers of The Truth are employing the Western Tradition of Rationality and Realism which goes right to the Mother Lode. However, both sides are relying on representation to convey reality, both sides are unalterably on the same side—the side of the signifier, the side of the spin.

The tail has been wagging the dog since the moment our cerebral cortex pushed us to telling or showing someone what we meant or what had happened. Now we can point to a dead body to convey the idea of the reality of death but someone believing in an afterlife and a resurrected body hooks up with a different notion of the reality of death than does an atheist. Of course, if we are pointing to a dead body in a room filled with atheists, a common reality of death is shared. Politics is easy here. But if the room is divided among Hindus, Christians, Muslims, and agnostics, as well as atheists, politics can be said to begin. In fact, some group may go out and hire a spinmeister to represent their view in the most compelling way simply because they think it's a life-and-death issue to get folks to see the "real" meaning of life and death. In our present world, power and profit are our life-and-death issues and the most high-powered politicking goes on here. At the same time, for instance, that *Wag the Dog* leads us to think that we should get "reality" back into politics and kick out the spinmeisters, we are convinced of the "reality" of market ideology to convey to us the "world as it is and ought to be." Now while DeNiro represents one spin doctor brought in surreptitiously to work in a dark basement room of the White House and is known only to the president's assistant, the Fortune 500 spends more money on advertising than it does on product development and improvement; the spinmeisters of Madison Avenue come up with "product" that bombards us in our own living rooms, connecting the "reality" of this "fully loaded" suburban, four-wheel-drive vehicle with the "reality" of our human needs, desires, values, dreams, purpose, meaning, future.

If we want to consider the "reality" of anything and how far we can be sidetracked from reality, we certainly have to consider that here we are openly and globally engaged in spinning consumers in the name of profit and yet wondering how the spin doctors crept into politics. A plausible or at least debatable answer to this odd situation is this: While there is very little for politicians to gain at this present moment by attacking the market's use of hype and simulacra, there is a great deal to be gained by the market's attack on the political use of the same. Indeed, it would be looked upon as sheer lunacy to question advertisers' claim to reality-connecting and truth-telling. *Caveat emptor:* Let the buyer beware. Of course, since "awareness" is already shaped within advertisers' designs, all consumers are ever aware of is what they "need to buy" which is the same as the "need to have." If we lose faith in our federal government, especially its honesty when it comes to using our taxes wisely, when it comes to impeding global-market competitiveness in the name of the environment, or workers, or aiding the old, the sick, the poor and luckless, or an antimonopolistic economic environment, or democracy itself, then that turning away from government is automatically a turning toward market rule, a globalized rule that can only be challenged by taxation, by regulation, by federal suits.

DeNiro is a mythmaker in *Wag the Dog:* He needs to fabricate a myth in order to take media attention away from the sex scandal. He decides to "leak" stories denying any trouble in Albania and the possibility of American troops being sent there. He decides to present the question: "Will we be at war with Albania?" as the next "hot" headline, knowing that the question itself will sell papers and attract viewers and therefore get the presidential sex scandal off page one. He goes to Hollywood and hires a producer, Dustin Hoffman, to produce the war and then the two work in tandem as the mythologizers of the war. DeNiro is a doctor of the cultural psyche; he knows how to read it and also how to move it. But he knows he doesn't have the forces to implement what has to be done; he's a theorist and strategist but he's not a producer. For that, he needs a Hollywood producer who knows what will play and what won't, who can deliver the lines, the song, the merchandise. Hoffman knows who to hire to write the script, who to hire to direct the needed images, who can do the casting, when and what kind of hero is needed to win the hearts of his audience. He is, in effect, a producer of "seems," a man who, unlike Shakespeare's Hamlet, knows only what seems to be. Reality is not his province; only the manipulation of it.

The same day I see *Wag the Dog,* matters with Iraq and its unwillingness to comply with the terms of the 1988 Gulf War regarding UN inspection have turned so bad that there is talk of renewed bombing of that country. A few days later Paula Jones and President Clinton sit across from each other in a deposition hearing regarding what the press calls the "Paula Jones sex scandal." It is difficult for me not to think of a DeNiro and Hoffman-like duo producing and directing our possible war with Iraq for the sole purpose of getting the Paula Jones sex scandal off the front page. Of course, if the makers of *Wag the Dog* didn't have that sex scandal in mind, it had any one of a number of others connected with Clinton. Mythologizing here serves ignoble ends. Or, rephrased, it serves money and power. Unlike when? So the uses to which our story making is put is not as discussible an issue as whether or not we can rise above mythologizing and live in "truth statements." Now this is the same thing as asking whether or not we can get outside what we say about the world and ourselves and live in the world directly. On a prereflective, prepredicative level, we are in the world directly because we are never for a moment outside the world; "we are the world" is not just an annoying refrain to an annoying song. But we are not part of the world which is totally silent and empty, or worse, triggered for millennia by instinctual impulses, like cockroaches, ants, and bees; we are sentient beings, aware of a world enframed within our gaze as a world apart from that gaze and from our thoughts which always distinguish where we are and where the world is. And we are aware of ourselves as being capable of filling that world in the light of our own needs and desires, our own dreams and hopes. Thus, although we are always already embedded within the world, socially and culturally we live only in that part of the empty vessel of reality that we narrate, a reality that has gone through the human process of "worlding."

Personally, we may, like Wordsworth, have our imaginations reenkindled by Nature, or like the visionary Blake we may "see a world in a grain of sand," or like the Buddhist monks, meld with the universe. And all these personal experiences may be represented, but the representations are not the experiences but only a record of knowledge of those experiences. Therefore, when we attempt to communicate with each other, we inevitably partially narrate the empty vessel of reality, as well as ourselves, the past, the present, the future, the social order, and the culture we are in. And before we can do that, we have already been "narrated" by a society and culture filled with narratives. Mythologizing is one step beyond mere narrating: Here we make a deliberate, defensive effort to convince ourselves that reality is not empty outside our own impositions upon it but in such and such a condition and responsive to such and such a series of events. Cosmology and ontology are at stake here and thus the need to mythologize is great, especially at those moments when resident mythologies are waning, time seems to be running out, and spinmeisters seem to have replaced mythologizers.

We are all Hollywood producers of the real, not just Dustin Hoffman; how you wind up producing your own life and filling up the scenes of your journey from birth to death are all matters of production, although numerous films already playing are the horizon for your own production. While we are occupied with nine-to-five schedules, or monitoring our investments via computer round the clock, or running a country, or taking classes, or taking care of the kids, or whatever, our world is so overproduced, so chock full of scenes waiting to be played that we have no time for, that we don't contemplate that this world is such and such because our minds make it so, not just "our" mind but all the minds around us and all the minds who have ever been. There is so much that you would think there never would be a moment when we would run out of material, either personally or socially, with which to be engaged. But one of the plights of the retired elderly today is how to fill the empty vessel of reality now that the old stories don't apply and can't be used.

In *Wag the Dog*, the fact that there was no war in Albania other than the one fabricated by a Hollywood producer meets our postmodern suspicions; there is no sound outside the office building, beyond the street leading to the subway, outside the aircraft, beyond the orb of our spinning planet. Depression sets in and the ultimate stone-cold silence of death seems to be the meaning of it all, always lurking, always there, but unrecognized. The journey ends in death precipitated—the ontologist who is called in says—by a disastrous collapse of mythmaking power at the sound of nothing beyond the victim's own voice.

I am not happy that mythmaking serves the machinations of power and money; but I know that myths challenge each other for dominion and that we suffer in the present not because we tell stories about the world but because one story—the story that says capitalism and the market are the answer to all problems that matter—has enervated our storymaking and mythmaking talents. It has, in fact, done what all myths are designed to do but seldom do: Convince us that it is not an intellectual totem but a testament to the essential truth and reality of things, and that what opposes this reality and truth is always the work of spin doctors and Hollywood producers hired to make us believe in "make believe." I also know that there are spinmeisters and Hollywood producers working on environmental concerns, and workers' rights as opposed to property rights, and on equal opportunity, and the limitations of a doctrine of "self-interest" as opposed to "mutual aid," and the need to lessen the gap between rich and poor globally as well as nationally. The danger we face is not that spectacle will replace reality, but that only one myth will seem to be reality and all the others, only spectacle.

Snow White: This surely is a fairy tale and not a myth; but for my purposes the distinction—that fairy tales are told to entrance children and myths have real cosmological intent—is not important. In imagining our journey we are as inspired by fairy tales as by myths, and, perhaps, since fairy tales are familial tales, tales told by mother or father when we are young, they may do more to affect that "unconscious which is shaped like a language" and therefore the way we imaginatively live in ourselves and in the world than traditional myths. There is a design and purpose behind cosmological mythologies that reaches far beyond the mere personal level, while fairy tales engage us directly and, beneath the guise of good cheer, ominously. Dark dream-works are narrated here, irrationalities fully accepted, compression and expansion of time and space lawful, identities crossed, reversed, uncertain. For all the blood and guts, the heroic combat, and mythic feats of mythic legends, there is more to be feared in the Brothers Grimm than in the shenanigans of the Olympic gods.

I am interested in *Snow White: A Tale of Terror* because it reminds me that political and marketing spinmeisters are not the only ones who narrate our journey for us, conjuring up illusions and playing to our delusions. They are, after all, covert operations: Politics is ostensibly the art of the possible and not the art of illusion, and marketing is ostensibly the art of persuading and not the art of deceiving. But fictionalizing is an overt operation: Literature lies openly. And while the classics doubtlessly play a large role in making it seem as if the empty vessel of reality was "really" filled with all sorts of noble stuff, I suspect that fairy tales reach more deeply into our psyches earlier on and they are never brought into the light of critical inspection in the fashion of our literary classics. Pulp fiction, you might say, has a gut-level, dark-recesses-of-the-mind hold on us because it often marks time the way fairy tales do, stresses the "and then . . . and then . . . and then" style of fairy tales, sets up its moral dualities clearly and distinctly like fairy tales, and throws everything into an over-the-top rush of primary colors, primal fears, basic lusts, and definite endings.

It was Nietzsche's view that art, unlike mythology, possessed the same commitment to honesty that science does but that science led to a "graveyard of perceptions." Art, on the other hand, pushes toward an honest revealing of the ultimacy of illusion in human affairs. Correspondence to reality and truth description—the aims of science—are untenable notions of truth and knowledge and lead to skepticism and nihilism as these aims elude us. The knowledge Nietzsche praises seeks links between the dissimilar, between things that are not the same, and thus a metaphorical reaching into the world enlivens our human condition: "The drive toward the formation of metaphors is the fundamental human drive, which one cannot for a single instant dispense with in thought, for one would thereby dispense with man himself" ("The Philosopher" 150, p. 51 in *Philosophy and Truth*). And again in "On Truth and Lies in a Nonmoral Sense": "Truths are illusions which we have forgotten are illusions; they are metaphors that have become worn out and have been drained of sensuous force, coins which have lost their embossing and are now considered as metal and no longer as coins" (1, 84). Reality is not so much an empty vessel to be filled as a vessel to be transferred from a nonhuman sphere to a human sphere. In other words, we are to give it a human connection through metaphor; all the universe stands as metaphor or plays a metaphorical role for humans. When the metaphorical connections dry up and fall out of sight, truths are born and, in Nietzsche's view, we fall into the "graveyard of perceptions."

So what is it in this *Snow White: A Tale of Terror*, a film of a fairy tale, that redirects that fairy tale to us here in the present, here on a particular journey to the new millennium? First of all, I think that the Brothers Grimm are fitting scriptwriters for this millennial moment; their subtextual darkness befits the subtextual darkness of the moment. Time is growing short; there is not enough of it to bring all the meanings and implications of our present journey to the surface. And, besides, we have had a thousand years to do that and all we have are footnotes countering other footnotes in an endless pilgrimage to something that eludes our approach. This is a time for fairy-tale capture, for tales that capture the movements of our imaginations, filled with dreamscapes punctuated by holocaust footage, bodies at risk, minds losing hold. Fairy tales don't pretend to fill the emptiness of the silent universe we are spinning in; instead they evoke our plight, their full presence, their too sharp *mise-en-scène*, their unhesitant performativity is laced with precariousness, instabilities, false logics, rootless actions, frightening absences, urgency, and futility. They mean nothing but that they are what we come to when we plot our journey to mean something more than what we can say the world means. They manifest bizarre linkages between what we can recognize as real and what seems fantastical, thus uncovering or revealing something recognizable in the fantastic and something fantastic in the recognizable.

Here then is the tale of Snow White as a metaphorical evocation of the present: An accident on the road precipitated by wolves causes the death of Snow White's mother and the sudden Cesarean birth of Snow White in order to save her life. The husband/father marries again and this time the wife lives but the baby dies, his body retrieved from the fire and kept by the new wife, Claudia. The deteriorating body of the stillborn mirrors the deteriorating mind of Claudia. An actual mirror ensconced in a wardrobe reveals to Claudia the thoughts her own mental collapse are projecting. She turns wolfishly against Snow White, demanding to see her heart and lungs as evidence of her death. But she is fooled and dines only on the heart and lungs of an animal. Snow White runs for her life and winds up in the hideout of seven, hardluck and disaffected "masterless men" who are illegally mining on a nobleman's property. We witness what one would barely recognize as "love" scenes between Snow White and one of these men scarred both on his face and on his back. Claudia succeeds in poisoning Snow White but, just at the moment of burying her, her odd lover shakes her and the poisoned apple is loosened from her throat and she awakes. What follows is an assault upon Claudia's evil domain and a victory by Snow White, who stabs at the mirror, destroys Claudia's power and her life.

Snow White's father is no more than a body to be dragged about; Claudia's brother a mute with skill at sleight of hand; Will, the scarred lover, embittered, soul-scarred, with his wolf pack, sullen, driven to hard labor in a lost mine. There is a Dr. Gutenberg who should have been the prince who awakens Snow White but he is stupid baggage thrown out a window to his death. He is seduced like a schoolboy by Claudia, the would-be lover of the step-daughter detoured to the mother's lips. The mute brother who dies from a spider's bite, a spider summoned by his sister. Hoffman and Gutenberg—meat to be devoured. The most haunting image of the film is at the very beginning: carriage overturned, the Hoffmans spinning in the carriage interior until it reaches the bottom and the wife lies there with a carriage spoke through her body, the husband ministering to her. And halfway down the slope the driver, on his back fending off the attack of the wolves. The camera pans away as wolf jaws snap all around the doomed man. Eaten alive. Later we will see a manic, wicked Claudia dragging Hoffman around the castle bound hand and foot like so much meat being carted to slaughter. And how do the "seven dwarves" live but as in a lair like wolves; only one a dwarf, the other six themselves scarred and maimed as if they barely survived an attack of wolves. Not yet fodder for wolves, crippled and twisted, angry and brutish, but not dead, not easy to drag about, to eat, to throw out of windows, to seduce. Think of Claudia's stillborn boy, rescued from the fire before the little swaddled bundle is consumed by the flames and then set up on an altar by Claudia. The stillborn male, half-burnt, consumes her own imagination; she does everything in the name of her own creation, stillborn, and therefore not created, dead at the moment of birth. But this never-born, uncreated male replaces all other males in the fairy tale, except the seven masterless men, four of whom Claudia manages to kill off through dark incantation of Nature's forces, propelled forward in revenge for her stillborn son. And then it takes a sister, Snow White, to kill a sister, Claudia; no man can do this. The reign of men is now stillborn, no longer a creative force. And Snow White's life is now twisted around her love for the scarred, "masterless man," the man half-devoured. All energy and charisma reside in the mind and body of the woman who goes up in flames, Claudia, while Snow White is a pale parchment, an empty whiteness, whose deepest moment is when she lies in her coffin with a bit of red apple, a poisoned bit of redness, in her throat.

Something is being brought forth from concealment to unconcealment here, what the Greeks called *Aletheia*, but it only starts its journey; this is a tale of a new ontology, not yet brought into presence, unlike Costner's hopeful mythologizing of a dystopic future redeemed, or *Wag the Dog's* parodic display of mythmaking itself. We are on our way to arrival here but the way itself has no greater presence than that of a fairy tale and the time and place of arrival lie hidden, as in a dark dream where we are journeying to a place we don't know at a time we can't quite calculate.

Side Tracked: The President as Bad Subject

February 21, 1998

February 21, 1998
Doesn't TV news have something better to do than spend
24 hours a day salivating over a pile of tawdry, unproven
allegations?
No.
TV news has never had anything better to do than this.
Furthermore, you have never had anything better to do
than this. Big hair, sting operations, Presidential DNA
analysis? This is why miners risk lonely death by suffoca-
tion hauling ore for copper TV cables. This is why God
made electromagnetic radiation. This, my friend, is why
God made you.
    —*James Poniewozik*, "Bring me the head (and more
                                    important,
        the body) of Monica Lewinsky!" *Salon* 2/18/98

. . . since when is the search for adventure and thrills anything other than average? . . . Among my contemporaries,
it isn't all that shocking to sleep with three different partners in a weekend, not all of the opposite sex.
—Jenn Shreve, "The Lady is NOT a Tramp," *Salon, WWW*

There's definitely farce and wit, wit and farce, still coming out
of Monicagate one month from when the first report of Clinton
having sex with a White House intern named Monica Lewinsky
surfaced. "[T]he leadership of the free world may hang on the question of whether a blow job equals a 'relationship'" James
Poniewozik writes on the Net; "Al Gore is only an orgasm away
from the presidency!" Jay Leno monologues on "The Tonight Show."
Then there are the barbed and disturbing observations: "Thirty
years after free-love counterculturalists and bra-burning feminists

supposedly liberated female sexuality from such archaic constraints, America's aging, mostly male media hacks continue to fall
back on the tired old virgin-or-whore model to explain it all." And
more from Jenn Shreve who sees a real split between Baby
Boomers and Generation-X'ers on this "scandal": "And for parents
outraged at a fifty-year-old man 'taking advantage' of a girl not
much older than his own daughter, then I'd say you don't know
very much about your own daughters." But maybe she's fighting
another war here because polls show Clinton with a 79 percent
approval rating at this point. If there's outrage out there Clinton's
not the target. And for those who want to distinguish moral outrage from suborning perjury rage—that too would show up in the
ratings. And it doesn't. Besides, as Bill Maher says almost every
night on "Politically Incorrect," nobody's interested in the perjury
thing; it's all the sex.

> [I]f Americans are going to be the laughingstock of the world
> in the biggest postmodern joke since the Spice Girls, we all
> need to examine this vague, highly subjective turn of phrase
> ["sexual relations"], upon the definition of which the fate of
> our government may hang.
> —Courtney Weaver, "Unzipped," Salon

Is a blow-job (an act with no reciprocation?) a "sexual relationship"? The semiotics of the blow-job are actually reel first and
then real; it's an issue in Kevin Smith's film *Clerks* where the clerk
discovers that his girlfriend has given blow-jobs to multitudes.
When he expresses his outrage at her lying to him about who she's
had sex with she tells him that giving blow-jobs is not a sex thing
with her. She's not even intimately involved in the act. So if the person being blown isn't involved sexually because he isn't reciprocat-
ing and if the person giving the blow-job doesn't feel the act
involves any intimacy, then nobody had sex; and if Monica Lewinsky visited the president thirty-seven times in the Oval Office and
gave him thirty-seven blow-jobs, it was about as sexual as if she had
come in to vacuum the carpet.

Sexual relations means intercourse; without intercourse, sexual
relations didn't happen. This is funny stuff but, *pace* the semioti-
cians in the crowd who are pulling their credentials out of mothballs, whether 79 percent of the American public figure sexual relations includes every sexual posture your ten-year-old kid can surf
on the Net or whether they think it means only sexual intercourse,
those 79 percent approve of Clinton as president. Caressing a lady's

Side Tracked

leg in the nineteenth century might have meant sexual relations; a French kiss might mean "Oh hello!" in France but lead to a shotgun wedding in America.

Clinton smoked some dope—but he didn't inhale; Monica may have "fellated" him—but he wasn't having a sexual relationship with "that woman." He's a Southern gentleman; he's trying to spare the country a moral examination. He wants to leave them with a way out of that painful process. Unless another Abraham Zaprudder turns up with a video, a Zaprudder for the '90s, we always only have one person's word against another's. And at this date, Monica is sticking with her sworn affidavit that she did not have sex with the president. Does she think a blow-job is not sex? I'm sure Ken Starr will ask her that. Maybe it will be a way out for Monica: She thinks not, so thus her sworn statement. Being able to say that she and Clinton did have sex, some kind of sex, will free her to spend the rest of her life telling her story for money on TV, on the page, on the Net, on the radio. She'd have something to really tell Larry King. And Oprah might be able to get every woman in America to empathize with her. There's some bucks waiting on Monica if she can just find a way to go public without going to jail.

Need Clinton have spared our feelings? This is where the suborning to perjury comes in. Regardless of whether or not the country is morally where Jenn Shreves says she and her contemporaries are at ("three different partners, not all of the same sex, in one weekend"), the suborning charge would grind in the wheels of justice and Clinton doesn't want to start those rolling. Kenneth Starr will have to do that on his own and so far after thirty million dollars and six years, he can't get a thing rolling. So Clinton has to hedge and finesse and spin on the sex thing; give us all a way out so that we can say it's all alleged, media speculation and pundit hypotheticals. And that gives us further room to say he's a good president anyway and who cares about his personal life. That's between him and Hillary. If it's okay with Hillary, why should we care? Is this really an issue of public concern? An issue in the national interest? It's rather like a variation on a Pro-Choice argument: Why should we care what Bill and Monica do with their bodies? After all, this is private matter, not a public one. That argument, of course, reaches some and enrages other.

Now let's say Clinton does what naive realists, Enlightenment rationalists, and born-again Christians want him to do: He tells us what we already know (the classic realist's take), he tells us The Truth (Enlightenment dude), he confesses (born-again). He goes on

Larry King and Larry leads him through a painful confession to all of us: He's a sex addict. He names names and places and acts. Would he still get a 79 percent approval rating? Well, we would get a chance to see just what the split is in this country regarding sexual attitudes (same thing as saying moral attitudes here in America). Those working through three different sex partners in a weekend might call in and tell Larry and Bill that sex addiction isn't an addiction: It's normal human behavior. Just like fat people should not be made to feel that they're sick because they're fat, people who have a lot of sex shouldn't be made to feel that they're sick people. Those who have internalized the sex = AIDS = death syllogism might be already so deeply into virtualized sex (isn't this why pornography on the Net fits so well with the sexual needs of the '90s?) that the idea of the President of the United States having face-to-face sex, flesh in flesh, might send them into hyperdrive reactionwise. For this crowd, Bill and Monica are either both from another planet where people do inconceivable sexual things; or, Bill and Monica are projected into a home-viewed porn movie where they become sexual catalysts for a repressed yet sexually obsessed American cultural imaginary, one that has made the postmodern leap toward spectacle over real contact, visuals over flesh, Baudrillardian simulacra over the "real."

But what about the "cheat on your wife-cheat on the country" crowd, the crowd that says, in effect, what Goethe said: "What is inside is outside." Wouldn't a president who is sexually reckless—sneaking a twenty-one-year-old intern into the pantry of the Oval Office—project that recklessness outward, say, in his political decisions? If the man lacks a moral compass—a favorite Cato Institute image—how can he chart the whole country toward what is right? How can he uphold the noble and sacred traditions of this great democracy? And so on. I present this as as a mapping of the moment in regard to Blowersgate, the President and the Intern scandal involving blow-jobs blown up by the media to the irrational, fantastical, mystifying realm of the cultural imaginary. Let's trek further down each of these roads.

Take the last road first: Somehow sex with Monica damages Clinton's role as president. This is broadly put; it covers a lot of ground, from the notion that Clinton is so damaged in reputation that he can't summon the kind of moral force that he needs nationally and internationally to the notion that he's become a president we can't trust to tell us the truth about anything. We can't package him as honest the way we packaged Washington, Jefferson, and

Lincoln; maybe he's lost the heroic charisma that JFK had. But of course all that packaging is being unwrapped and repackaged to the point that we're not quite sure whether any of our presidents display as a clear view of how sexual behavior, moral character, and leadership interrelate. Look at the ratings of Nixon and Carter postpresidencies: Despite Nixon's clear criminality and Carter's clear charitableness, Nixon is out front in our estimation of leadership qualities. Carter carries around a huge moral compass; Nixon had a resentment compass; Clinton has Dick Morris's polling techniques. So the matter of who's got the biggest moral compass doesn't necessarily win in the presidential reputation ratings. There is obviously some sense of presidential character not limited to what we mean by moral character and some power of image and imagery that occludes our moral estimations.

We confuse sexual behavior with total moral worth; and at the same time we are aware of confusing the two, are uneasy about that but, given the loaded nature of the confusion, we don't know what to do about it. So Blowersgate hits us where we hurt, where we are most vulnerable, the hot spot in the American cultural imaginary. It is not just in our inherited Puritan imaginary that Sex Is Sin; I partake not at all in that Puritan inheritance. Mine is Roman Catholic, via Baltimore Catechism and the moral lessons of the Brothers of St. Francis Xavier. When my conscience was troubled, it was troubled over sex. When I confessed, I confessed about sex. When I was absolved of my sins, it was of sins of sex. My soul had been purified, my conscience freed of guilt. Sex was forgiven; I had repented. I don't know if I had a moral character outside that Sex Is Sin frame. I don't know if you could have trusted me more before or after I confessed my sex sins. I don't know if I exhibited a different sort of overall behavior before or after confession. Was I more likely to get into fights when a sex sin was weighing on my conscience? Was I more likely to thieve, or cheat, or lie, or drink, or speed, or not do my homework, or sleep on the job, or display a "bad attitude"? The years I lived in Oxley Hollow, West Virginia, I was invited to Revival any number of times and those inviting me were all always on the wrong side of drink and women, as they put it. Holiness evangelicism, the kind that Robert Duvall evokes in his film *The Apostle*, is about saving souls when the body is always yearning. And *The Apostle* doesn't lay the dilemma to rest for us or himself. No, I don't think we can limit our sexual hangups here to Puritanism; this is a byproduct of Christianity's soul/flesh hierarchy. Christians have never known quite what to do with bodies. And that lack shows up in the dark recesses of the cultural imaginary.

We are, as I say, not unaware of our American perspective on Blowersgate, and enjoy telling ourselves that the Europeans are not so burdened in their cultural imaginaries with this psychic schizoidism of repression/obsession in regard to sex. The difference in attitude they display can, of course, be broken down to a multitude of differences as the French don't handle this exactly the way the Dutch do, nor do the Germans the way the Italians do, nor the Portuguese the way the Swedes do. But European culture, generally speaking, has been working at this morality = sexuality thing a whole lot longer than Americans have. And they've worked their way to the other side, beyond the letter of the law to living a life. Italians, for instance, have for centuries been able to observe close up how the clergy puts its own restraints on the flesh into a liveable, détente sort of relationship. The French may be more obsessed with morality being expressed socially and politically than sexually, which is, after all, personal, inevitable, wonderful, and ineffable. French rationalism will extend into the political and social and stop at the gates of the sexual.

Experience exceeds knowledge is one way of putting it. But not so with we Americans. Americans are more literal minded, miss the ironies and the subtle tones, bureaucratize and legalize and pragmatize into every domain. And our advertising and marketing capacities are like elite special forces that invade personal space, obliterate privacy, not only geographically and spatially, but mental, spiritual, emotional, imaginative space. In fact these forces target the inner life; they go after the cultural imaginary with an intent far different from my own. Smart bombs are launched every second of the day into our inner space, into our privacy zones. Once that space is under control, product can be most successfully developed and marketed.

Marketing efforts reach our inner lives so that you cannot properly say we seek to rationalize things like sexuality, or bureaucratize them into a public space, but rather we marketize sexuality and everything that has to do with it. One of the repercussions of this is that we think because a scandal is being blown up for every possible profit motive that we are dealing with it. We even talk about The Truth being told and justice being served and all the facts coming out. But meanwhile we're only handling this on as a market level. Nothing will come of that except the market will dry up and then the issue will go away. No Big Truth, resolution, wisdom,

Side Tracked

lesson learned, further disclosures. Just dried up. There is neither an intellectual nor an emotional, psychological, or moral engagement here. And though the cultural imaginary has been targeted for market reasons, it has been left in the same quandary, the same schizoid state in regard to sex, that it has been in. Why? Because this cultural pathology is profitable; our obsession with what we cannot get right in our own minds turns a profit.

Look at it this way. Say Americans didn't have a pathological cultural imaginary in regard to sexuality. And then stories of Clinton having sex with a White House intern show up on the Net, or on TV's "Hard Copy." At the same time the State of the Union address is given and the bombing of Iraq seems imminent. Now remember: no American psyche hangup regarding sexuality. Maybe we wonder whether Hillary is going to leave Clinton. Maybe we wonder what kind of reward Monica got for her services; or why she got in the White House in the first place, or why she went to the Pentagon. Maybe we shake our heads and smile when we think of how the Bubba never got out of the Bill. And then we pay close attention to what Bill has to say in his State of the Union, what the Republican response is, what he hopes to accomplish by bombing Iraq yet again. In other words, we leave the sexual as a private affair and scrutinize closely the new proposed political moves on the board, where the advantages and disadvantages of this new round of proposals will be.

What happens? Bill Maher's ratings are not going to go up; Geraldo won't be saved from cancellation; Kenneth Starr won't have a bone to chew on; a new line of products with Monica's face on them won't be forthcoming, no "tell all" book deals, Larry King won't be able to say "But it's the sex, isn't it?" when guests wander off and talk about issues other than sex, Hollywood won't be able to do all those young girl/older man blow-job-involved films that are now in production.

A mystified, dark sexual psyche prompts the Dow upward; if it could be suddenly relieved and released, the Dow would undoubtedly drop. The market would go limp. And we want to be Bullish.

Other roads taken here: Our affront at Blowersgate is felt by the old dudes but not by the young; and, sex has gone virtual as it keeps morphing into new and more arousing manifestations of what we can no longer deal with in the "real world." Let's start with the second: sex has gone virtual partially because of our fear of AIDS but more for market reasons. In fact, the market has invaded the fear of AIDS and turned a profit on it. My first hint of this came in 1997 when during a class discussion regarding love, sex, AIDS, and death, the majority of students indicated that AIDS was an issue of the '80s; it was old, over, and adios. It wasn't '90s! Sort of like fad and fashion; it had come in for a time, had its play, but now it was played out. And this attitude had nothing to do with "cures" or "better treatment." They didn't know anything about medical progress here. I was momentarily shocked. This sort of response was sick, scary, depressing. And then I realized that the market necessity to generate new desires by rendering the old ones dead and gone, tacky and trashy, had shaped a whole mental disposition toward not only products and services but toward AIDS. And why not after all? Hadn't death itself been repressed and then dealt with as a market matter?

You have to step back and see how the layers are being stacked here in the cultural imaginary: Fear of real sex which is now always reckless leads to reckless eye balling, which is safe and rewarding because market promotion of products and services intensifies its use of sexual spectacle on every level. Apparel attracts because it's sexy; leisure is sexualized; cars continue to fulfill sexual fantasies; TV tells the nightly news of sex; Hollywood plots sex: "First you get the money, then you get the power, then you get the women"; celebrities have sex appeal; money surrounds one in the spectacles of sex; the future promises sex; careers show us the money which opens the private doors to sex; power is access to sex; private offices, including the Oval Office, allow for private sex. The next layer is very Baudrillardian: The fear of AIDS pushes us away from real encounters toward surrogate, virtualized sex; from flesh to spectacle of flesh. But if the REAL fear of AIDS can then be repressed, spectacle seduction can go on blissfully. Everyone is propelled toward the imaging of sex but has forgotten why. And the flow of traffic from fad to fad can go on without a lurking sense of escaping from something that should be faced.

Capitalizing on our sexual hang-ups is a smart market move, and so Madison Avenue and Hollywood and TV make an enticing spectacle of sex. We even have celebrities of SEX, from Marilyn Monroe, probably the first body turned into a commodity fetish, to whoever we have at the moment, probably Pamela Anderson and Cindy Crawford. Sex is sold via imagery and now with the Net it just may stay there. Look at the Net as a purveyor of nominal reality, of virtual rather than face-to-face contact. As as a postmodernist I think that we live in stories of reality, in all sorts of personal, social, and cultural mediations of the world. But I don't think

Side Tracked

transnational corporations have an exclusive license on mediating the world for us. Our stories emerge from our encounters with real people and the real world we are always already a part of. A postmodern view of things does not urge us into a movie theater or onto the Net because spectacle should be our steady diet. Mediating the world, narrating and imaging it, are things we necessarily do as humans but they result from our efforts to respond to real existence, to real being-in-the-world. We may wind up with only clashing mediations of the world, rivaling narratives, but we start with trying to match story to reality; we don't have anything to say until the world sets us in motion, and that world is not simply what we say or have said about it.

I like to dig up Samuel Johnson's rebuke to Berkeley: Johnson kicks a stone and thus refutes Berkeley's idealism. Of course, Berkeley would say that in Johnson's mind the stone was there so why shouldn't it move when he kicked it? More recently, Alan Sokal has invited postmodernists who he SAYS don't believe in the real world to jump out of his fourteen-floor window. The stone is there and so is gravity. But what we might have to say about that stone will never be that stone, nor will it probably be safe from rebuttal; and what we SAY about gravity is not gravity itself: Words to describe a word is what it is. And I don't think we have an uncontested story of what gravity is at this moment. The stone and gravity haven't vanished; they're there; they're here. They're here with us humans to experience as humans, and not as computers or androids however much some of us might want to make the switch. And what we humans do is talk about everything, including stones and gravity.

All this to say that virtualizing sex and capitalizing on turning sex into spectacle is market motivated, turns a profit but doesn't help us really imagine where we are at when it comes to sex. And marketizing morality doesn't help us see what morality is, beyond what we do sexually. In this market-generated confusion, we wind up bewildered in the moments when we're not hoping that The Truth will be revealed. In a "Dear Mr. President" posted on the INTERNET magazine *Salon* in which Andrew Ross's refrain is "you should go quickly," Ross finally writes: "Frankly, I don't know what to make of you. How, if you did what you've been accused of, can you face yourself, your wife and particularly your daughter?" I don't know what to make of Bill Clinton either, but then again I wouldn't know what to make of a lot of people if I were positioned somehow, for example like an Olympian god, to see and reconcile their private and public lives, their sex acts and all their other acts. I wouldn't know what to make of Al Gore or Newt Gingrich or Dick Armey or Ronald Reagan or Jimmy Carter or Abraham Lincoln or JFK or Michael Milken or Ted Turner or Bill Gates or Rupert Murdoch. I'm not in that position even though putting me there is a marketable move. The fact that it's a move condoned by Enlightenment presumption doesn't help at all. This presumption spurs us onward, deeper and deeper into matters that neither "reasoning methods" nor "moral compasses" will bring to any conclusion other than what satisfies us at the moment in the way of reasonableness and morality. And in the meantime, the longer we are fixated on what we think we can handle but shouldn't be handling, TV ratings go up, papers sell, whole product lines are developed. We're at an easily targeted place and it pays to keep us there until the market is drained. Sadly, the very way the market consumes Blowersgate, blowing it to marketable proportions, further distorts our already repressed/obsessed hang-ups with sex. We're getting deeper into market titillation and further from what sex may be when Hollywood and Madison Avenue don't hype it.

The longer we stay surfing the more we may be seduced into clicking on a product or a service we need. There is profit in keeping us surfing the Net; it's almost like people voluntarily sitting in front of a TV and just looking at commercials. The price we really pay for a steady diet of virtuality, in regard to sex that is, is that we are detoured from facing our sexual repressions and obsessions and are simultaneously getting deeper and deeper into contrived, artificial, totally preposterous spectalization of sexual relations.

What about the idea that we are now seeing a kind of sexual progress wherein a new generation is sexually liberated, relative to the older generation? I recall my '60s generation saying that about what we called the Establishment generation. "Love the one you're with" may be a refrain that Jenn Shreve and her contemporaries agree with but they didn't create it. Pat Robertson, Jerry Falwell, and Ralph Reed have become forces since the '60s and constitute a more vocal and powerful born-again Establishment than what we faced in the '60s, so there is definitely a need to revolt yet again. But market influences have grown considerably also and SEX is packaged for easy consumption by the mind more than ever. Those shackles have to be resisted also. But rebelling against market and religious contortions of sex doesn't necessarily take us to the best place. I don't think that the free-love impulse of the '60s reconciled the sex/morality dualism or made us any less vulnerable to the

Side Tracked

seductive spin of market spectacle, more resistant to the market's use of sex to titillate us for a profit. And it didn't save us from the flood of divorces that were just up the road. Nor are Shreve and her companions on the liberated side of sex now since the number of sex crimes continues to rise.

If we resist turning sexuality into a marketable site and keep it private but not repressed, we are not thereby becoming promiscuous. Sex does have a connection with morals and moral behavior; Blowersgate has both a sexual side and a moral side and the two overlap. Now if we can't see or make the distinctions here because as soon as SEX is pictured in our cultural imaginary everything else fades or blurs, it may be because over time we don't have a moral sense that isn't keyed to SEX. We certainly don't have a market-inspired moral sense. "Winners" play "hardball" and show "tough love" and possess the "will to compete and win," sort of the dark side of Nietzsche's "will to power." Those who "get caught" breaking the law are not guilty of a moral lapse but of not having enough brains and talent not to get caught. What we regret about Nixon is not his murky moral sense but his brainlessness in taping himself, of providing the prosecutors just what they needed. You note that Bill makes no such mistakes; it may have been beyond reckless—how about taking pleasure in being a "bad subject," a rebel, an outlaw within an order of things that you yourself are the president of??!?—but Bill neither taped nor videoed himself. And he doesn't give evidence against himself, especially I think in a situation that he can easily compartmentalize as having nothing to do with being a good president. Seventy-nine percent of the country is on his side when it comes to him implicitly saying "it's not the public's business." Now he is upholding a moral view here: A politics driven by the market and the interests of profit has no right in invading private life, and SEX is private. That much we accept; but if market supremacy has already invaded private space, swept it clean of non-market values, and filled it with bottom-line values, isn't SEX, whether as a private or public matter, still caught in the a "bigger, better, more" market sort of mentality?

What is Jenn Shreve saying when she boasts her contemporaries have at least three different partners, not all of the opposite sex, in one weekend? Isn't this a sort of "affluenza," a sort of shopping around in which more is better, variety is the spice of life, and "the person with the most toys" before, now, and later is winning? I want more sex the same way I want more money and more stuff. And what are the tactics we can draw upon here?

Why, I think the same sort of tough competitiveness, the same sort of pursuit of self-aggrandizement grounded in a consideration only and always of one's self-interest that we see displayed and admired globally. Sex is acquiring a good body, a good blow-job, a top-of-the-line lay, a wardrobe of sex partners, a maximization of one's investment in the body of another. The clever player, the Gordon Gekko of SEX, is a short-term player, a no-risk player, a player who knows that winning is everything and that the journey to winning doesn't matter, it gets covered over with smoke, it becomes just mirrored images. The goal is not in the relationship, but in the having, in the possessing, in winning something and then going on to win something else. Maximization of sexual pleasure is like the maximization of profits: It knows no limits; it takes no prisoners; unstoppable, inevitable, right and good. I don't know how a cultural imaginary steeped in this could wind up producing anything but a president looking for a blow-job wherever and whenever he can get one. The hypocrisy displayed by those who are morally repelled by him but uphold self-interest as an indisputable ground of being lies in this: They too are committed to market ends justifying any means, to a moral sense grounded in self-interest, but they find it profitable to pay lip service to a nonprofit moral sense. Clinton pays the same lip service, but like Nixon he's given us a glimpse of how hollow that nonprofit moral sense is. But he's obviously not alone and Jenn Shreve is openly and honestly telling us that her contemporaries aren't playing the hypocrisy game any longer. Sex is a marketable commodity, a service that everyone wants on a top-of-the-line level; it's pure consumption. Restricting it is like restricting one's goal to increase profits. There's no such thing as "steady state" sex, or "sustainable" sex. Those who choose to live as if there is, that is, faithfully and monogamously, are just like those who don't want to get rich. They fear entering the arena and competing for what they want. They ultimately don't have the will to win, the stuff it takes, the competitive edge; they can't play hardball. Being married is like having lost. A married man and a married woman who don't seek to maximize their sexual life are losers, victims. They wind up leading lives of quiet desperation and sexual frustration; they get bored, they don't have enough product, they can't catalogue, they don't know what top-of-the-line service is. If one of them were president they probably would turn down Monica's offer for a blow-job in the pantry. Jimmy Carter probably did; and he

Side Tracked

Side Tracked

only got one term in the White House as as a result. Filled with an incomprehensible malaise, he failed to show the voraciousness of appetite for stuff and services that overwhelmed everyone else in the country. Bill may be a bad subject in his own country but he's right out of the American cultural imaginary of the moment. He's a bad subject—but a pure product.

Side Trip: Timing Our Journey, Setting a Moral Compass

Suppose you know the length of your journey, not in miles but in time. And then the journey is over. Your mortality claims you but you know in advance when. You have one hundred days and after that you close your eyes for the last time. But let's say you can't be sure your eyes won't open again. You can't be sure you might not have another hundred days to live. And no memory loss, which is what you suffer in the case of reincarnation, or mostly the case. Every hundred years there is someone, like Bridey Murphy, who claims to remember her past life. But in the myth I am here creating, if you open your eyes, you remember who you are, where you are, and that you're back, that you've got another hundred days to live. Let's say you're fifty-four, my present age, and you've been living like this your whole life, one stretch of a hundred days after another, with no reason to believe that at the end of this present hundred days, you won't wake up in this world yet again. Or, you might believe that if you do wake up, you're not in this world but in some sort of spiritual world: either the good antipode of that world or the bad one. Regardless of whether you are a person of faith or not, you still may be facing divine judgment. You may be held accountable for what you do in your hundred days, or hundred times a hundred days.

How do you set out to live your hundred days? Remember, you may segue into another hundred days and then another, so you may just be around long enough to face the consequences of your actions right here on earth. You might decide to live recklessly and fearlessly; you might decide to hold the *Rubiyat of the Omar Kyam* as your Bible. The person with faith in a spiritual afterlife may spend his or her hundred days earning indulgences, doing good works, preparing, in other words, for judgment day. But a person who doesn't believe in a spiritual afterlife may just try to get as much of whatever happens to float his or her boat as possible. Without being picked up by the police.

221

Now—chapter three—let's say that there are some people in the country who know they've got another hundred days to live, with possibility of renewal indefinitely, but these people are living "normally." What is the "normal" living like? Why, if they're like me, they're living as if they had more than one lifetime, living as if another hundred days were guaranteed when they know they're not. I may not have ever said something so ridiculous but when I look back I see that I have lived this way. (I'm actually not looking "back" but merely scanning what's available in the old memory banks at this moment through the filter of this moment). Here's what I review: I'm in my mid-twenties before I finish with school (I "professionalized" but more of that later); right after my B.A. I'm drafted and ready to be packed off to Vietnam just before the Tet Offensive but because of a misreading of my medical tests, I'm 1Y'ed, deferred indefinitely. Some years before that I step out for a smoke and wind up with a gun pointed at my head. Somebody who knows me comes on the scene by chance and talks the gun-man out of shooting me. My savior had forgotten something in his car and had come out to get it. Chance. So I live. Some years before this event, in the '50's when my neighborhood in Bensonhurst, Brooklyn, and the surrounding neighborhoods were filled with rival gangs—no semiautomatic weapons just knives and what we called "zipguns"—somebody puts a knife to my throat because I'm invading his gang's turf. I'm not invading; I'm just lost. The guy with the knife at my throat is the same guy who several years later will talk the guy with the gun to my head out of shooting me. Now someone else intervenes and talks the guy who will save me in the future from cutting me at that present moment.

I should at some point be impressed with how much of a Thomas Hardy universe it is, although Hardy tends to see Chance as gloomy Fate and not as pure contingency. Contingency is neither Destiny nor Karma but simply the disruption of human ordering by what human ordering has no control over but is in fact subject to. I should at some point begin to think that life insurance company mortality statistics are not a promise of seventy-six years of life but merely numbers that have nothing to do with an individual life, just as the results of any statistical survey winds up not precisely representing any one individual surveyed. The further I go down the path of formal education the more in control I think I am of everything, including my own life. Both explanation and interpretation move me away from a real confrontation with my mortal time/space predicament at any moment—the pumping of my heart, the rise and fall of my lungs. Time is abstracted and distanced; space is internalized, spread out on a mental landscape. Here there is neither sudden ends nor catastrophic disruptions; with my books around me and my words in front of me on a computer screen, I master time and space. There is no end to thinking, no limits on intertextual journeys. I am immortal in reflection. For me, there has to be a reason for all this to end; I can foresee no reason. One thought leads to another; one sentence to another. I am knowing all this, writing all this, reading all this in preparation for living a life in which I need to be and to have all this. I am living as if there will certainly be a time when I will need all this, will use all this. And with all this I'll be properly prepared to live. Another one or two lifetimes.

I'm still living as if I'm just prepping in this lifetime and after this I'll *really* be living. I can't find the present moment; it eludes me. I am caught up in theorizing the present moment so that I can one day live in the present moment. I defer the present moment; thought defers the present moment. That it was just Chance that kept me from being in Nam in 1966 as a second lieutenant didn't get me to take a closer look at the way I had my life timed and what Chance might have in store for me. If I really have lost the impact of that, I am not without constant reminders. This Christmas at a friend's annual gathering of two hundred of his closest friends, I meet his former brother-in-law, a road musician who hasn't made this scene in years. He's the center of the party; all his old friends want to greet him. There is something particularly alive about this man, who is slightly younger than me. He has greying shoulder-length hair like mine; he seems very happy; he seems to really be enjoying himself. About a month later, my host calls me and tells me that the road musician has been killed in a car accident. I immediately think of drunk driving, or drugs, or speeding home from a gig dead tired in the early morning hours. But no, his car wasn't in motion and he wasn't behind the wheel. He was seated in the back seat with his girlfriend at a toll both when a drunken driver crashed into their car, climbing over the car trunk and then landing on the car roof, crushing to death Nick and his girlfriend.

What are you doing when you're sitting in the back seat of a car and it has just stopped at a toll booth? Not looking behind you probably; not thinking of having the life crushed out of you the next second. What was Nick thinking at that moment? Where was he going? What plans had he? I see him now at that party, standing by the door, saying goodbye to someone, being asked whether he too is leaving? No, man," he says, "I'm hanging till the end."

Side Trip

Side Trip

While my daughters are young, I'm always thinking that there will be plenty of time to give to them but right now I have to finish this essay, this chapter, this book, this project. I'm deferring their youth into another lifetime. Sometime ahead, all this that a dad does with his daughters will be done. Ditto the time I share with my wife. Right now I'm living out a lot of abstract thoughts in my head and when I work through those and see them in print, my wife and I will reap all the benefits of my having done all that—whatever—first.

This is too painful to continue.

How many people live their lives this way? I have no idea because I've mostly been lost in my own internal configuration of the road ahead. When you live as if this life were mere preparation for a "real" life ahead—and I'm not talking about a life after death—you defer real contact with the present. And that sets this type of person up for another type of person—the person who knows they've got just one hundred days—with possible renewal—to live. These are the short timers, the short-term players, the players who don't have time to live in some interior drama, who don't do monologues in front of their mirror, who don't lose themselves getting ready for the journey. They have no interest in self-observations, self-reflection, self-reflexiveness, or any of that. They know that whoever they are, they have one hundred days to live. There's no time to probe the conscience, to see whether they've got a moral compass or not, whether they're making progress in one area and not in another, whether they are their own worst enemy or whether or not they should clean up their act. What's in this world during this hundred days with these people in these places that will give them more bang for their buck? More minutes to the hour? More laughs than tears? More orgasms than headaches? Where's the best steak in town? The best martini? Whose company do I enjoy the most? What's out that I haven't seen? Haven't heard? How do I get what I need to travel fast and easy? How can I pollinate the most flowers in this garden in this short season? Who can I get to pay my ticket and then run out on? Who can I get to shoulder the burden so I can coast through? What does it take to get this person to do what I want? How do I get what that person has quickly and without trouble?

A personal and social moral sense is grounded here, in the way we time our lives. Maybe there is a text that sets the timing in motion: the Jewish Old Testament, the Christian New Testament,

the even newer Muslim testament, The Koran, or the even older
Bhagavad-Gita, or any religious sacred text. But the text could be
secular: the texts of the law for lawyers, medical texts for doctors,
Shakespeare for literary critics, Paul Samuelson for economists, Fed-
eralist Papers for political scientists, Newton, Einstein, and Bohr for
physicists, Weber and Durkheim for sociologists. The texts, secular
and nonsecular, replace individual experience of life with knowledge of living and nonliving things. It moves those involved from
experience's space to knowledge's space. And here personal living
time is deferred while it is replaced by knowing time. The believer
in an afterlife who defers present time may seem to be a greater
deferrer of time than a secular deferrer—give them their most
recent appellation—"symbolic analysts." But both can be struck out
of their deferring time mode and brought into a present-time
mode, a "I may only have one hundred days to live" mode, and neither, I think, is more or less susceptible to this. When either the
religious deferrer or the symbolic analyst deferrer gives up living
outside the moment and seizes whatever the present has to offer,
they think they have either gone off their moral course or relapsed
into unstructured, untutored time. They think they have either
gone off into sinful space or into nonsymbolic space. Which gives
greater pangs of conscience? Unknowable. Sin darkens the whole
being, cuts one off from the spirit that really matters; but life not
taken to an abstracted, symbolic level, not either quantified or
interpreted, is superficial, transient, banal, literal, raw, and thus
denigrates the mind, dulls consciousness, and cuts one off from
knowing matter and not being reduced to matter oneself. Both
move from controlled, deferred time and space to the flux and
chaos of the present, to experience seized as the lion seizes the
haunches of the passing buck.

Strangely, the present moment provides us with two examples
of what I'm talking about here, one in the headlines and one in
film—the Bill Clinton of the Monicagate story, and the Apostle E.F,
Robert Duvall's Southern holiness evangelicist in the film *The Apostle*. Clinton, as we all know, has been shaping his résumé toward the
presidency almost since birth; he has carefully and shrewdly
mounted a life campaign toward that end, strategizing each and
every political campaign toward that 1992 presidential campaign.
There has never been a more public example of time deferred, of the
present as no more than an occasion to move toward some goal in
the future. What must he have denied himself that the present

Side Trip

offered on his way to a Rhodes Scholarship? What opportunities that the present offered must he have neglected for the sake of maximizing his opportunity to be President of the United States? His whole life moves on a chessboard; the present orchestrated to achieve a goal in the future. The past is nothing more than moves already made, pieces already won. Life is only and always life to be lived within a story of life: He can become the President of the United States. When what furthers the plot of this story is separated in present time from what deters it, then the aspirant, Clinton, is being true to his moral compass. He is on course; he is holding the course.

Sonny Dewey, who later becomes the Apostle E.F., is just as clearly a deferrer of the present. He is out to save souls, bring them to Jesus, bring them out of sin and into the light of salvation. He is an ecstatic evangelicist; it seems as if every moment of his life is filled with redemptive force, lyrics praising Jesus on his lips at every moment. The unseen spiritual world permeates the present world and puts the purposes and distractions of that present world aside. Jesus calls us to praise the Lord, to see ourselves as divine as fantastically more than what is bound in this mortal body. He is happy doing the Lord's work; this day will end, this day in all its delusions and seductions can never matter in the face of Eternity; eternal time and eternal space reduce to nothingness mortal time and space. When Sonny is not distracted from this mission, he is being true to his moral compass. He is on course; he is holding the course.

Both men go off course and in doing so they give us a reading on our American cultural moral compass, a new reading. Clinton's life is wrapped up in his political life; Sonny's life is wrapped up in his preaching life. If you want to explore what their individual human natures are, what kind of men they are separate from their roles, you have to first separate them from the stories they live in. Is this possible? My postmodern view questions the possibility of we humans living independent of the stories we have created for ourselves—personal, social, and cultural stories. At the same time, no one story encompasses the reality of what we are and what our lives have been, are now, and will be. There is space, in other words, between story and life at any given moment. Now when Clinton as a teenager decides to go for the presidency and narrates reality toward this goal, he is not concealing or replacing or denying his moral nature. Rather, moral decisions come through to him through his aspiring-to-be-president reality frame. He begins to create his moral sense through what this story offers him or puts in his path, which is, in this case, considerable. But since this presidential story defers a lot in the present in order to achieve results in the future, there has to be necessarily a lot in any present moment which does not come into his moral field of vision. It's outside his privileged story and therefore it has no existence. So the personality, including the moral sense, is constrained by the story. But paradoxically no one can have a moral sense unless it is constrained or filtered by some story or stories. More stories will create more filters, more filters will pick up more of what the present offers. If one story wants to defer something in the present, another story might need it then; it's part of the plot to need it then.

Sonny Dewey as a Pentecostal preacher is totally into a story about bringing people to moral awareness but, paradoxically, the preaching story overwhelms his capacity to develop a moral sense that goes beyond bringing other people to moral awareness. Like Clinton, his own moral frame is mastered by the dominating force of a story that has a stranglehold on his life. He misses whatever is in the present that does not seem to apply to his goal: To bring others from present-living to future-living, to bring them from attending to the moment and what it offers to deferring that moment in the hope of something greater to be gained in the future. Though Clinton's presidential story doesn't have a deferring plot, it is nonetheless a plot he imposes upon himself. The presidency, in the eyes of the teenager Clinton, lies in the future as desirous and wonderful as Salvation lies in the future in the eyes of Sonny Dewey. They are both committed, deep deferrers of the present. The moral sense they develop is reality filtered through once and in only one way.

Culturally we are caught within the same deferring sort of filter—Protestantism rewards deferral of present pleasures for future rewards—but it is one surely cracked by the flagrant successes of those "players" who live as if they had only a hundred days to live, with the possibility of renewal. So when Clinton deviates from the presidential story and acts unpresidentially or Sonny deviates from the preacher story and acts unpreacherly, those actions pass through a complex cultural mediation before they are given a moral slant. Both presidents and preachers should be moral leaders—that's the moral sense through the deferral lens. At the same time, however, everybody should maximize the opportunities that present themselves in line with the continuous pursuit of self-interest.

Side Trip

When you live your life as if you only have one hundred days to live, you not only take what you can to enrich those days but you go around looking for new ways to expand the quality of your living. One of the things you don't allow to get in your way are the stories which urge you to postpone the present moment for the sake of a future moment. On the other hand, when you live your life within the boundaries of a certain, fixed story that picks and chooses from the present based on what use anything may have in the future, you go around contracting the present within those plot parameters.

When Sonny's jealousy breaks through his preacher story and he becomes violent, or when Clinton makes a grab for big-haired, big-breasted women and acts adulterously, they are repeating the same sort of "moral lapse" that has been around since the Fall. Everyone continuously breaks through a story of deferral—whether religious or professional (symbolic analyst) postponement—and makes a grab for what is in the present moment but not within their story. What's new with both Clinton and Sonny is the fact that the culture is now apparently ready to openly declare that stories of deferral are okay up to a point—to the point where they ask us not to maximize profits in the present. There's no credible story that can now make us long-term players; all the credibility lies on the side of short-term plundering. And the idea of self-interest, a signifier ready to go in any direction, is now not defined as giving up what you can have in the present but taking as much as you can in the present. When everybody lives this way, the Dow Jones goes up. It's a current market belief and it has its moral counterpart in our reaction to Clinton's behavior.

The market story, however, is a story; it does create players who prey, like carnivores in a jungle, on what turns up NOW. But the story blocks off any real interaction with what the present has to offer except in terms of gain, of profit. Those who think they only have the present moment have the edge on those who think that they have endless time, that the present can be deferred for the sake of the future. They have the edge because they're paying close attention to people who are really attending what isn't here yet. Or, attending only to what will have significance at a time that is not here yet. The only moral sense that can come out of preying on the present moment is a rapacious predator's moral sense. They feed on everything that comes in their path. The only moral sense that can come out of deferring the present moment is what the story of deferral will allow. Clearly, the task is to attend to the present but not through a predator's lens and at the same time multiply the number of lenses through which we engage the world, counterbalancing deferring story lenses with nondeferring story lenses.

What kind of moral apprehension would we humans achieve then? I don't know. I was raised within a Roman Catholic reality frame, a story of deferral that left me with little understanding of what I was as an embodied being, although I had a good sense of how much better something that wasn't my body was. I was also caught up in a "symbolic analyst" story early on: The son of a man who had had the immigrant's experience although born in this country, I wanted to "professionalize," and education was the path to that. I almost deferred my marriage to an "after I get a tenure track position" moment; we seized the moment however and married because my wife has always been able to balance deferral with present living. I have encountered many like myself; I have encountered those who live already in the sweet hereafter; and those who think they are living in the sweet here and now because their investments are soaring, their stocks dividing, their salaries ballooning. I have encountered those whose lives are so seduced by products and services, by games and toys, by sex, drugs, and rock and roll that they think they are living in their sweet here and now but are only living in what Madison Avenue, Hollywood, Walt Disney, TV, and the Internet produce for a profit. I also know that while some have the luxury of choosing what stories to plot their lives within, most people on this planet live out the plots that profit others and have scant opportunity or reason to see sweetness in the present here and now.

It is virtually impossible to live in the present if Heaven or some Ideal World fills your imagination; impossible to live in the present if living for you doesn't begin until you are a doctor or lawyer or preacher or president; impossible to live in the present when the present is always only an occasion to profit. Each and every one of these has its moral complement; a moral sense that goes with it, so to speak. They represent the moral of the story. Not the moral nature of humanity, which is, as I have said, paradoxically always and only available through the mediation of a story. Proliferation of stories may lead to an expansion of the moral sense, a remapping of the moral terrain upon which we journey.

Side Trip

Permutations on the Act of Saving
in A Sliding Door Action World

> *... the endlessly and happily expansive discourse of thought ...*
> *... the more styles of intellectual discourse cultures find the*
> *room and time for the healthier.*
> —John Sturrock, "Le pauvre Sokal,"
> *London Review of Books*, July 16, 1998, p.8

> *He told me to live a good life and be a good man. I have led a*
> *good life and been a good man, haven't I?*
> —Tom Hanks as Private Ryan
> in the film *Saving Private Ryan*

The quoted fragments above are in the ballpark of what I want to pass on to you preliminary to writing about the thoughts and memories that the film *Saving Private Ryan* has drawn me into. I want, in other words, acceptance in your mind, at the outset, of the wanderings of my own mind. This film about World War II evoked Vietnam for me, and how so many of us then were not trying to save Private Ryan but ourselves.

I received a notice to appear for an Army draft physical in 1966, right after graduating from Brooklyn College. I failed that physical because the Army thought I was diabetic when in fact I had an innocuous congenital condition that showed up on their tests as diabetes. But they were suspicious; other test results belied the diabetic diagnosis so I was sent to St. Alban's Naval Hospital where I spent a week, undergoing tests. I was put in a ward with the wounded from Nam. Half of them couldn't get out of bed and those that could promenaded with blank faces up and down the center aisle of the ward or wandered into the TV room, through swinging doors just three beds down from where I was. You could go into that room at any hour of the day or night and see the same figures, smoking cigarette after cigarette, watching the TV screen. No one seemed to ever change the channel; maybe if they had a TV remote control the channels would be forever changing, clicking a new screen every two nanoseconds, making the long run from 2 to 99 in six

230

seconds flat. But this wasn't a digitalized generation; all the channel surfing then went on strictly behind their eyes. It didn't matter who Johnny Carson was talking to or what the weather was going to be. Hands clutched glasses of Kool-Aid.

I wasn't allowed out of the ward because I refused to wear the naval issue hospital garb: blue PJ's and a blue robe. I was a civilian and I didn't have to take orders. I don't like the way nurses, doctors, orderlies, Junior League volunteers, death-and-dying counselors, and soul-savers and everybody else hanging around a hospital as a vocation can take the high ground with you, the patient, simply because you are a patient. The sweet ones infantilized you and the not-so-sweet ones bullied you with a certain tone of voice, the kind my grammar school teachers would use. I admit to having a problem with hospitals; I had an extended stay when I was ten and then again when I was eleven. 1953 and 1954. Back then hospitals were white walls and white metal beds and shiny bed pans. Someone screwed up with my meal plan and I wound up eating Jell-O for a whole week, breakfast, lunch, and dinner. I had my leg in a cast and my stomach taped so I couldn't move much. I was totally dependent on the hospital staff. Long nights of calling out for water or the bedpan and only laughter in the distance and the sound of coffee cups. Someone would come eventually. Time passes differently for the patient; it's the one thing you don't have: patience.

I wasn't treated badly, just turned into "the patient in bed five." I was part of someone else's shift. I was never feeling good and could never summon the strength to show them what I was really like. For me, being in a hospital was being some sort of victim, someone at the mercy of folks who only knew you as always less aware, less mobile, less real, less human than themselves. It's a strange form of oppression. And being just a ten year old didn't help. You might say I was doubly infantilized, dehumanized, turned into no more than my illness, no more than what my medical chart at the foot of the bed said I was. Visitors looked at me as if I didn't have long to live. I dreamed I had hundreds of days to live. Hundreds was a ten year old's way of counting to infinity.

So at the age of twenty-three, there in that ward at St. Alban's, I had all that stored up resentment in me. I was the only one in the ward who could fight back; these guys, hurt in body or mind or both, had to accept their role as lesser beings. I didn't. Everyone who came up to me in hospital whites was a face from the past, a pair of efficient hands from the past, a coaxing or domineering voice from the past. But now I wasn't a patient; keeping my own clothes and refusing to wear that hospital garb was the first and necessary step to declaring my independence, to show a rebellion that this time I could back up. Very weird vibe but it was mine and I hadn't thought about making this connection for all these years. I never understood why I bucked everyone in that naval hospital for that long, long week.

To put my rebellion down they wouldn't let me go to the mess hall and eat. I don't remember what I ate or if I ate. Probably candy bars. Everyone had candy bars. It was like minds that had gone beyond the "endlessly happy and expansive discourse of thought" into the nether zone needed a lot of sugar to run on. There wasn't much curiosity as to why I was there—jeans, T-shirt, and boots—sitting in a chair by my bed and reading. I guess I didn't compute within a mental frame in which things that didn't compute were okay. I was an aberration in that place and that time but that was okay; the world for these guys was only aberration. Aberration was the norm. I fit in.

My cousin Billy meanwhile had gotten married and then drafted. But he didn't go to Vietnam. He was saved. He spent his whole tour of duty stationed in the states. I never talked to him much about those years but I remember seeing him after boot camp, lean and muscled, all the baby fat gone. Now here in the present, he sits in a wheel chair and can only say "Yeah" and can't move his legs or his right arm. He was saved for this odd, totally disastrous disease of the brain cells, a slow erosion of the body's command post. Not so slow as it turned out because his doctors say his condition is deteriorating a lot faster than they expected. They offer no hope of saving him from this attack. A rare attack; very little research funding and therefore very little known.

In between Billy's being saved from a tour of duty in Nam and this disease there is some thirty years of life: a wife, two children, grandchildren, a fine career with AT&T, a truly impressive home in the oldest part of Staten Island among even more impressive homes. You can say he was saved for that life, for that span of time. And then his luck ran out.

I think of this when I see Tom Hanks and his comrades in search of Private Ryan in order to pluck him out of danger and set him down in a safe zone. Wherever that might be.

If the medical staff at St Alban's Naval Hospital had been able to say "what he has looks like diabetes but it's not," I would have gone down that road a sergeant in a recruiting kiosk on Flatbush Avenue had pointed out to me. More than pointed out. "Whatya want to go in as a private for with your college degree and all? I can get you set up for OCS." I agreed. I liked the thought of myself as an officer. Second lieutenant. As it turned out second lieutenants doing a tour in Nam in those years had about a thirty-minute shelf life and then they either got fragged—shot from behind by their own soldiers—or blown away by the real enemy. Of course, this was a war in which it wasn't quite clear who the real enemy was. Later on, in graduate school, I would hear that the real enemy wasn't Ho Chi Min but had been McNamara and Johnson and then Nixon and Kissinger. No, someone more cynical would say, the real enemy was the Fortune 500 who stood to make a bundle on government war contracts. And once that Fortune 500 crowd found their spokesman in Ronald Reagan the view that the real enemy had been Liberalism soaked through with socialist leanings swept the American mental landscape. If it wasn't for the leftist-indoctrinated student protesters, we would have gone into that "war" to win and not to empathize with the enemy. If we weren't saving the whole world for the sake of democracy, we weren't saving anything. Kind of thing. Now, thirty years later, few can doubt that a few came out of that war with ample savings to invest in a world laid out for investors by Mr. Reagan. The domination by the top 1 percent of the American population began back then. Government contracts make fortunes.

What saved me from my short career as a second lieutenant? The same force that rolled craps thirty years later for Billy—the play of Chance.

A week or so after seeing *Saving Private Ryan*, I see a movie I had read little about: *Sliding Doors* with Gywneth Paltrow. I don't know what to expect. I'm in the theater to escape the heat and humidity, to escape the damp air that my fans at home are circulating and the even less bearable life without fans. The theater is air-conditioned and is my escape for a few hours. The movie follows through on a bright idea: What if we show Paltrow getting to the train just as the sliding doors close, going out into the streets to hail a cab, getting mugged, getting home too late to see her live-in boyfriend in bed with another woman and the story that follows from that, and then show an alternate reality story of her getting to the train just in time to push open the sliding train doors, meeting someone, and the story that follows from that. What's the most immediate cause of her missing the train? She has to go around a small child coming up the stairs. When the mother has the child step aside and Paltrow goes directly down the steps she makes the train just in time. The child is climbing the stairs with some purpose, not his but his mother's, but still a purpose. But in relation to Paltrow's life, the child being there is a random event. It's just by Chance that he's in the way or not in the way. Even though Chance has been a major player in Paltrow's life, Paltrow is "free" to take an entrepreneurial view of life: "I'm free to choose and I assume personal responsibility for my life. I am therefore entitled to all the rewards accrued or all the losses." The attitude seems reasonable, in the face of what we know. But then again what we know and how we know is already subject to a sliding-door action.

Both Paltrows go off and live in the aftermath of opened sliding doors and closed sliding doors *as if they are where they have placed themselves*; they are choosing amid the many choices before them. And there is an interesting entrepreneurial aspect to the two lives that develop. The Paltrow who misses the train winds up working menial jobs in order to pay the bills for herself and her novel-writing-but-no-income live-in, cheating boyfriend. The Paltrow who arrives on time to see what a cheat her boyfriend is summons up enough courage to take out a small business loan and start up her own public relations firm. And through a bit of social networking she winds up with a very big account and succeeds in business. And with a new love. But once again Chance intrudes and she is hit by a car and hospitalized. The loser Paltrow winds up discovering her boyfriend's duplicity, falls down the stairs, and is hospitalized. One dies and the other lives and in the final scene, new love once again emerges. Happy closure of a film that wound up troubling the hell out of me.

I begin to dream that night of the sliding doors at St. Alban's Naval Hospital. They slid open and I left a civilian. But they easily could have remained closed. In fact, if they had diagnosed me properly, I would have been drafted. Who I am now is a person who went on to graduate school and not to combat, to writing these pages and not to a grave perhaps in Arlington. The self I am not interested in fostering is a self grounded in Chance. The self I am interested in fostering is "free to choose," free to pursue self-interest, a pursuit that will somehow lead to my saving those who have limited resources to tap in pursuit of their own self-interest. Or, in a different scenario, the selves of others need me to put aside my self-interest and save them, or they need to put aside their self-interest to save me. We are all on shaky ground, in shaky lives, getting to the sliding doors just in time or a second too late. We are aware within circumstances disconnected to our intentions and our choices. There is a climate to our perceptions and realizations that is as stochastic as the weather.

In a world riddled by the play of Chance, some act nobly or cleverly amid the choices they have, and some do not. But as it is impossible to say to what degree Chance plays in a person's life, either for good or ill, it is not possible to say that as we all face Chance, factoring it in politically or ethically is unnecessary. We do not all experience the play of Chance equally; all men and women may be born equal but only in the eyes of the law we try to maintain in this country. There is no law binding Chance to an equal treatment of everyone. But what is hard to deny is that Chance treats everyone in one way or the other. No one is self-saving then; everyone is somewhere, in good or bad circumstances, because at some point in their lives, or at many points, they reached the sliding doors before they closed or they didn't.

In my own life I have been saved numerous times without my having any memory of it. My mind was saved from a life of deadening redundancy by words, heard or read, that sparked my desire to know, to think about a world I was already in. Sometimes, only a desk positioned so no one could see what I was reading or writing saved my spirit. I was saved from cigarettes by one late-night game of half-court basketball that left me vomiting. And a wrong diagnosis saved me in 1966. Who knows, perhaps a wrong diagnosis will one day kill me. I want to say if our science was better, the play of Chance would be negated in our lives but I don't think we have ever imagined a future world in which the science, however wondrous, is not also subject to Chance. I've read too much history to think that Chance can be programmed out of existence. I've seen Chance at work in our *Star Trek* future.

I recall going back to see that recruiting sergeant and telling him of my stay in St. Alban's. "Kid," he said to me, "you gotta be half dead to get a medical deferment the way things are going now. And you don't look half dead to me." "What do I do now?" I asked. "Have a life kid is what I would do," he told me. "The Army's through with you." "OCS?" "Forget about it. You're out. You're a free man. Uncle Sam doesn't want you." I left there bewildered; I didn't know then what I later found out. That I wasn't sick, that I wasn't half dead. I couldn't trust the way I felt. I felt okay now but maybe I wouldn't feel so good a couple of months from now. I didn't know what I had been saved for.

In my whole life since then I've felt I went to Nam and met my Fate and that I was living in the aftermath of that, that like the guy in the film *Jacob's Ladder*, I would one day wake up and realize I was someplace in Nam dying and while I was dying my mind was spinning a story to prepare me for being dead. My whole life was a gradual transition to the moment of death. I've been trying to fit myself comfortably into the thought that I did go to Nam and I died there. No one saved me but I got the chance to live as if I had been saved, a chance to get used to the fact that I died there, that I wasn't saved.

I think about my cousin Billy breaking apart and dissolving into nothing more than a heartbeat and an expansion and contraction of lungs until they too cease. It's not something I can think about without wanting to save him. His present state is sufficient cause for serious doubt in the existence of a caring God. I wouldn't let Billy suffer like this, and I've got more animal passions than spiritual yearnings. I wouldn't use him to teach anyone a lesson about the preciousness of life while you've still got it. And though this may be a fallen world, it is surely a fallen God who allows torment to exceed any transgression by a thousandfold. If I had the power, I would save Billy. I would replace the play of Chance with real spiritual purpose. But then I think differently: Perhaps there is something unresolved, unclear, unfinished in his life's journey that only this bitter ending can vanquish, convert into true salvation. And then an eternal tour of duty in a spiritual world that no human imagination can conceive. I would not save him from this eternal reward.

The roads are not clear ahead. I see no enemy ahead, above, or below. I want something more to blame than the play of Chance. I want a chance to save Billy from this cruel Fate.

Spielberg's camera has an easier time focusing on the Germans. See the villains here. Look at the scene when the American Jew Mellish is wrestling with the much brawnier German. The German now on top, the bayonet pushing into Mellish's chest. "Wait," Mellish says. "Let's talk about this. Hold on." Obscenely, the German whispers for him to close his eyes and be calm as he pushes the bayonet further and further into Mellish's body until it rends his heart and he dies. The German on top of him like a lover, the bayonet like a penis, the slow penetration. Mellish sighs, he dies. The German lover dismounts and disheveled makes his way down the stairs, past the American intellectual who cannot bring himself to act, who has listened to it all and done nothing. The terrible sin of omission. Whose is the greater sin? The German's or the fear-paralyzed intellectual?

I don't begrudge Spielberg this personal journey, this digging into the unspeakable obscenity of what the Nazis did to his people, the Jews. In the same fashion, he cannot deny me my own personal journey via the thoughts his film arouses in me. But our journeys intersect when Spielberg, in trying to save Private Ryan, loses most of the men who set out to save him, including the man of steadfast duty and honor, Captain John Miller, played by Tom Hanks. Hanks tells his men he's really pursuing self-interest in trying to find Private Ryan and save him. He figures if he completes this assignment he can go back home. They can all go back home. Why he thinks completing this special mission will save him and all his men is not quite clear. Maybe at the end of that mission they will have put in enough combat time. Or something like that. Anyway, he says he's not being an altruist; he doesn't believe in mutual aid. He's just pursuing self-interest. Like everyone else in this 1998 American audience is supposed to be doing. The days of worrying about the next guy are over with. Cooperative efforts, except entrepreneurial networking, consolidating, merging, and brainstorming, have gone out with the collapse of political socialism. Nobody is busy saving anybody but himself or herself and maybe their kids. I say maybe because I recently read an investment analyst's note to future parents and the bottom line was this: Given the cost of raising children (computed to a cent), it would be a far wiser use of financial resources to invest in the stock market. Better returns.

Having said all this, why do I still feel that these men are giving their lives to save the life of another man? After two men are killed in the pursuit of Private Ryan, Private Reiben, a guy from Brooklyn who lacks all the tact and restraint that Miller (who has the air of a Midwesterner) possesses, decides to walk away from the mission. But he doesn't. Clearly he would be serving his own self-interest better if he were to walk away. Miller tells him he has his permission to go. But he doesn't go. Maybe he won't desert his comrades in arms. They are leaning on each other. The mission doesn't make anything but political sense but they overlook that. I think they overlook that because that mission is encased within a war that makes sense to them: They're saving their families from Hitler. Risking all their lives to save the life of one man may not make sense but being in a war that is attempting to save Ryan's mother and everyone's mother, everyone's family, from the terrors of the Third Reich makes sense.

Imagine how this mission to save Private Ryan would transpire in the Vietnam "conflict." Here's a war where the young, as always, are being called upon to protect the old. Or, another way of looking at it, those not yet on the road to prosperity are called upon to protect the already prosperous. In 1966, when I was drafted, there was enough young people in universities and aware of disingenuous politics driving that "conflict" to protest being sacrificed by their country. Instead of answering the call to duty, they sought to save themselves. Spielberg's *Saving Private Ryan* only gets close to this Nam profile when Miller and his men are sent on their special mission to save Private Ryan. At that point, the reason to be fighting a war turns from clear categories of good guy/bad guy to something that doesn't quite make sense, something that smells of politics, not war. The enemy may be heartless in every way, including its disregard for mothers, but the American military aspires to something nobler. At least the image of something nobler. It will return this fourth and last son to his mother. At the cost of others' lives.

This is war as spectacle to be transmitted into millions of homes; that's the war reduced to one heroic mission to save Private Ryan; that's the war reduced to a photo-op that will play large in the media; that's the war being packaged for a Spielberg film, just the kind of special mission that stands out amid the monotonous sameness of the war's continuous dead, dying, and horribly wounded. It may very well be that Spielberg has filmed the most "realistic" account of the blood, mayhem, and chaos of battle. But it is the heroic gesture of Miller and his men to save Ryan that Spielberg focuses on. The mission as special event, as action with box office potential. In the end, just as the Holocaust was reduced to what excitement its own extremeness could generate, here in *Saving Private Ryan* all of World War II is the mere occasion or field upon which Tom Hanks gets to play an ordinary American called to a patriotic act and summoning all his strength to fulfill his responsibility.

I don't think we can get to see war for what it is until we stop trying to find heroic photo-ops that will bring us to a heart-rending realization of how horrible war is and how unselfish we humans can be when occasion requires. I mean I'm tired of seeing the human race stroke itself at the very moment we should be wondering how a cerebral cortex and an oppositional thumb necessarily lead to madness and atrocities. So I say what this movie may be all about is what every war movie has been about: We're trying to save our image of ourselves for ourselves. We want to see ourselves in the midst of bloody slaughter and yet find some Captain Miller on a special mission to shine as a fellow human being before our eyes.

There are certainly causes for my cousin Billy's illness but Chance has put those causes into play. Maybe he was exposed to something that led to this strange and lethal deterioration of his brain cells. Maybe he did something, went somewhere, ate something, drank something, was injured at some time—something that set this hard, slow journey to death in motion. Maybe something happened to him out of the blue. Fifty guys living the same sort of life and he gets the short straw. Chance. Isn't the question: How do we save ourselves from Chance? And because we can't, we think about saving ourselves from the perils we can see and think about whether the wisest course to saving ourselves is to make the lives of others equal to our own and set about saving us all. At a moment in the American journey, we stop on the path of self-interest and think about a special mission to save someone else, someone we don't yet know.

Those who really knew how to pursue self-interest didn't go to Nam and probably arranged to stay stateside during World War II so they could fulfill needed government contracts. Captain Miller turns out to be nothing more than a high school teacher, a teacher of English composition, a man of no great importance back home. I mean in 1998 dollars; consider the salaries of high school teachers compared with, say, Wall St. brokers, or investment bankers, or accountants, or systems analysts. Now, back in the '40s, he's not a guy in a "loser's profession" but just an ordinary American tested and equal to the test. Nevertheless, while he and his men, all equally ordinary Americans, wrestle with the dilemma of giving their lives to save another, those who have already answered that question without thinking twice are outside the war zone. They may in fact be maximizing profits as usual, eventually extracting marvelous stories out of the war for future commercial packaging. Only Chance may stop them cold—but not on a battlefield in this war.

I often wonder about those from my Bensonhurst neighborhood who died in Nam or who lost their minds there and I wonder about those who made a profit on their deaths, who wound up taking that profit into the new world of investment that Reagan opened up for them. No twenty-something today wants to "lose" the way my long ago buddies did in Nam; the role models of the '90s rather are those who came out of that "conflict" with large investment portfolios. They were saved for the glories of an ever-rising Dow Jones; they were saved to see the Third Technological Revolution. They were saved to write the story of those who were not saved. They were, in short, simply The Saved.

And I can't get it out of my mind that I wasn't saved; that my mind was lost then, a bitter rebel since then, unsaveable amid the blessed Saved. I was saved for this. And my cousin Billy was saved for his own bitter ending. Or, more exactly, it took all these long years for him to know for sure that in the end no one could save him.

Being saved in a medieval world had all to do with the state of your soul, whether you were in a state of grace or not. It's not part of global-market values for anyone to deeply ponder the state of his or her soul. It doesn't appear in the Dow Jones; it isn't traded in New York, London, or Tokyo. There is no futures market in people's souls. We want to save the whales, and the spotted owls, and the mountain gorilla, and the rain forest, and the bald eagle, and our teeth, and our hair, and our money, and our minds, and the planet, and your grandma's bread recipe, and first editions, and Beanie Babies, and stamps, and energy, and time—and Private Ryan. But our souls have sort of faded from view. And because we can never know who has been saved and who hasn't, can never know whether bad acts that yet reap a profit tarnish the soul while good acts that reap no worldly profit polish the soul; we have lost interest in the matter altogether. Easier to save money, to save time, than save something we can never know we have saved until it is too late.

That's why saving Private Ryan while losing almost everyone in the platoon's lives, including Captain Miller's, seems such a bad bargain. If all those men had earned paradise by doing what they did, then it was a good bargain. But paradise now means no more than the possible name of a club or an island or a mixed drink or a drug or a designer label. We simply no longer think in terms of eternal salvation. And at a time when we think only in terms of two-column bookkeeping, of profit and loss, Spielberg shows us ourselves doing nobler things than pursuing self-interest. As I have said, we have a gift for elevating ourselves during the times we're acting like pigs. Americans have not only been acting as pigs and promoting the beneficial effects of such but have been elevating pigs to role-model status.

In going back to World War II to find young men who have a self-sacrificing capability, Spielberg has had to bypass not only the war in Korea, but Vietnam and the Gulf War. In order to find a stage upon which he could impress his story of human nobility emerging from the act of saving Private Ryan, Spielberg has to leave the '80s and '90s when global-market values are discarding lives, not saving them, throwing more and more people on the trash pile as "losers" in that most important and stochastic game of all: competing for dollars. And just maybe the film is not about putting aside self-interest and reaching out a hand to someone else. Maybe the film is all about how the many should be sacrificed to save the one. All for one kind of thing. All those kids working in Dickensian factories in Asia in order to give Kathy Lee Gifford financial security. American citizens sacrificing themselves for shareholders. Ten thousand workers building up a sweat so that the dividends of one shareholder can divide at year's end. We don't ever know what old man Ryan has become. It could be that he's tended a nice investment portfolio over the years and is now spending his days sitting in front of the TV watching the endless screening of stock quotations and financial analyses. And his initial investment was tied to wartime government contracts. Right now we certainly are sacrificing the very many for an infinitesimal few. And the guys in Miller's platoon do more griping about it than we are presently doing.

The hookup with the present may be messier than first appears. The need to go back to clearcut good and evil in World War II is meant to make things less messy. Maybe Korea was just not as clearcut in regard to who the bad guys were and who were the good guys. And Nam, as I have said, was clouded in moral ambiguities. Half of the folks I speak to now regarding Nam think the lesson of that war was never fight a war except to win and never tie one hand behind your back. The other half think that the lesson was never let a paranoic mass psychopathology spewing something like a Domino Theory get you to send troops where they don't belong. The Gulf War had a demonized personality: Saddam. The perfect name for a sadistic despot. But the idea lurked that we were in the Gulf to protect our oil interests. Not as much moral murkiness as Nam certainly, but a good amount nonetheless.

The problem with the Gulf War as a setting for saving anybody was that the '80s just wasn't producing the kind of youth generation that would perform such an act. Let's morph the '40s soldiers into '80s soldiers: Start with Captain John Miller. When he tells the audience of the '80s that he's an English teacher everyone in that '80s audience computes his net worth, wonders whether a guy who's not in the competitive entrepreneurial ring can be trusted to make "hardball" decisions, and knows for sure why his arm is shaking. He's out of his league. His Sergeant, played by Tom Sizemore, is a loyal, let's-get-the-job-done-and-keep-the-bellyaching-down sort of guy. He's The Sidekick, the trusted companion who's "got your back," doesn't say much, understands what you're going through, and will follow you into hell. He's not as well spoken as Miller; his emotions are on the surface; he's volatile; he doesn't suffer fools gladly. He gets the job done and doesn't bitch. Why, he's a "working-class hero"! What's the '80s version? The guy who wants your job. The guy who is playing you till he gets another rung up the ladder and then you're history. Or, he doesn't compute at all. They don't hook up with him at all. Why? Because the idea of a "working-class hero" is inconceivable in the '80s we have created. Edward Burns's Private Reiben, the cynic from Brooklyn who speaks his mind, would have become in the '80s a guy angry about his job going to foreign shores and his girlfriend wanting a bit of what she was seeing on the TV show "Lives of the Rich and Famous." Corporal Upham, the Bible-quoting sniper? Probably more into upsetting the American federal government than the Third Reich. Private Mellish? He would be kicking German ass the way the Israeli's were kicking Arab ass. And Medic Wade would be selling his supply of drugs to the highest bidder.

You just can't put together a post-Reagan platoon that can measure up to the standards of Reagan's own Hollywood mythos. You can't put together a bunch of guys held together by the common interest of saving someone else. You'd have to find a platoon of Forrest Gumps here in the '90s that would run back and forth saving everybody and not thinking about their own self-interest. And if they were all Forrest Gumps they wouldn't be thinking about self-interest because they wouldn't have the brains, cleverness, insider information, networking skills, résumé, stock portfolio, and toys necessary to pursue self-interest to the max.

And note one other neat trick in jumping back to World War II to stage this reenactment of American valor: There are no women. There are no African Americans, or Chicanos, or Asian Americans. There is no multiculturalism. No sop to diversity and difference. You shouldn't pursue the interests of your own difference but instead blender mix yourself into the platoon. It's easier for the market to target you if you're The Platoon. After all, let's face it, only the rich are really different. Implicit in this planned absence is a certain critique of all this present-day political correctness. We can't get back to good old-time acts of courage and unselfishness if we hold on to the politics of identity. We're not a tossed salad of ethnic and racial and sex differences. We're all Americans. In the same platoon. Saving Private Ryan.

We can be good socialists when we're in battle; cooperative efforts, a sharing of the danger, the horror, the pain. And if we have a mission to save another soldier, we do it together. Nobody grandstands, nobody walks off and does their own thing, nobody worries about whether they have all the equality they need, all the opportunities they deserve, all the freedom accorded to them under the law. Nobody in our platoon makes a stock market killing on the mission, although all are equally vulnerable to being killed. There are no winners and losers in our platoon; when someone is killed, they did not lose. They fought and died valiantly for their country. They gave their lives in their country's cause. And those who return are not the winners, but merely the survivors, filled forever with the memories of their comrades in arms who died.

But this '40s platoon must return to a '90s world, dissolve the binding fluid of mutual aid, of watching each other's backs, of looking out for your neighbor as he looks out for you. Now we return to the world of winners and losers, of toys, not actions, determining one's worth. Return to the far more horrific war of All Against All. And ironically, in this global-market world, the Germans are not losing nor has the notion that, on a far different battleground, they lost, signify. Perhaps, in the end, that is what Spielberg has set himself against: this global-market restaging of what it means to win and lose. And in seeming to want us to return to valuative criteria other than economic, he may be urging us all on to a mission to save our neighbor, Private Ryan, before we think of saving ourselves. In a world that is both grounded in Chance (what else is market play but casino play?) and intent on hiding the play of Chance in the shaping of winners and losers ("I Did It My Way"), there is great need for all of us to engage in a mutual effort to save each other from the cruelties of Chance and a social order willing to leave our salvation to Chance.

When I think of the film in this way, I know that the journey to that past war, the second world war, was a journey we needed to make now. Perhaps America can be redeemed by more such journeys into its own past, not especially because that past is so noble, but because the present power of the global market and all its priorities have far less force there. And we desperately need to see beyond and through the curtain that hides the supreme power of global-market wizardry.

It is a journey we must make to save ourselves.

That Rug Really Tied the Room Together

[A]ll the brothers' intelligence and skill can't make up for the sense of vacancy in their movies. Until they find a way to let a little real life in (grownup reality, that is), Joel and Ethan Coen will somehow seem stunted—no more than the brightest kids in the class.
> —Daphne Merkin, "Smart Alecks,"
> *New Yorker*, March 1998

The Big Lebowski is an empty frame.
> —Stuart Klawans, "Sex and Bowling,"
> *The Nation*, March 30, 1998

Through this bewildering landscape . . . wanders our addled Philip Marlowe figure, toking herb, swilling White Russians and, truth to tell, looking increasingly heroic relative to the dysfunctional world around him.
> —Andrew O'Hehir, "Everyman Must Get Stoned," *Salon*

I'm still running
Against the wind . . .
> —Bob Seger

One of the consequences of friends knowing that I may be writing about films that they've seen and don't quite know what to make of is their asking me what do I make of this or that film. Now they know whether they like or don't like a film but times are such—postmodern I mean—that just what they especially don't like about a film may yet be their hidden access to the whole film. What unsettles us and holds us off could possibly provide an epiphany. A transformative moment. Hold on another second and maybe the opaqueness here will attach itself to the Dark Holes of our postmodern age, move us into new figments of old figments like cause and effect, linear time, noncontradiction, nonrandom order, external reference points, and grownup reality. I take it for granted that today everyone is holding on another second to see if their command of reality isn't going to be pulled right out of their hands, flung high in the air so that all the new movements, all the new revelations of an ever-changing us-and-reality relationship can be clearly seen.

That's not to say that everyone is ready to go along with the new swerve. Refer to our "culture wars" here: On one side you have an army digging in and ready to hold on to grownup reality in the finest tradition of family values as displayed on Nickelodeon cable TV, and, on the other side, you have any number of radical, guerilla-like factions more than ready to admit that reality has moved on, say, from adultery or suicide or same-sex marriages or abortion or transexuality as destructive on all counts to the same as new constellations being brought to recognition for the first time in the firmament. We are never at play on a planet rotating on its axis and spinning in the heavens when we belong to the conservative cultural army but quite seriously grounded in Truths, Laws, Imperatives, Explanations, Equations, and Investment Principles. Bend one knee, please. They are, of course, opposed by those who see themselves at play with reality, bending it, rather than a respectful knee, to fit the contours and dimensions of an infinitely flexible and varied human nature.

If you invest the spirit of one side with the spirit of the other, and vice versa, you get the sort of awareness each side needs of the other in order to have a really good intense cultural war. You also get a cultural climate in which the two attitudes are to be found at all settings on a good blender. And, ironically, market imperialism—which on one hand demands an inert social order which offers stability—makes its profits by pulping reality to push product. The market is at play with a pliable reality; Return on Investment is the only immoveable part.

When events—like Princess Di's death or Clinton's sex drive—become like a movie we can't get control of, they now fall into this culture wars' miasma, a La Brea Tar Pit, which is our minds, in which white bones of all sizes swim about, and it's our job, as reconstructors, to put it all together. This is the sort of occasional acid-trip scene that Dude, of *The Big Lebowski*, might have. Which side is the Dude on? Why he's clearly at play with reality, skirting all the necessities that bind our present entrepreneurial society. Market players don't play the way the Dude does. They get into a competitive global arena and they make sure they come out winners. The fact that in getting to be winners they are willing to obey no laws but those of profit, no principles but those of profit, and no tradition but only what profit requires at that moment does not turn them into Dude. His disrespect is for self-aggrandizement, his unconcern is for being rich, his rebellion is against self-interest. And because he is so startingly atavistic, so disturbingly nonentrepreneurial in 1998, after some twenty years of ascendant Dow, he activates a new clash of the culture wars but at the same time he and his crew of masterless men push the postmodern envelope a bit further. I mean to say that *The Big Lebowski* pushes us to wondering whether we can't command its subject because we're right and there is no subject, there is no rug that brings the whole room together, or that the fact that we can't command its subject and are wondering why is precisely what the film's subject has led us to.

Dude and his friends are bowling outside our lanes and we've already rented shoes and are trying out bowling balls in preparing to join them. I'm not saying that we're all prepared to score this game according to rules we can't even begin to fathom. Nor that once we see the kind of game the Coen brothers are rolling here, we don't try to close it down at once. All I'm saying—and I sound like the Dude when we can't wrap things up or follow all the in and outs of the "case"—is that at this moment in America, market imperialized as we are, this is a postmodern flaunting of reality making and we're all bowling on those lanes, just scoring the results differently.

Let's explore the "sense of vacancy" that the *New Yorker* film critic mentions. Who possesses this "sense of vacancy"? And does it arise from a "sense of realism"? And, indeed, don't we reveal what sense of realism we hold when we begin to talk about "grownup reality," whose antipode surely must be infantile reality? Within this particular "sense of realism" a certain "sense of vacancy" arises when not enough "grownup reality" is let in. But what if, say, we adopted the "sense of realism" of an eighteenth-century fruitcake like William Blake, who, because he was a fruitcake, confounded the realms of Innocence and Experience, childhood and adulthood. Because he was a fruitcake—sang on his deathbed, for instance—his "sense of realism" wanted to "let in" to "grownup reality" the joy, imagination, spontaneity, exuberance, emotions, playfulness, the dreaming and irrationalism of childhood. None of this appears particularly appealing when viewed by those already in the realm of Experience; it all appears frivolous, childish, disorderly, lunatic, and ludic; and where there should be grownup thought there is only a failure to achieve cognitive grasp, a prepubescent assertion of the will, a bombardment of cognitive dissonance. In short, when time and space are not filled with the priorities of what now passes socially and culturally as "grownup reality," then the observer notes a "sense of vacancy."

This "sense of vacancy" is, however, a presence in this movie. It is not, therefore, the byproduct of *failure* to bring something into being but rather the result of the film *bringing* something into being. What does it bring into being? Well, from where I sit alongside you in our present "grownup reality," I'm not quite sure because it all first registers as unplotted, less than purposeful, fractured, disconnected, ludic, mazelike, discordant, surrealistic, incoherent, a jumble, a farrago. What does it appear like to the Coen brothers? I know from their film *Fargo* that they have a real grip on grownup reality as presently being manufactured in the Midwest. And they can't see the whole of it without seeing the ludic, farrago dimensions of that reality. For them it appears that grownup reality is always already filled to the brim with unstoppable mania, is always tending to bring its own sobriety and control onto the snowy drifts of the cockamamie where the hard, cold edges of grownup reality finally melt away in the sun. In *The Big Lebowski* all of the grownup reality the Dude becomes entangled in gives way to a musical number à la Busby Berkeley. And when the Dude is hit over the head and things grow dark as they do for Dick Powell in *Farewell My Lovely*, the Dude doesn't fall into a deep, dark pool and wind up running through a dark corridor of endless doors pursued by who knows what. Instead, he flies like Superman with arms spread wide over Los Angeles at night with all its lights fluttering below. He has a great, happy smile on his face; he surely dreams he can fly away. And then he's embracing a bowling ball, a look of surprise on his face, as he plummets downward, his flight canceled. He's weighted down and it's the weight of real-world gravity.

As in *Fargo*, all real-world gravity passes through human mediation, which gives it this role or that, assigning it wherever our "sense of realism" sees fit. Oddly enough, what the force of gravity is—often cited as an indisputable component of and proof of the "real world"—contributes to our "sense of vacancy." It is a vacant force in a realm of vacancy. It's so real we bring to it nothing in our daily lives, living as if it meant nothing and didn't exist. It is so powerful a force in the real world and at the same time lies unmediated in human life. We bring to it no meaning and no value, unless of course we are working for NASA. I am merely trying to point out that a "sense of vacancy" inhabits all the "hard" stuff we connect to the "real world." Observations of a "sense of vacancy" in a film which is—whether it's a film you like or not or the critics like or not—is a ludicrous claim, because all films film human mediations of reality. They film "worldliness," the movements of people within the world they are already part of. Electricity, nuclear fission, the synapse, photosynthesis, $E=mc^2$, LaPlace Transforms, and so on, are vacant lots in everyday human mediation of the world; we greet them with a "sense of vacancy," even on exams where the only human transformation they have is in terms of grades, a symbolic enterprise whose meaning and value are socially and culturally manufactured.

So the Coen brothers greet grownup reality with a "sense of vacancy" and rather than put on gravitas they try to take a look at things as if they themselves weren't obliged to obey the laws of grownup reality. And they literally film their attempt as a point-of-view shot from inside a bowling bowl. What sense of realism do we get from inside that moving bowling ball? If you're inside that bowling ball do you project a "sense of vacancy" out there in the lanes, with the bowlers and their world? Or, do you take your gravity-bound "sense of realism" in there with you and hold on to the notion that vacancy is here inside the bowling ball and anything from this perspective results in a "sense of vacancy"? Who's going to mark the frame empty? From inside the bowling ball every frame is filled with action, every frame is a roll down one or another lane, and the sights along the way vary—pace, time, and speed locked into a new equation each and every time.

The flight of the bowling ball, like the Dude's flight over LA, are metaphors of travel Coen brothers-style and it seems to me a profitless endeavor to object to their style of travel. Unless, of course, you are thoroughly convinced that grownups can and should travel only one way across a reality that allows for only that perspective of travel. Once you settle in for the ride on the Coen brothers' terms you can see that every character in the film, not just the Dude and his bowling buddies, are coming at reality from separate lanes. And every dude on every lane has his or her bowling style and perspective. Now I don't know about you but when I bowl, I'm glancing at who's bowling on the right and left of me. I watch the lanes on either side. I distinguish mature bowling styles from amateur ones. I engage in bowling chatter and listen to that around me. I am on lane four and way over to my right someone is bowling on lane fifty; noise and movement blur where I am from where that bowler is. You might say that the reality of lane fifty lacks interest for me, but that's only an effect of where I am on lane four. I don't know how much I could say about life on lane fifty without filling you with a sense of vacancy.

Let's find a way to wander from lane to lane, although this sort of lateral movement doesn't take place in a bowling alley because we stand side by side, lane by lane, focused on the pins in front of us, moving toward them, releasing, and then returning. If reality is only ahead in our lane and if we are the only ones with the proper bowling form, we're the only ones bowling like grownups, then the plot and perspective on lane fifty shouldn't mean a whole hell of a lot to us. On the other hand, if you take a postmodern view of things—and the Coen brothers do— then you're going to bowl laterally. Maybe your game will improve and your "sense of realism" expand; maybe your empty frame will get filled in and your "sense of vacancy" shifted back out to empty space.

Let's journey cross-alley in this film. Let's put the Dude in the center lane. The film opens with him strolling down the dairy aisle of Ralph's supermarket, stopping to sample from a carton of milk. The Dude is caught in a time warp: He experiences the occasional acid flashback, listens to whale song while soaking and toking in his bathtub, listens to the music of Creedence Clearwater Revival and passes time at the bowling alley with his buddies Walter and Donny. Reagan never happened for the Dude; he missed the film *Forrest Gump* so he doesn't know he's been declared extinct by Newt Gingrich, a wrong turn in American history. The Dude's misadventures begin when he is mistaken for another Lebowski, the Big Lebowski, the Lebowski who has won, who apparently has all the toys. The goons that piss on the Dude's rug have been sent by Ben Gazzara playing Hollywood's creation of the porn and drug sleaze-kingpin behind the sleaze. But the Dude doesn't cross his path until later. Now he is set on getting restitution for his rug because this rug really tied the room together, a thought not his own but his friend Walter's. Walter has the gift of all true paranoiacs: He can tie together the most disparate things and he certainly knows what the key piece is when trying to fit things together, trying to make sense of things. The counterpresence here is Steve Buscemi's Donny, for whom the whole world is just a series of sentence fragments and conversations only partially heard. His constant interrogations elicit the same response from Walter: "Shut the fuck up, Donny." Donny is not privy to the real workings of things and in Walter's view can't possibly be brought up to speed.

There is, however, a home base to Walter's thoughts: Vietnam. Everything, no matter how unrelated on the surface to that conflict, is inevitably linked to it. Nam is the rug spread out in Walter's mind which ties the room together. The discrepancy between that sense of order and what is in the world leads Walter and those who follow his "logic" into strange conflicts and many casualties, a sort of microcosm of Nam itself. But no Tet Offensive daunts Walter whose absolute certainty and determination never falter; no matter how distant the points may be on the map, Walter can connect them. He never experiences a sense of vacancy. Or, more precisely, he never experiences a sense of vacancy he can't fill.

Seduced by Walter's logic that he needs to be compensated for that rug which really tied the room together, the Dude pays a visit to the Big Lebowski. Lest we ourselves forget that it's the '90s and Dude is all that's left over from the Counterrevolution, the Lebowski of the '90s— the BIG Lebowski—a fatcat in a wheelchair, describes the Dude to the Dude's face early in the film. He tells the Dude how in spite of being crippled he has succeeded in becoming a winner, a success, and he did it because he was relentlessly, competitively entrepreneurial. In other words, he represents the shtick of the last twenty years to the Dude. He won't give the Dude a handout; did he personally piss on the Dude's carpet? No, then he's not responsible. The Dude insists that he's suffered a great loss by being mistaken for the Big Lebowski. But the Big Lebowski doesn't share the Dude's sense of order and throws him out. The Dude nevertheless leaves with a Persian rug, which gets taken back later by the Big Lebowski's daughter, Maude, for whom it holds cherished memories of her mother. Maude will later mate with the Dude because she wants a child but she doesn't want anyone connected to her life fathering that child. So she picks the Dude; the lane he's bowling on is so far removed from the one she's on that even sex can't really bring them together. She fills the Dude in on the real success story of her father, the Big Lebowski: He has no money of his own; the money was her mother's and now it's in a foundation administered by Maude. She once let her father invest some of the foundation's money and he lost it all. He's an incompetent, lying, vain man who bought himself a trophy wife. He is, in short, a fraud; he didn't earn millions; he can't take the high ground with the Dude. In fact, the Dude is his moral superior: He's down but he's not a hypocrite, nor is he vain and selfish. He doesn't make people trophies; a bowling trophy would suffice for the Dude.

On his way out of the Big Lebowski's, the Dude meets the trophy wife, Bunny, who later may or may not be kidnaped. As the Dude glances over at the pool, he asks "Who's that?" "Oh, that's a nihilist," Bunny responds. "Oh, a nihilist," Dude says, nodding, as if a nihilist sleeping on a rubber float in a swimming pool was per usual. Bunny has been painting her toenails and now she holds up a foot and wants the Dude to blow on it. "Oh, you want me to blow on it?" the Dude says. But then he drifts off, following his rug being carried out. When he visits Maude in her studio she isn't painting her nails; her own body isn't her art as it is for Bunny the porno star now trophy wife. Maude swings naked over a canvas below and splatters paint on it as she flies by. Some of that paint gets on the Dude who is as unperturbed with the expression of "high" art as he is with "low" art. Art is not his passion, nor lust, nor money, nor ambition, nor nothing itself. Neither a committed artist of life or of profit or of nothing, the Dude carries on at his own pace. There's something stubbornly heroic about the way the Dude feels called upon to not only attend to all the ins and outs of the plot he's wandered into but make some sense of it, come to some kind of conclusion. It's not a committed intent, a serious drive through the main street of this bewildering landscape. The Dude's command of the ins and outs of life's intricacies—and the bewildering landscape he's wandered into—never goes beyond his knowing the way to the In & Out Burger Shop.

You might say that while everyone else has an abstracted sort of connection with the world, the Dude's remains concrete and particular. But he does take it as it comes; I mean he takes it as serious as life gets. He doesn't dismiss it as vacancy on his way to nobler ground. He hasn't, for instance, adopted a posture of scornful and amused aloofness as David Thewlis does in a brief cameo. The Dude has come to see Maude and finds only Thewlis sitting there, amused by not only the Dude's appearance but seemingly by his very existence. Later, when Maude shows up and answers a phone call there's a three way "inside" joke that the phone caller, Maude, and Thewlis share. Theirs is a world in which avant-garde art and living life like art disdain the mundane, especially a figure such as the Dude, who represents all the messiness, disorder, and confusion that art seeks to transcend. Ironically, it's not aesthetic detachment that will impregnate Maude. For that she has to turn to the Dude. Quite interestingly, Thewlis is one of the only people in the film who provokes the Dude's wrath. "Who the hell are you anyway?" the Dude asks him after Thewlis has treated him to reeking condescension. Who indeed is Thewlis here but the aloof, scornful critic who will soon write about a "sense of vacancy" pervading the film?

Even though it is the Dude who has the occasional acid flashback, he lives without illusions. But he's surrounded by the deluded. Jesus, the Latino bowler, takes vanity to a new high; he is in his own mind the cock of the walk, all posture and braggadocio. He promises great harm but will never deliver; his delusion is harmless. But when the Dude winds up in the hands of a Malibu police chief he winds up smack in the middle of a law and order, "tough on crime" worldly outlook. It's suddenly "Giuliani time," allegedly the words New York City police used when they were brutalizing a hapless victim. This sort of neo-Nazi barbarity and brutality is part of the nihilists' approach also; they throw an attack marmot into the Dude's bathtub as he is soaking, toking, and listening to whale song. Their violence finally runs up against Walter's, the Vietnam vet, calmly telling the frightened Donny not to worry because these guys are amateurs. And Walter does go through them as if they were paper bags. A black leather, German skinhead, Sprocket look makes a good photo-op, but it's nothing but '80s and '90s hype compared to the violence Walter has seen. But the clash is too much for Donny whose weak heart gives out and he dies on the spot. Later, his ashes will be flung out of a two-pound coffee can into the wind and back into the Dude's face.

I can't help thinking: Who in this film is living as if they were mortal? As if they had one and not more lives to live? Do you counter mortality by committing yourself to something, like art or sex or wealth or power or anger or service? The Golden-age TV scriptwriter that the Dude and Walter visit, in the hope of getting back a million dollars from a fourteen-year-old thief, is in an iron lung set up like a casket at one end of the living room. Maybe every script he's written is now being replayed in his mind to the rhythm of the iron lung bellows. It's as if the reality of the present continues on unscripted. There was always life going on outside the script; and the script was less enduring than the life. Was mortality held off by a script, no matter how Golden Age? Or does that all inevitably lead you into thinking that you can't follow the ins and outs of life and world but that you are getting the most you can out of it? The Dude is not entrepreneurial; he's no symbolic analyst; and he's certainly not shaping his own destiny. He is in fact being led through a maziness that confounds grasp. But maybe he's here in a way that no one else in the film is. Maybe the Dude is leaving his frame empty and that's an accomplishment whose skillfulness we just can no longer recognize. But I see it as a reminder that while we may need to journey, the world doesn't journey. There is no journey but only movement, and that movement, foundationally, has no order or causality or time or speed or space. I am not claiming that the Dude is enlightened in the way of the Dalai Lama or has reconciled in himself the paradoxes of consciousness immersed in what merely exists, what is outside of what we humans make of it. And yet the Dude is a pause on our journey here; perhaps a pause, received as vacancy, but a pause in our entrepreneurial rush to "return on investment."

Side Trip: "And the Sun Set . . ."

Side Trip

And the sun set, and all the journeying ways were darkened.

—The Odyssey

I found a message from my father on my answering machine.
When I called him back I could tell immediately that this would be
one of those conversations where I would be trying hard to make
him laugh, trying hard to get him out of the dumps, as my mom
referred to his periodic dips into a dark sun mood. I wasn't bringing
him around this time and then he told me why: My mom had gotten another allergic reaction, this time so sudden and frightening
that he was still shaking. She was alright now, all the swelling slowly
going down, but she had refused to go to the emergency room
because she didn't want anyone to see her like that. "I've never seen
anything as bad as that," my father said. "I didn't know lips could get
so swollen. She didn't look human. And then she threw up all night.
But we got pills from a doctor's assistant that saw me. Benadryl. She's
doing better. It's all going down." I questioned him about what she
had eaten; I covered up my fear with a method of approaching
causes. My father goes along with me on these coverups; he does it
for my sake. My mother-in-law once told me I was "overeducated"
and I think she was referring to the same thing: the retreat I would
make from experience to some file of knowledge, some recipe of
treatment. The "over" part, I think, came in because the dead files in
my head overwhelmed the experience and if that went on for long
my head would be like a car left in the sun too long with all the windows closed. She told me that when she herself was slowly dying of
leukemia. She was her in her eighties too, like my mom and dad.

"There's only two of us here by ourselves," my dad tells me,
"and when one gets sick, the other one can't handle things anymore. I didn't know what to do last night. I wasn't thinking clearly.
Or fast enough. Your mother . . ."

He let that trail off. Elaine, my wife, tells me afterward that my mother could easily have died of shock. She's eighty-three, hypertensive, and has an irregular heart beat. The phone call could have been the one that I dread, that I wait for, that I put out of my mind, that I try to face.

My mother has just gotten over a bad flu that not only knocked her out physically for weeks but dropped her into a depressed state that she is not used to. Religiously charismatic as she is, she interpreted the strangeness of her mood as the voice of God summoning her to the afterlife. I spent long telephone conversations trying to bring her back: You can't will your own ending, Mom, I told her. You can't give in to hopelessness and despair as long as you're alive. I wanted her to be upbeat for her sake but for my sake too. I didn't want to think that my mom who had given so much joy and enthusiasm to other people in her long life would go out of this world dejected, forlorn. I didn't want her to lose heart at the end of the journey because that wasn't the tone of her whole life. I wanted her to hold on to what people half her age needed "products and services" to simulate.

"I have to tell you what you would tell me if you were in my place," I tell my dad. "You're eighty-four . . ."

"Eighty-five," he corrects me. "I was eighty-five in November."

I keep track of his age by adding thirty years to my own but we are really thirty years and nine months apart.

"Time to move out of there and into one of those assisted-care hotels."

He tells me he had planned to do that later. Why does he at eighty-five think there will be a "later," especially when he and my mom have already outlived most of their friends and relatives. It used to be that every year brought the death of someone close to them but then it was every month and now there are just a few, mostly back on the east coast, holding on. The father figure in my father's life was his grandfather, who lived to be ninety-nine. My father's own father was killed in World War I in Austria, fighting for the Italian Army. He was given the silver medal for valor, his last words printed on the official papers presented to my grandmother, along with a pension from the Italian government that was paid to her every month for over sixty years. Twenty-seven and a half, my father told me was his father's age when he was killed. I have always thought then that in my father's sense of the time a life takes to make it's journey, one doesn't die young unless killed. Strangely my father wasn't sent into combat in World War II because he had skills in steamship transport and was needed on the New York piers. But his closest friend, in his twenties, was killed days after armistice when his jeep struck a land mine. Maybe that sealed it for my father: Death comes in war when you are young but if you get passed that then the longevity of his grandfather awaits you. Within this imaginative mapping of life's temporality my father could think that at eighty-five he wasn't yet ready to leave his retirement community in southern California, give up the two retirement properties he had there and all their "stuff," and move into an assisted-care residence.

But now he was shaken; he realized that my mother might have died because he hadn't done the right thing soon enough, that he wasn't up to doing what had to be done as a "provider" and a "caretaker." These are no longer roles that males, husbands and fathers, adopt, or ones they now shy away from because they are elitist, hierarchical, and we have moved gradually toward an equal sharing of responsibilities and power in a marriage. My father was born in upstate New York but from the age of three to seventeen he lived in Patti, Sicily, the place his father was only returning to for a visit but Chance drafted and killed him. It wasn't until my father was seventeen that there was money for him to return to the United States, with his older brother there to help him adapt to a language he didn't speak and customs that were far different from those in the small Sicilian village of Patti.

My father's journey to total Americaness, which he identified variously, depending upon what and who crossed his path, is the classic immigrant's journey. And I, like my brother and sister, were pointed in the same direction: toward all things American and away from all things European. I can only indicate how powerful this direction was and how well etched the mapping by saying I never stopped until I received a doctorate in English. Perhaps my father and his brothers always felt that this meant I was a specialist in the English language, that somehow my mastery of English (which neither of my father's two brothers ever succeeded in speaking without heavy accents) gave me the control over all things American that eluded them. The language unlocked the mysteries of a country whose customs, whose history, whose meanings and values, would always be alien to them. But I would be able to unlock those mysteries; I would be more than comfortable with what they were uncomfortable with. The sly comments that they could not fully understand but could sense were ridiculing, as well as the open insults that they endured because their reactions were

Side Trip

"foreign" in situations they could never anticipate, would never be made in my presence. I, indeed, could reverse the situation and shame the persecutor. Every son and every daughter of immigrants is sent forth as their champion, while they live and after they live, a champion to recoup the honor they have lost, redress the insults they have endured, to win on the battlefield they came to late and never could assimilate within their "foreign" personal, social, and cultural imaginaries. The world had already come to meaning within a Patti, Sicily way for my father and although his great natural intelligence revised and amended that originary mapping, it has always been an abiding reservoir, a dominating way of hooking up with the world for him.

When he first hears of my youngest daughter Brenda's desire to have dual citizenship, he immediately responds to the irony: So long a journey to success in this country that he has made and that his children, dispersed in widely separate parts of the country, have passed on to his grandchildren, two of whom are already college graduates. And now a desire to return to the "old country." I myself am confused. Brenda asks me if I had ever thought of obtaining dual citizenship and I confess that the thought never entered my mind. More than that, I tell her, all the thoughts I did have defended themselves against thinking of doing something like that. "Going back" to the immigrant's son is a sort of retrogression, an admitted defeat, a collapse backward to what we have been trying to distance ourselves from. Patti was our "primitive" beginnings, not the place where we were heading back to all along. I have never felt like Odysseus, that I was fighting my way back home. At the same time, since leaving my birth place, Brooklyn, in 1968, and wandering around the entire United States, living an adjunct academic life everywhere, the idea of what "home" is to me has become more and more puzzling, disturbing. "Where's your home?" people ask me in the South. "The old country?" a young Black girl in West Virginia asks me. "Where are you originally from?" "You going back home for Christmas?" "Your family still in New York?" "I bet you'd like to get closer to home?"

My oldest daughter, Amelia, leaves home as soon as she graduates and takes up life in Tucson. She goes there with only the hope of finding a job, but she does. And she is happy. About leaving "home," the town in Michigan we bring her to when she is ten, after she has lived in five other states, she shows no remorse. The place is not "home," just a place we wound up. She has never been able to abide the sunless days here. The Southwest, on the other hand, has called

Side Trip

to her ever since her first archaeological summer work. She first traveled to Europe by herself when she was nineteen and, as a student with a double major in studio art and in archaeology, I think she found there a feast for the eye and surroundings which evoked what has been called, in regard to the Romantics, the "antiquarian spirit." Her American cultural lifeworld, a bricolage of having been moved all around the country and jerked in and out of schools, could now be contrasted with her first glimpse of Europe. The next year both she and her sister traveled with me on my "Is This a Postmodern World?" program, railing across Europe from Amsterdam to Naples. They were both developing an émigré attitude, the reverse of my father's immigrant one. And now, through them, I was moving from that son of an immigrant mentality that had brought me time and time again into a clash with "mainstream" cultural values and meanings and those of my Italian-American neighborhood. My failure to ever find a place where that conflict could be reconciled, a place where I didn't have to suppress and repress my "foreignness" in the name of a privileged yet nebulous American Identity, had made a nomad out of me. And I passed that on to my daughters. They were not haunted by where they had begun, or on a journey "back home." It seemed to be that they were seeking from the outside what was most compatible with what was on the inside, just as those nomadic people so fascinating to Bruce Chatwin moved from summer digs to winter digs—for the weather, for the grass, for the beauty, for the quality of the sleep, the incentives to dream, the inspiration to create.

The precedent for the nomadic life had, as I say, already been established for Amelia: She doesn't come from that Italian-American neighborhood in Brooklyn. She was born in New Hampshire, in a hospital in Concord where the nurse who asked my wife what name she had picked for Amelia, wrote Amelia Natoli down and then said "You certainly have enough vowels in there." Years later, Mario Cuomo, when asked whether he thought he had shot at the presidency, responds that for most of the country he was afraid he just had too many vowels in his name. Call it too much European connection, or just too "foreign." A man whose name I cannot recall but who was prominent in the Southern Appalachian Leadership Conference told me in a small café in Bluefield, West Virginia, that if I had been living down in Oxley Hollow before Kennedy was president, I might just have been too "foreign" for folks down there. Instead of being welcomed I might have been rousted. And we were welcomed down there; I don't think any one in those hills knew just how different we were. They hadn't a clue.

I have taken America's '90s assault on immigrants in this country personally. Market values do not value diversity because unwelcome differences come with that diversity and because tax money has to be spent in public education, unemployment compensation, emergency medical services, welfare—on a social "safety net" that a conservative ideology wants to take apart. The whole argument that diversity and its accompanying differences strengthen a social order by forcing it to meet new challenges and reorganize itself on a higher level has no force from a market perspective. It is not the social order that needs to expand so as to avoid redundancy and entropy but the market itself. The social order need only maintain stability through redundancy, through the maintenance of a clearly marked identity. Difference is only an assault upon that identity and therefore upon that stability that the market needs in order to maximize profits to shareholders. The argument that diversity and difference, what immigrants offer, revitalizes our culture, expands, for instance, what I call the "cultural imaginary," the options and possibilities of living life under other conditions, putting into play different values and meanings, also has no force from a market perspective. In fact, the whole concept of a cultural ferment being a necessary antagonist to the complacency of a social order is an unhealthy concept marketwise. What other purpose does this cultural turmoil serve, this constant battle of narratives of truth, but to counter market values and meanings, the imperialism of such values and meanings, with other, forgotten, silenced, marginal, denied, dismissed, left-out values and meanings?

If immigrants are liable to bring other cultural imaginaries into this country, then they are liable to upset a country now trying to impose only one cultural imaginary, the one in which we all see ourselves at war with each other, my self-interest here against yours, all of us trying to amass a private fortune and then retreat behind a gated community so that the "losers" can't follow us. It may very well be that immigrants now already possess this market imaginary, that immigrants have always come to America to get rich, that only budding materialists, anxious entrepreneurs ever come here. However, since market imperialism is so unencompassing, so stunted, so reductive and limited, there is so much that human, everyday life connects itself to that is "not costed in" by the market, that even the introduction of those who already make other than market connections with the world is sufficient to shake market imperialism. We in this country are progressively losing hold of anything and everything that is not "bottom line"; we are educating the young into a very limited apprehension of themselves and the world. We desperately need the influx of difference.

But from difference's side of the street, where it winds up, on the margin, on the periphery, adjunct status, what future is there in living always "as if different"? My grandfather began the voyage here, and my father and myself have fulfilled its promise, but now I think my daughters will return.

I see now that I had signals all along the way, right from the beginning, if you will. My father, for instance, was born in Olive, New York, a town now extinct. His mother and father had bought a house there but upon return my father found neither the town nor the house. His American beginnings had vanished. For one who has been so fascinated by poststructuralism, I was strangely unaware of my own name as a signifier. Upon return from Sicily the first time, Brenda said to me that our cousin Paolo had said the name pointed to peasant roots: Nato li, from *natus,* to be born, and *li,* there. She said Paolo pointed when he said this "born there." I was, in fact, born and raised in Brooklyn, moved to Albany for my doctoral study, then to Massachusetts, then to New Hampshire for my first teaching gig, then back to Albany, then back to Brooklyn, then on to West Virginia, then to North Carolina, then to California, then to Michigan. We stayed in Michigan only because our daughters had reached the "we have friends and we don't want to move stage." I never stayed in the "heartland" because it was the place I had always been journeying toward, the adopted "home" where my heart was. For me this is a place where all my Italian-American Bensonhurst past, and all the whole European flavor of that neighborhood and the qualities of my family life, don't connect. It's all a disconnect, all useless; in a xenophobic "heartland" such different connections give you no welcome. Stranger in a strange land. I get mail addressed to "Jonah Tolley," what is heard when I say "Joe Natoli" on the phone. It is more than dispiriting to think that I must be feeling the same sense of alienation that my seventeen-year-old father must have felt. It drove him toward bridging the gap, toward becoming what held him off.

For the last few years I have been thinking about where we will retire. The word *retire* also prompts the same response from me: "From what?" A boxer retires from the ring, a race horse from racing, a bank teller from the bank, a salesman from sales, a hairdresser from hair, an entrepreneur from the "business," a hooker from the "life," a preacher from preaching, an actor from acting—

but how does an "adjunct" retire? I mean someone like me who has had a long series of temporary gigs, from teaching, librarying, farming, editing, selling, cooking, landscaping—and all that time was looking for a place to start. In a career that has no beginning, there is no retiring. And yet I have been looking for a place from which to begin, and from there I will be on that lifelong journey to arrival. And now I know that I was "born there"—in the name, in the word, in what I am writing, as well, I think, as the place my grandfather Pietro left at the beginning of the century, traveling to a future where he was told the streets were "paved with gold," the land of opportunity for a man just "born there," a man locked into the place and status of his ancestors in a society in which most men and women are the hands to do the work that is "there" and a privileged few reap the harvest of those hands.

The globe has moved; the American middle class, which served as a comfortable place to aspire to and reach in the mind of a Sicilian laborer like my grandfather Pietro, is fast disappearing in this country, replaced by a working marriage, where both mother and father work eighty hours a week in order to have a life previously made possible by the wages of one, working forty hours a week. We may continue to call that middle class because these folks have two cars, and payments, and a house, with a mortgage, and all the new electronic gadgets that the market promotes as "needs." But it is hard to see a real difference between the hard work and poor pay that Pietro immigrated from and the multiple Mac jobs, the endless hours sitting at a keyboard looking at a monitor emitting perhaps harmful radiation, the humiliations of making "cold calls" to strangers who are in the same financial straits you are in trying to coax them into purchasing something they "need," the innumerable menial jobs serving the "winners" that you can have and keep if you look clean, follow instructions, and don't talk back.

What has clearly happened in America is that we now have a whole generation rising to majority that identifies their lot with freedom of choice, with the American Dream, with social mobility, with entrepreneurial necessity, with inevitable progress, with, in short, a rising, aspiring middle class. If the Dow Jones at this moment breaks 8000, something significant only to shareholders— a minuscule percentage of the population—and only benefitting everyone else from a market perspective, it is now misinterpreted as a sign of the felicities of middle-class life, of the continued dominance of America. Misleading and false signs of well-being are everywhere: The possession of a CD player, a VCR, a four-wheel-drive sports van, timeshare, a lawn to be serviced, season tickets to one's favorite sport, buying through catalogs, credit cards coming in the mail, the freedom to ignore the carnival of a presidential campaign, or mock the commercialism of the media, or boast about the superiority of our global-market capitalism and the sacredness of our democracy, and so on, are taken to mean that here there is power, freedom, success; here there is life being lived on the most civilized and expansive human terms possible. We're "fully loaded" with choices. Who's better than us?

A disquieting counter to this: In an essay titled "Was Democracy Just a Moment?" Robert D. Kaplan asks: "Is it not conceivable that corporations will, like the rulers of both Sparta and Athens, project power to the advantage of the well-off while satisfying the twenty-first century servile populace with the equivalent of Bread and Circuses?" (*Atlantic Monthly* Dec. 1997, 80). Kaplan describes democracies as existing "within a thin band of social and economic conditions, which include flexible hierarchies that allow people to move up and down the ladder. Instead of clear-cut separations between classes there are many gray shades, with most people bunched in the middle." Do clear-cut separations exist at this moment? Here is Michael Walzer in *The New Republic* (Feb. 2, 1998, 9):

> We are awash in statistical studies of income inequality, but even the best of them under-estimate what is happening in this country. Last month, the Center on Budget and Policy Priorities, a Washington-based research group, released state-by-state comparisons of family income, showing what seem to me astonishing disparities between the wealthiest and poorest fifths of American families—20 to one in the state of New York, almost 30 to one in the District of Columbia. And yet, since the center used Census figures, which do not record incomes above $100,000 or pay attention to capital gains, the actual disparities are even larger.

We are already, in the last decade of the twentieth century, not democratic but merely told that we are, and all the imagery of media and government, imagery more and more dominated by corporations, is designed to convince us that we are as well as keep us placated. It is not just a matter of Bread and Circuses, of being titillated and entertained, being more than happy to have sports the glue of community life. We are living within the mythologies producing this imagery and produced by them, seduced into repressions, misidentifications, "machine" dreams, "show me the money" fantasies, while at the same time, losing track of human values that market values excludes. "We must be wary of market *ideology*," James B. Rule writes in *Dissent* (winter 1998, 35), "as a Trojan horse for all sorts of schemes that are ultimately subversive of humane values." The numbers of the Dow, like the things bought and displayed in the home, conceal the erosion of what has been called, for market purposes, "quality" time. "It used to be that the middle class," James Atlas writes in *The New Yorker* (Feb. 2, 1998, 36), "could take for granted certain basic things in this life: light, space, quiet. Now those things are considered perks." Everything that the market places no price tag on and does not promote has fallen into invisibility, inconsequence, replaced by the false signs of prosperity and well-being. No one can miss or mourn or hope to redeem by whatever means necessary what they no longer can see, or even conceive.

I understand that this scenario does not simply apply to America, that the play of the global market is urging a nationalist Europe toward a European Union that can prosper as a global "player" and not be subsumed and consumed by the Asian Rim or the Americas. The gulf between rulers and ruled in the ancient world had much to do with "literacy," but our literacy now is "computer literacy," technological expertise, a fast-changing literacy dependent upon costly, sophistical technological innovation. "Analogous gulfs between rulers and ruled may soon emerge," Kaplan writes, in comparing the ancient world and our own, "not only because of differing abilities to process information and to master technology but also because of globalization itself. Already, barely literate Mexicans on the U.S. border, working in dangerous, Dickensian conditions to produce our VCRs, jeans, and toasters, earn less than 50 cents an hour, with no rights or benefits. Is that Western democracy or ancient Greek-style oligarchy?" (80). And that force of free-market globalization propels the oligarchic elite elsewhere as well as here. The processes of seduction, of mesmerization, repression, and exploitation are transnational processes.

Immigrating and emigrating are meaningless acts here. Our technological literacy has honed in on global financing, on global profit making, where it is not the presence of an individual who can read and think that makes the system work but rather an individual with capital and computer. Intelligence is harvested through "networking," through "independent contractors and contracting." Human intelligence is assigned, given "work for pay"; a meritocracy

Side Trip

of symbolic analysts reap possessions and gives itself over wholly to protecting those possessions. Whether or not this symbolic analyst class ever rises to power within the capital and computer financial network is undecidable in the present; whether this mobility, if possible, serves democracy is highly questionable. Transnational corporations network within and through the ever-expanding network of computerized telecommunications. The only journey here is through electronic pathways, neither linear nor cyclical, nor human.

What is an individual journeying through one lifetime to do? I have here related what I think. But what to do? If the effects are global, why journey? Or is the necessity for us to journey, to immigrate and emigrate, more essential than for capital or information to flow, more essential than the dissemination of an industry's "message," or a politician's?

Cul-de-Sac: Seductions and the Wellsprings of Loneliness

> *I was born here and I'll die here, against my will*
> *I know it looks like I'm movin' but I'm standin' still*
> *Every nerve in my body is so naked and numb*
> *I can't even remember what it was I came here to get away*
> *from*
> *Don't even hear the murmur of a prayer*
> *It's not dark yet, but it's getting there*
> —Bob Dylan, "Not Dark Yet"

I'm beginning to feel more and more like a lonely traveler in America. Where does the feeling come from? Maybe it's just a continuation of having reached (believe me, I wasn't reaching for it) fifty-five this summer; I've been calling it my "Double Nickel" state of mind.

Last night, November 3rd, 1998, I went to Ann Arbor for a "Reading and Reception." I was going to read from my book *Speeding to the Millennium*. For the past couple of days I had been rehearsing—reading various parts and finally deciding on what I was going to read and then reading those parts out loud, pretending I had an audience. We had just pushed the clock back a couple of weeks before so although it was 6 P.M. the darkness of 7 P.M. was the reality. Three days into November but it was already classic November weather: a kind of Michigan cold, filled with dampness that goes right through you. It was worse in Ann Arbor, almost the feel of Manhattan in the winter when the tall buildings block off whatever sunlight there may be and pavement absorbs no heat at all. Dave was thinking of coming along but discovered he had business in Kalamazoo.

I took the ride by myself and when I got there, there were numerous copies of my book for me to sign and to be sold and about sixty folding chairs set up and facing a podium where one copy of the book was perched for all to see. I was supposed to begin speaking at 8 P.M. but by 8:20 there was no one there. The bookstore guy who had arranged the thing, Paul, had just been on the job a couple of months and he kept looking at his watch. We finally sat down in the "audience" section and talked about the book. In a half hour two other people joined us, Steve, who told us later when we were eating the cheese and bread and drinking the wine that had been laid out for the "audience," that he "was between jobs and not able to buy a copy of the book. Jeff, the other guy, admitted he didn't know who was speaking that night but always came by because he didn't have anything else to do on Tuesday nights. Steve had the kind of look I envisioned when I wrote a piece in *Speeding* called "Ghosts with Résumés." And from the comments he made as we chatted about this and that, he was obviously some kind of sci-entist. He clearly had a résumé but he had the haunted look of a guy with a résumé and no place to go with it. Jeff spoke with a heavy accent, so heavy that when he said his name I heard "Jeff" but I know that wasn't it. He was dark, balding, portly, nicely dressed with a scarf—November 3rd and already a scarf!

Paul read a very flattering introduction which he had written after reading the book on a couple of his lunch breaks. I took the introduction with me. After all, it was meant to be read up there at the podium to a seated audience of about sixty. It was part of my fifteen seconds in a Midwestern bookstore limelight. Very pathetic but you can see how the lonely traveler in America mood is aug-menting. Paul then asked me a couple of questions and I filled in the spaces. And the time. After all, I had come all this way. Steve the scientist was mostly unresponsive; I don't think he was in a recep-tive frame. A couple or three times a faint smile appeared and then vanished. His enthusiasm came out when Paul said "Well, let's open the wine and eat some of this food!" I think Steve was hungry. For the food, not for what I had to say. Even Paul's flattering introduc-tion hadn't whetted Steve's appetite for postmodern thought. He was busy elsewhere. Okay. Steven is the loneliest traveler in Amer-ica. But I'm second. "Jeff" talked a little bit more after a few glasses of wine. He knew old movies. "Did you ever see *This Gun for Hire?*" He asked me. "Yeah. Alan Ladd's first screen role," I replied. "Well, his first major screen role," Jeff corrected me. "Do you know the name of the character he played?" I confessed I didn't. "Bill Gates," he said. I had been talking about the antitrust case against Gates. "Maybe, in your postmodern view," Jeff said, "The real Bill Gates saw that movie when he was a kid and adopted a story of cold ruthlessness, of gunning for everyone who gets in his way. The fierce entrepreneur as a gunster. Kill or be killed. The war of all against all." Okay, Jeff knew more about the movies than I did and he was an agile concocter of quirky cultural connectedness.

About 9:30, we four shook hands, I waved goodbye to two bookstore clerks who had joined us in eating the cheese and drinking the wine, and I went out into an even colder, darker Ann Arbor night and took the long highway ride home. There wasn't much traffic but I continued to use my changing lanes signals although no one else did. Cars going 85 and 90 will pass you and cut back in front of you without signaling and barely a car length away. I continue to drive on the highway the way I learned driving the New York State Thruway some thirty years before. I thought signaling lane changes, not driving closer than several car lengths away, not driving at high speed in the left lane bumper to bumper, not passing on the right, not running high beams into coming traffic, and so on, were part of a civil code of highway driving. Nobody is in that reality frame here in Michigan. I am driving on Michigan space but in the time frame of thirty years ago and someplace else.

Strangely, cars pass me in close herds, like speeding packs of chase dogs at my heels, their lights reflected in my side and rear mirrors and blinding me. After they've passed me at 85 mph as if I were standing still, I am once again left solitary, the highway is deserted except for me. And then in a certain amount of time, another angry pack is at my heels. They are all cutting in and out, jockeying for the open space, for a front position where they can have nothing but open highway before them. But as they are all doing this, each accelerating past the other in his or her turn, none succeed in freeing themselves of the pack. They go off into the distance and disappear, still accelerating, jockeying back and forth, taking that particular time/space zone that they are in with them. They take their speeding, competitive, hyperaccelerated reality with them. I think of them like fierce asteroids caught in some orbital interplay for all eternity. While all around them is empty, silent space. If only they could break free and be alone, be in their own time, at their own speed for once.

Back here in my time/space zone I am alone. The moon, which was full and looming on the horizon when I left, is now no longer visible. All I hear is the sound of this 1986 Nissan Sentra four-cycle engine churning. Maybe if I had a 1998 car I could live at 1998 speeds. The way I wrote about America speeding to the millennium is a way, I see now, that America is speeding within, like the fierce

Cul-de-Sac

swarm of speeding cars that overtake me at erratic intervals. The way I am driving doesn't reach, doesn't connect with the way they are driving, and I think it has all to do with their equation of their self-created highway world with reality as it is. I am observing how we press the pedal to the metal ourselves and then assume what ensues is what there is. I am, this night, feeling lonely in that knowledge. This is my private fifteen seconds in the limelight of my own self-appreciation. I don't think you ever break out of that; even when you write about it in a self-deprecating way, you are basking in the limelight of self-awareness manifested in self-deprecating ways.

But it's not this self-constructed reality trap I want to deal with—mainly because I don't know how to deal with it. I think I know something of the distance between me and the highway speedsters. Look at the reality they are bearing with them and that is bearing them down the road: While I am hearing my engine, they are listening to a CD through maybe four speakers. Cars in the '90s run silently; you can hear your music. The sounds of outside are muted and even silenced. You travel within a comfortable womb in which you have little sense of being at high speeds; the more expensive the vehicle, the more you are self-contained and cut off from the highway you are on, the landscape you are in, the world going on not being played on your CD. Your car is "fully loaded." It's one of the dreams of almost every American, and the Cool Beans generation is no exception.

"Fully loaded" has a magical sound. It's what you've come for. You get that fully-loaded car and then you take to the highways. High speeds, soundproof interior, your own music, a Coke or a hot coffee in the beverage rack, and the gratification that comes when your eyes wander across the multicolored, hi-tech dashboard. Travel has been commodified is what any self-respecting leftist would say. And since you are not the only one produced within this market-driven reality, you will have companions alongside you on the highway. You will, in fact, be a part of that speeding cluster, anxious to speed past everyone, and winding up in that endless game of speeding past and being sped past. Until you reach your destination, your journey's end. And at that point, when St. Peter, now working for CNN, asks you to describe that journey, you say, "You've got to get in that arena and compete; you've got to see that nobody is going to do it for you but yourself. That you're alone on a speeding highway and nobody is going to get you where you want to go but yourself. You see losers on the side of the road all the time. They've given up. Or what they want is what you've got and you've got to protect what you've got. Maybe the government wants to take it away from you and give it to them. So you learn to protect and guard what you've got. My life has been fully loaded and I'm the one who's loaded it. We can all do the same thing and not blame society for our failures. Society doesn't make or break us. I'm responsible for my own life and the other guy is responsible for his."

And then the commercial: This has all been brought to you by your global market at work on the minds and hearts of everyone. Pushing products has an attendant politics and it's this: Make a consumer out of everyone, convert rights and responsibilities of citizens to rights and responsibilities of shareholders, seduce the disenfranchised with Bread and Circuses, now appearing as "fully-loaded technology and channel and web surfing," demonize all possible opposition, including the federal government, the underclass, the coming "slacker" generation, feminists, politicians of "identity," multiculturalists and postmodernists, and all manner of liberals and socialists who question global-market imperialism, and, lastly, never step back and observe how your own observations are socially and culturally constructed, which in the '90s means never look for the Wizard of Market Values hiding behind the curtain pulling the levers controlling your life.

If we are in an America in which how we know America and ourselves as Americans are already shaped by this market way of knowing, how do we journey away from this? How does that angry swarm of cars on the highway break out of their time/space mental zone and journey in a different way? If the problem is not just a Sherlock-Holmes type, three-pipe problem laid out on the table before us and awaiting our analysis and critical reasoning faculties, but a perceptual problem, what do we do? By perceptual I mean that if we already perceive our interaction with the world as throwing before us "a three-pipe problem laid out on the table" then the game, if you will, is over. The outcome is already laid out in the approach; what we wind up with is only what the prescription of our perceptions enabled us to wind up with at the outset.

Cul-de-Sac

No Sign of Loss on the Horizon

November 1998

A film entitled *Meet Joe Black* is previewed at the Saturday showing of *What Dreams May Come*. I've seen the preview before and recognized the film as a remake of *Death Takes a Holiday*, an eerie film with Frederic March playing the part of Death. Taking a holiday. He's taking a holiday from his death duties. In the preview, Death is Brad Pitt in a tuxedo; he's got a sort of Southern Cal look to him. In response to the question "Death comes in a suit?" he says, "This is just the suit the body I took had on." In the original movie, Death falls in love. The scene we all imagine: When death announces its love—is part of the preview. And why not? It's a marvelous clash; it's got built-in power and fascination. We don't know how to put Death and Love together. The one cancels the other. But which one? Surely, Death. Death puts an end to love. Or does it? I mean it doesn't in Hollywood because it doesn't in American culture.

The preview is an unplanned segue into *What Dreams May Come*, a film all about love and death.

Death seems to make all the moves in this film. First, the children die in a car crash. Then the father and husband, Robin Williams, is killed in another car accident. He winds up in his own particular version of Heaven—life on a canvas his wife once painted, the world they were to retire to—if they managed to grow old together. But they don't. And though death is finished with Williams, it still reaches him through the suicide of his wife, Annie. She can't join him in this picture-perfect paradise but has to remain in the hell her own mind has created. No suicide so lost in his or her own delusions has ever broken free and ascended from hell to heaven. But Annie and Robin are soul mates; there is a bond between them that even the angels in heaven do not understand. Heaven has never seen the force of such love—as this film would have it, *pace* St. Anselm and his view of heavenly omnipotence. It is the force of that Love which will trump Death and bring Annie to paradise, to a timeless existence in the retirementscape of their earthly dreams.

Computer-generated graphics puts this heavenscape on the screen; the film could not have been done any time before our computer revolution. Without the computer revolution we would have had to put yet another character recently dead—*Here Comes Mr. Jordan* and it's remake *Heaven Can Wait, A Guy Named Joe,* with Spencer Tracy as your ghostly copilot—among the cloud machine's clouds. The colorless clouds. What dreams may come in 1998 come because we now have the technical knowhow to screen dreams. Or at least we think we do. How do we represent what we imagine? Is this purely a technical matter? We all can visualize what heaven and hell are but we just don't have the technical means to do so. Is this true? Or, do we visualize, do we imagine only within the stories and depictions of what our imagined worlds look like, fanciful as they may be? How we imagine anything is already out there to be seen. Or read about. For instance, the 1998 hi-tech version of hell in *What Dreams May Come* comes mostly out of the Hieronymous Bosch hell tryptic (that hangs over the suicide-prone Annie's bed), Homer, Dante's *Purgatorio*, and the Surrealists. Where else would they come from in our Western culture? And Robin Williams's heavenscape doesn't go anyplace that Walt Disney Productions hadn't already gone.

This point confounds the point the movie makes in regard to what awaits us after death. The movie wants us to believe that heaven and hell aren't extrapolations of Disney, Madison Avenue, and cable TV. Rather, they are opportunities to imagine beyond earthbound constraints. What the imagination conceives is necessarily true—an observation of William Blake's, a man you might say who tried to depict both poetically and pictorially what imagination could conceive when free of the limitations of what he called "single vision." Single vision is looking at the world with the eye and not through the eye, by which Blake means it is a physical, earth-bound, thing-bound viewing of the world. We must see *through* the physical in order to view, in Blake's view, what is *really* there. This is what Cuba Gooding, Jr., Robin Williams's guiding angel, urges Williams to do. Being in heaven is being given the opportunity to imagine your heaven; being in hell is being denied that opportunity and instead being caught within the nightmares of Blake's single vision, lost in bad Karma, upholding only "bad faith," taking the seductions of this world into the next.

After death comes the real journey of imagination, of being free of earthbound stories of what it is and what is conceivable and not conceivable. It is a total departure from a way of seeing and being that was anchored to the world and to the body. What our cultures narrate and what our societies bring to order are not narrated in those ways after

death nor is anything ordered in those ways after death. And yet, paradoxically, when we imagine this journey—as it is imagined in this film—
we do nothing more than computer upgrade the "classic" cultural narratives and rescreen the "classic" hierarchies of worldly order. We
inevitably see heaven and hell and our lives after death with the eye and
not through it; we see culturally, socially, and personally. The greatness
of Blake's art, poetry and pictorial, lies in his dissent and anger at this
state of affairs and his attempt to break the boundaries of his own being-
in-the-world through the force of his imagination. What we get is a lifelong record of a courageous and energetic struggle to reach beyond an
imagination mired in the world to an imagination free of that world.
And the entire effort is made from this side, from our side, from the
world's side. He never escapes nor can he escape his imagining-in-the-
world. But that endeavor itself becomes a classic cultural narrative. And
it shows up here in this state-of-the-art display of computer hijinks.

   As much as Blake sought to escape the eighteenth century, he yet
remains in that century, establishing for us a more incisive awareness of
that century's "order of things" and doing so by contesting that order
with every fiber of his being. Does he do what Cuba Gooding, Jr.
advises? Does he break the boundaries of what is and configure what
could be? Does he take a finger, as Gooding does, and draw the shape
of a window and then punch it through and reveal a new and previously
unknown and unnarrated world? Blake doesn't. He's at his best when he
shows us the lopsidedness of what is. And Gooding doesn't either. The
view we get through the new window is right out of Disney Studios. It's
Disney's pastoral world where bright times dawn and creatures frolic.
Until things grow dark. Death comes for Bambi's mother. It's *The Wizard of Oz* at the moment it is transformed into color. If it's like Oz, it's
not like death because you can always click your heels and go home.

   So what exactly is the journey we take after death? I mean as Gooding tells Williams it is. There is no judgment of good and evil he tells
Williams. There's no high moral drama being played out; no scales are
being weighed; no authority separating the chaff from the kernel; no
recriminations, no censuring, no vindictiveness, no spite; no judgments.
God is not taking his pound of flesh, extracting his due. There is in fact
nothing personal about this life after death; Gooding doesn't know for
sure but he thinks God is into his own imaginescape. His only connection with life after death is making it possible for those who have died
to live forever in their own imaginescapes. This appears to be a very '90s
afterlife.

   And why wouldn't it be? The film has been done in the '90s. Why
should we expect the film depiction of the afterlife to sever itself from

life now, here in the '90s? In some ways, this is a global-market freeplay life after death where no absolutes exist except the absolute to pursue your own imaginings. But as those imaginings cannot escape the priorities of the culture, heaven and hell turn out to be places where you can continue to "reality make" as usual. Only now, since you've died to reality, you are "heaven making." Or, "hell making." If there is no heaven or hell beyond what we imagine, and we always imagine within the constraints of culture and society, then what can heaven and hell amount to but an eternal playing out of what we already are and where we've already been? Williams imagines heaven as the place in the painting his wife did of their retirement world, a world rooted in the Swiss Alps and lakes where they first met. Annie's world, on the other hand, turned dark; despair and hopelessness filled her vision. And this is where she winds up in her hell.

So our past lives are not witness to our afterlife; we weren't earning or losing heaven by our actions. When we die we get a chance to pursue what we imagine to be our self-interest. And that self-interest has already been imagined in life. Only most of us never get a chance to see it enacted. Now in heaven we all get what we imagine to be our just desserts. The only folks who don't are those who give up the will to live, which is essentially their interest in their own self-interest. Self-interest is first of all interested in preserving the self. And in aggrandizing whatever interests the self. We have been living in a world in which self-interest is the bedrock of being. Suicide not only cancels self and therefore self-interest but it merits an eternal life in hell.

The sin one is guilty of is giving up any interest in imagining a heaven that is in line with one's interests. Annie is a loser because she has lost the desire and the will to project her desire upon the world, upon not only life but afterlife. Williams gains his heavenscape by choosing to pursue his own self-interest and live rather than cut his wrists after his children die in an auto accident. But Annie cannot assert enough self-interest to stay alive. Only Williams's own will to live and to assert his interests in living above all else coax Annie back from her death-in-life state. And he does this twice: Once when they are both alive and she is in a psychiatric hospital and once when they are both dead and he visits her in her hell to bring her back.

Pardon me, but I don't see anything but market conservatism in all this; nothing more than "Show *Me* the Money!" extended into the afterlife. Maybe Robin Williams's imagination extends to life in a painting, a timeless sojourn in the place he first fell in love. But I'm sure he's surrounded by self-created heavenscapes pulled right from episodes of the "Lives of the Rich and Famous," heavenscapes pulled from full-page advertisements in *Fortune, Cosmopolitan, Country Homes, Glamour, GQ, Esquire*, centerfolds from *Playboy* and *Playgirl*. Maybe JFK has set up a dreamscape with Marilyn Monroe; Sinatra is forever Chairman of the Board of his rat pack; John D. Rockefeller has everything in his heaven-scape he had on earth *plus* a good stomach; Alexander the Great is getting a chance to enjoy his conquests; Nixon is beating the Watergate rap; Teddy Kennedy is plunging into the Chappaquidick creek and saving his secre-tary's life; Abraham Lincoln is reconstructing the South the way he wanted to; John Garfield can have all the sex he wants without worrying about a heart attack; Nicole Brown Simpson is getting her revenge on O.J.; Jimmy Carter is having sex with all the women he's had sex with in his head; and William Blake is living in the dreamscape he always imagined.

My point is that if we are not held to someone else's account but merely left to fantasize our own heavens, we merely extend our present reality frames into eternity. And of course our present favored way of cul-turally shaping reality naturally produces heaven and hell in this way. We want to confirm in the afterlife the values we hold in the present: that we will our destinies, but that will and those destinies have no Nietzshean force or scope. Heaven is the place where we endlessly gaze upon our own image and continue to be what we behold; we never break the spell. Nor do we want to because we cannot imagine anything more heavenly than endlessly pursuing our own self-interests, endlessly maximizing our prof-its, endlessly winning and endlessly consuming the fruits of our winning. And to drive the point home that there is no difference between pursuing self-interest in life and pursuing it in the afterlife, Robin Williams and the Annie he brings back from hell decide to be reincarnated. They once again enter the arena of life knowing that pursuing desires there is like pursuing desires in heaven. Their heaven has given them no sense of grand fulfill-ment, of glorying in the sight of God, of shuffling off the mortal coil, of finding that peace to which they had always yearned, of finally coming home. Heaven is a place where self-interest imagines only within the con-text of self-interest; those who cannot imagine but are caught within a delusion they accept as a fixed reality are in hell. Life offers the same pos-sibilities: of pursuing self-interest but also the possibility of denying one's own interests. Williams and Annie decide to return to life clearly because they do not fear delusion. They will pursue their self-interests and then return to heaven to continue pursuing them. All of a sudden what we've got here is heaven already. It's just that some people don't know it. They don't know how to imagine the world in their own interests.

What a self-satisfying vision of heaven and hell! The wealthy have nothing to fear if there is a life after death; it will not be one of judgment and damnation but merely business as usual. And who better able to pursue self-interest and imagine a wonderful heavenscape for themselves than the rich? Heaven was made for entrepreneurs. And just think of it—no matter how much you sacrifice others in the pursuit of your self-interest, you won't be sacrificed after death. Only the non-entrepreneurial, those who don't "think big" or dream of having it all, or wield self-interest like a virtue, need fear the afterlife. They will enter depressed, or angry, or in despair, or "disaffected," or beaten down to their very soul and thus will earn only what they imagine—hell.

As a kind of thought experiment we could configure the afterlife of this film in line with our own earthly pursuits of self-interests. Instead of, for instance, separating the dreamscapes of Israeli and Palestinian, Belfast and Dublin, or Serb and Albanian, or Tibetan and Chinese, or Clinton and Newt, let's put them all in the same heaven. Or hell. Let their desires run into each other; let their self-interests collide. Heaven would soon turn to . . . our own world.

No, the heavenly nature of heaven as conceived in this film is that you can imagine your own desires into reality and not have them bump into anyone else's. In other words, heaven is a hangout for solipsists. People who imagine that they are imagining everyone's existence but their own. They are for real. Once the Annie you imagine is free to be what she herself imagines herself as, you are going to inevitably get conflict, tension, trouble in paradise. In the Christian story, such conflict is erased in Heaven by a miraculous transformation of mortal imperfections into immortal perfections. You become, as St. Paul says, a "spiritual body," not the old body and mind of desire and self-interest, of endless yearning and ceaseless competitiveness, not a tortured soul riddled by the Seven Deadly Sins. Not any of that old mortality but a new, risen body, at once of spirit and flesh.

The entire Middle Ages saw this sort of transformation into something different and brand new as a relief, something to look forward to, a change for the better, a release from the endless woes that all flesh is heir to, a glad shaking off of the mortal coil, a joyful springing into a "glad day," a "new morning" of rebirth. A minute proportion of the population would like to have kept the toys they already had, the wealth and power they already enjoyed. They only hoped that the afterlife would allow them to keep their "winnings." It was, after all, God's will that set them above the multitude in worldly possessions. Surely in the afterlife God would not rescind his special blessing on them lest he subvert his own order of things. And yet what had the New Testament to say about needles, camels, and the rich?

I don't believe the wealthy and powerful today believe that they are wealthy and powerful because God has deigned it so. They all, each and every one, did it "their way." They faced the odds, made their choices, made their moves, forged ahead and won. If Chance was involved it was always something not like a wind at their back but something to be overcome, another challenge, like a competitor, which they vanquished. And they can go on winning in the afterlife if given a chance, if the playing field remains level. Or, better yet, if they can bring their wealth and power with them. Maybe if all you have to do is imagine that you have that wealth and power, you will have it. And thus the afterlife is imagined now in the '90s in this way: Things for us can continue Bullish if we imagine they are. And there won't be any constraints on our imaginings, or regulations on our desires, or conflicts we cannot resolve by the supremacy of our own imaginations. Heaven is a place were the Dow Jones is always rising because we wish it so.

I'm not surprised that we would construe life after death as business as usual, as an eternal advance of the Dow Jones. Heaven is a place where all life is Bullish; self-corrections are here truly self-corrections. We know the world in a thoroughly market way and there is no reason why we won't produce an afterworld in the same way. But why the interest in death coming for us now, at this moment, less than a year and a half before the new millennium? I suppose the answer lies in that: The approaching millennium brings us to end of the world scenarios. Eschatological films make the scene. Death is a guy named Joe Black and he's coming for us but, wait, he wants to take a holiday from the usual round. He wants to taste and sample our mortality. But I haven't met Joe Black at this point; the film hasn't been released. Could my own interest in death and what life may come after death, my own probing of the shallowness of what dreams do come of that afterlife, have their origin in my mother's recent telephone conversations, always settling back to one point—her feeling that she is preparing "to go home"?

"I tell your father that it's time for us to think about going home," she tells me on the phone and I know she means dying and to her "home" is where Jesus Christ is and all the saints, waiting with open arms for those who have sought that home all their lives. And my mother has. She tells me about finding my father busy at his computer trying to keep track of his investment portfolio. He doesn't have a stock broker and at eighty-four keeping up with all this is overwhelming him. My mother wants him to come away from all that and listen to someone preaching on TV. My father walks out of the room and out of the house.

"I tell him that all those things don't matter for us anymore. There is only time to think about going home. Our journey is at its end and we won't take anything with us but our spiritual capital."

She doesn't say "spiritual capital" but I think that's what she means. She just says we won't take anything with us, meaning stocks and bonds, savings, and all their possessions.

I remember once when I was with my parents at the Fiesta of San Luis Rey, which was their church in southern California, my father and I were talking to a Chicano cook who was standing over the buried carcass of beef. When we walked away, he said to my father, "Praise the Lord, brother," to which my father replied "And pass the ammunition." "No, brother. We don't need ammunition. God provides." "Amen," my father said, smiling. It was the kind of smile he used when people made what he thought were naive observations. My father has always been self-reliant, ready to defend himself and his family against the "slings and arrows of outrageous fortune." Now, years later, my mother was telling him to prepare for Death, that Joe Black was coming, that they were already living on holiday time. "We're going to God and we have to spend all our time preparing ourselves," my mother began to tell him daily now. But my father doesn't turn away from worldly matters. He has to make decisions daily. It's what he's done all his life; what comes after is a matter of naive speculation. What comes now he knows how to handle—if he attends to it, which is what my mother is calling him away from.

How do you prepare for the journey home? When I was a child, I spoke as a child; but now I am a man, and I have put away childish things. I don't agree with that but it serves to establish a notion of the progress we make on the journey. There are stages. Now my mother wants my father to put away his worldly concerns and think of what comes after that life. Not as easy as going from Blakean Innocence to Experience, from childhood to adulthood. We can't see what we are to be after death, beyond that rotting corpse sunk in a dark, deep hole in the ground. What the world shows us of death is that corpse, that silent, breathless body that will rot in no time unless drained of its blood and filled with formaldehyde. My father has always been from Missouri mentally; God would protect us but meanwhile let's pass the ammunition to protect ourselves. He and my mother should be preparing for that final journey home but meanwhile let's do all we can to delay that final journey and maximize our investments. My father is thinking in terms of a legacy, of a living trust that will provide for future generations. My daughters' children and their children and onward. It is a very Sicilian way of thinking and my father learned it growing up in Sicily. The family that is here now but also the family that is to come, the heirs that only gleam now in the eyes of those living but will arrive. And my father will have prepared for them. So I know that in his way he is preparing for those not yet on the journey.

Anthony Hopkins's Bill Parrish is actually the only one in the film who meets Joe Black. And he's the CEO of a communications company facing a buy-out from a "corporate raider." We don't find out until much later that the corporate raider wants to buy out his competition, break it up and sell the pieces. Standard competitive tactics, the kind of thing Bill Gates should have done with Netscape long before it got big enough to think it could take on Microsoft—with the help of an antitrust suit brought against Microsoft by the U.S. Department of Justice. The demands of global-market capitalism lead to a bloodfest; death to the competitor! It can be, of course, a death sweetened for corporate executives who face death with "golden parachutes" and for shareholders whose shares augment. But Bill Parrish has principles and a vision that he won't see die for the sake of a profit. He's not a "slash and burn" capitalist. Don't think of that other telecommunications power broker Rupert Murdoch! Bill Parrish came in with a noble purpose: To preserve our American way of life by keeping the people informed, not manipulating and controlling what they were to be informed about, but keeping them informed of The Truth. After all, isn't information in the hands of the people the bedrock of truly democratic decisions? Bill's a sort of a Charles Foster Kane for the '90s guy. Here is more dream-works coming right at us.

When Death comes for Bill, is it coming for the last of the true American capitalists who were not just out to line their own pockets but wanted to do their part in contributing to the greatness of America? The "slash and burn," Great Liquidator capitalists are waiting in the wings. Actually, Rupert Murdoch, who has bought his American citizenship, is out on stage, center stage. But in this film it's Good Neighbor Bill Parrish, a wonderful, caring, noble guy right out of a Frank Capra movie who is at center stage. He's Jimmy Stewart in *It's a Wonderful Life* reincarnated as a '90s CEO. There's no making saints out of working-class types anymore; nobody is going to buy it. You have to focus the camera on a guy who lives in a Versailles-like palace on Long Island (East Egg, probably, with Jay Gatsby as his neighbor) on the weekends and in a Park-Avenue penthouse during a "work week." He's got a pool in his New York apartment the size of the YMCA pool I swam in as a kid along with an entire apartment building full of kids sharing the pool with me.

Death coming for a guy like Bill Parrish has got to be really unfair: I mean look what he's got to leave behind! Contrast that with the West Indian old woman that Death finally "euthanizes"—what is she leaving behind but poverty, superstition, and a lot of pain? The rich are different than the rest of us; but Death is an Equalizer. Eventually everyone will hear a voice in his or her head saying Yes to that question one day all of us will ask: Am I dying?

This is a film about entrepreneurial fears, the eschatology of the fat-cats, the repressed haunting in the psyche of the Winners, a filming of that moment when the Haves have to give up what they have, when the guy with the most toys at the end wins—and then loses it all. This is a preview of the ultimate Wall Street Black Friday, the final, and devastating plummet of the Dow Jones into the darkness and oblivion of Death. Unless of course, our entrepreneurial winners have led good lives and have no need to fear Death. Like Bill Parrish. He doesn't fear Death. His conscience is clear: Acts of goodness far exceed acts of evil. The scales tip in the favor of salvation. I'm throwing in the Christian scenario; the film doesn't. In fact there's no interest in this film in conscience, in the state of Bill's soul as he stands just steps away from meeting his Maker. He's no Dickensian Scrooge slowly being brought by the three ghosts to an awareness of his failure to transcend selfishness and devote himself to the welfare of others. Neither are the fatcats of the audience being asked to review the state of their soul.

What does seem clear, rather, is the view that life is to be enjoyed to the fullest and that leaving it is the greatest tragedy, the greatest sorrow. Life is all. And it is to be lived. What comes after Death's arrival is not really on the spreadsheet imaginary of this '90s film. As Bill and Death stand looking down at the gala affair that is his sixty-fifth birthday party, they both agree that it is hard to leave all that. What "all that" is I can't really describe except to say there's a palatial dwelling with a long avenue lit up like Fifth Avenue at Christmas that leads to a number of rotundas erected for the party, also lit up, and looking somehow Roman, and then in the distance the waters of Long Island Sound. The orchestra is niched in what looks like the Hollywood Bowl and literally hundreds of partygoers in formal dress fill the screen. When we get inside either the palace here or the New York apartment, we have all the toys that money can buy to gaze upon.

Bill's daughter Susan tells Death that her father has, among other things, a first edition of *Bleak House*. Bleak House? Not this house. But what a contrastive imaginary journey thought of that Dickens' novel takes us on right at this moment! If inherited wealth, and even the notion that wealth brought happiness, is deeply interrogated in that novel, wealth is not given such a rude going-over in this film. It is an indisputable, grounding premise in this film that wealth makes a life a good life and that the wealthy therefore have a much tougher time than the rest of us when it comes to facing Death. We seem to be only steps away from the ancient funereal practice of throwing all the servants in the burial pit when the master of the house dies. What right have they to live now that the master is gone? What reason would they have? The powerful and wealthy need to take not only all their toys with them but their lackeys too.

No last-minute reminder to the Equestrian class that Death brings them to a Day of Judgment; this film, rather, reminds them that Death will one day separate them from their wealth so they better enjoy it now, live to the fullest. And for the throngs that have no wealth, seek to gain it before Death robs you of that chance. *Carpe diem*, brother! A film that begins in deep ontological dread of that last moment winds up celebrating all that money can buy. Death is not to be feared: You attend a gala party with Brad Pitt and then take a leisurely stroll with him across a bridge. And then the camera fades. Reconfirmation of '80s and '90s turbo-capitalism is the product here. And maybe it's also less a transnational turbo capitalism than a nationalist one: Bill Parrish won't be liquidated; he won't be bought up and swallowed up. He's going to remain competitive and entrepreneurial—or at least his company will after his death.

Is the real hot and disturbing issue here resistance to transnational corporate mergers? Is this the brave and noble challenge to corporate transnationalization? Not a reminder that it's hard for a rich man to get to heaven, not a warning to take stock of conscience and soul in the last hours, not an urge to simplify or renounce or repent. How entrepreneurial has the soul of Humankind become, how deeply market-affected is our self-awareness, our self-examination at the moment of Death.

I wake up with a pain in my chest and a strange numbness in my left arm. I sit up in bed and flex and unflex my left arm and breath deeply, trying to catch my breath and slow my heart down. Because I am somehow afraid. A nanosecond ago I was asleep. Now here am I in the first light of dawn thinking something is really wrong. And then I hear a voice: Yes. But there is no one around. It's a surround-sound voice; it's a voice-over for the ending of my life. Death's voice in Dolby. I go to the bathroom and splash cold water on my face and then return to bed. There was a pain; there was a numbness. But now it's gone. I lie back. And hear the voice again: Yes.

Yes, I am going to die. I'm in a movie theater, comfortable in my seat, in the darkness, watching someone else experience all this but it's not hard to see myself in the same plight. Bill is going to be sixty-five; what does he say at his birthday gala: "Sixty-five years. Don't it go by in a blink?" I'm fifty-five, no pain in my chest, no numbness in my right arm, no voice telling me Yes. I am not even looking back and saying "Fifty-five years. Don't they go by in a blink?" I'm still thinking of the days ahead; I have plans. I will go there and then here and then there. I will do this and that and after that I will do something else. And I hope to do this then and by then I hope to be there. And so on. I am full of schedule. I am full of the future. I am not in Bill Parrish's predicament. Death hasn't come for me.

Or has he? Is he waiting for me just there in the middle of the street, where he met the young man whose body he took? The young man is thinking of the young woman he has just met. They had spent the whole morning talking after an accidental meeting. Cupid's arrow has landed. First, he dodges an oncoming car he sees just in the nick of time; he does it like an agile bull fighter. But nobody stops to applaud. His quick move aside puts him in the path of a car he doesn't see and that car hits him, propelling him into the path of a car coming from the opposite direction which kicks him high, like a football kicked fifty yards. Death didn't show up looking like Brad Pitt with the news that his time was up. Death takes him suddenly, without warning, in a heartbeat, right at the threshold of young love. Love conquers all except Death.

If you put aside the entrepreneurial trappings of how we greet death in the '90s—all the stuff I said at the beginning—what you've got left is a whole lot of fear. Millennial fear I think. The end of the millennium breeds eschatology: thoughts of the last things. Of world and self. The Dow can be Bullish but we all eventually go Bearish. There's a drop; we drop out of sight; we disappear; we go with Death over a small bridge and then we're gone. Take a contemporary culture that for all its religious fundamentalism and born-again hype is still a culture whose materialism drives out all thought of spirituality. Or, spirituality appears on TV as Pat Robertson or Jerry Falwell; or in the tight-lipped assessments of Ralph Reed. Take this Dow Jones-obsessed culture engaged in a vicious war of all against all and get it for a moment to think about death.

You get fear. And this film plugs into it. That's why the beginning is hot and then when the alibi discourse kicks in and pushes the fear off stage, the film starts to die. Death comes for this film the more the film backs off from the fear that it has tapped.

Backing off, backing away, covering up, alibiing, hiding, putting some stuff forward while concealing something else. When Death shows up for us, this is what ensues. All that you see here is present. Or is it? There's a more courageous revealing of what happens when Death shows up in the 1934 film, *Death Takes a Holiday*, than there is in this 1998 film. In that film, Death, played by Frederick March, reveals his true nature to the young woman he has fallen in love with. As the two embrace, she looks into this eyes and he allows her to see in his eyes images of the Netherworld, images of that dark vale deeper than sleep, that swirl of no longer being-in-the-world but someplace without time or place. There is an expressionistic 1930s vibe to these scenes that

Death reveals to his beloved. They are "over the top" for the '90s; but I suspect the long, drawn-out scene in the '90s remake would have no force, no point in the '30s. Why don't dark scenes of Death unroll behind the prettyboy face of Brad Pitt? Susan tells Death that she's afraid—the precise moment in the 1934 film when Death reveals his dark side—but there is nothing but Pitt's blondish good looks to make her afraid. How does she know later that he is Death if he has not shown her, as he does in the 1934 film?

I have two possible answers to the absence of the most remarkable scene in the 1934 film—Death revealing himself in a dark montage of images. First, the commercial intent of the movie is to repeat here what Leonardo DiCaprio did in *Titanic*—enrapture Brad Pitt's audience with his good looks, sex appeal, and charisma. Somehow Pitt's eyes becoming the windows to horrific scenes may disrupt his heartthrob image. He may frighten the teenie boppers; Death is a bad note in the midst of idol worship. This is, after all, a movie that has decided to capture Death's personality by having him wander into the kitchen and lick peanut butter, which he has never tasted, off a spoon. Pitt's eyes light up in happy amazement and joy as he licks the spoon. That's the Death that this film wants to capture because it shows how cute Brad Pitt can be. *Titanic* didn't show Leonardo DiCaprio as anything but a young adventuresome Jack London type; no dark side to the vagabond, penniless life shown in that film. So why should *Meet Joe Black* show Brad Pitt as anything but a loveable, naive guy?

A second possible reason for cutting that dark-side scene has to do with replacing Love at that late stage in the film with Death. So far it hasn't mattered that the handsome young man is not really a handsome young man but really a personification of Death. It's been just another Harry meeting Sally film, guy meets girl and they fall in love and this is the course of that true love. Everyone in the audience who has ever wondered about how and when they are going to die, whether that numbness in that left arm really means something, what may come after death, what will happen to everything and everyone they love—everyone who has ever feared Death, would rather just keep looking at Brad Pitt's handsome face than look deeply into his eyes and see their own end. The culture isn't ready to face that. But it was more able to in 1934 when the young girl looked into Death's eyes and saw what even Love couldn't conquer. Maybe the Depression had already darkened the mental landscape, cast the American cultural imaginary into the shadows.

Maybe the journey from hard times in this world to Death wasn't something as feared or repressed as it is now in our Bullish times with the Dow Jones rising and no sign of loss on the horizon.

Index